SECOND EDITION

Unity Development Cookbook
*Real-Time Solutions from Game
Development to AI*

Paris Buttfield-Addison, Jon Manning, and Tim Nugent

Beijing · Boston · Farnham · Sebastopol · Tokyo    O'REILLY®

Unity Development Cookbook

by Paris Buttfield-Addison, Jon Manning, and Tim Nugent

Published by O'Reilly Media, Inc., 1005 Gravenstein Highway North, Sebastopol, CA 95472.

O'Reilly books may be purchased for educational, business, or sales promotional use. Online editions are also available for most titles (*http://oreilly.com*). For more information, contact our corporate/institutional sales department: 800-998-9938 or *corporate@oreilly.com*.

Acquisition Editor: Zan McQuade
Development Editor: Michele Cronin
Production Editor: Gregory Hyman
Copyeditor: Sonia Saruba
Proofreader: Kim Cofer

Indexer: Ellen Troutman-Zaig
Interior Designer: David Futato
Cover Designer: Karen Montgomery
Illustrator: Kate Dullea

March 2019:   First Edition
August 2023:   Second Edition

Revision History for the Second Edition
2023-08-03:   First Release

See *http://oreilly.com/catalog/errata.csp?isbn=9781098113711* for release details.

978-1-098-11371-1

[LSI]

Table of Contents

Preface

Welcome to the *Unity Development Cookbook*, second edition! Real-time 3D and game development tools have gone from strength to strength in the last two decades, and more people than ever are working on projects ranging from huge "Triple A" games to hobbyist projects built in the spare time of a single person.

We're incredibly excited to be able to update this book, and we're really proud of our work on it. We hope you find it a useful companion to your software development using the Unity engine. Unity has come a long way since we started working with it in 2007, and the more you use it, the more you'll come up with new ideas on how you can use it, why you could use it, and so on! It's all very exciting. Trust us, we've been there.

At Secret Lab, we use Unity to build most of our video games. We're best known for building children's games in Australia, the BAFTA- and IGF-winning *Night in the Woods* (*https://oreil.ly/JYBUZ*) (Finji), and the wildly popular *Yarn Spinner* (*https://oreil.ly/3Uhb5*) tool. We haven't stopped using Unity since we discovered it.

In this book, we've assembled a selection of recipes to solve common problems that we've found ourselves solving over and over as we build using Unity. This book won't cover every single tiny thing you want to know about Unity, but it hopefully covers the majority of things you'd be doing day-to-day in video game development. The second edition of the book adds a bunch of new material, based on changes Unity has adopted over the years since the last book, plus updates to everything that's changed. Unity doesn't move incredibly fast, but it's important to stay on top of things.

These recipes are about things we wish we had someone to ask about back when we were first using Unity. We really hope they help you!

It's a really exciting time to be using Unity. The real-time and game development world is getting bigger and more interesting every day, and the tools and technologies we use are better than ever. Go out and build great things!

Audience and Approach

This book assumes that you know a little of the C# programming language, or a similar language like C++, Java, Go, Swift, Python, or other common languages, but don't know anything about Unity. This book is intended to be a companion to get your games up and running faster.

 If you like our style, and want to read more Unity material from us, you can learn Unity from scratch in *Mobile Game Development with Unity*, also available from the fine folks at O'Reilly.

Our screenshots are taken with macOS, but everything we talk about is generally applicable to Unity on Windows, macOS, or Linux.

Organization of This Book

This book is arranged into 13 chapters:

- Chapter 1, "Working in Unity", introduces the fundamental concepts you need to know in order to use Unity: game objects, components, scenes, and how to work with the Unity editor itself.

- Chapter 2, "Scripting", covers the scripting interface of Unity, which is the way you write the actual code that defines how your project works. After we establish the basics, we'll dive into some practical examples, including how to write a save and load system, how to efficiently work with objects, and how to store your data in a way that both your code and Unity can work with easily.

- In Chapter 3, "Input", you'll learn how to get input from your user in the form of keyboard input, the mouse, and from gamepads. We'll also discuss how to set up game objects that react to input events, like the user clicking them.

- Chapter 4, "Mathematics", covers the fundamentals of some of the mathematical concepts that are useful to know about when developing games, such as vectors, matrices, and quaternions. We'll also look at some practical uses of these concepts, like detecting if an object is in front of the player or not.

- Chapter 5, "2D Graphics", discusses the 2D graphics and physics systems that are built into Unity. You'll learn how to display sprites, sort them, and make them bounce off each other.

- Chapter 6, "3D Graphics", covers the material and shading system of Unity: how materials and shaders work, how to build a shader in Unity, and how to get the best results in your scenes.

- In Chapter 7, "3D Physics and Character Control", you'll learn how to make the 3D physics system of Unity do what you need it to in order to support common gameplay tasks, like picking up and throwing objects, and creating a moving platform that the player can ride on.

- Chapter 8, "Animation and Movement", introduces the animation system used in Unity, and covers topics like how to set up a character to blend between different animation states, and how to integrate player movement with character animation. We'll also introduce the camera system in Unity, and discuss how to set up cameras that move to follow targets.

- Chapter 9, "Logic and Gameplay", is all about creating the gameplay that players interact with. There's a wide range of common gameplay tasks in here, like managing the state of a quest that you've given the player, tracking if a racing car is taking too much of a shortcut, and managing how damage gets dealt between objects in your game.

- In Chapter 10, "Behavior, Simulation, and AI", you'll learn how to add brains to your characters, including the ability to detect when the player can be seen, the ability to navigate a space and avoid obstacles, and the ability to figure out a place where they *can't* be seen. The chapter also briefly explores using Unity for simulations, using machine learning techniques for *real* AI.

- Chapter 11, "Sound and Music", introduces the audio systems in Unity. We'll cover the basics of playing sounds, and then move on to more advanced features, like routing audio to multiple groups, and automatically ducking the music when a character is speaking.

- Chapter 12, "User Interface", covers the tools for building an interface for your players to look at and interact with. This chapter also has a section on how to build your *own* tools in Unity by extending the editor.

- Chapter 13, "Files, Networking, and Screenshots", our final chapter, explores networking, fetching data from the web, and saving screenshots from code.

Conventions Used in This Book

The following typographical conventions are used in this book:

Italic
: Indicates new terms, URLs, email addresses, filenames, and file extensions.

`Constant width`
: Used for program listings, as well as within paragraphs to refer to program elements such as variable or function names, databases, data types, environment variables, statements, and keywords.

Constant width bold
> Shows commands or other text that should be typed literally by the user.

 This element signifies a tip or suggestion.

 This element signifies a general note.

 This element indicates a warning or caution.

Using Code Examples

If you want to download all our code from the recipes throughout this book, head to the book's GitHub repo (*https://oreil.ly/unity-dev-cookbook-code*). We also have a dedicated web page for this book (*https://oreil.ly/9b_pc*), where we keep the source code as well as other downloads and resources.

This book is here to help you get your job done. In general, if example code is offered with this book, you may use it in your programs and documentation. You do not need to contact us for permission unless you're reproducing a significant portion of the code. For example, writing a program that uses several chunks of code from this book does not require permission. Selling or distributing a CD-ROM of examples from O'Reilly books does require permission. Answering a question by citing this book and quoting example code does not require permission. Incorporating a significant amount of example code from this book into your product's documentation does require permission.

We appreciate, but do not require, attribution. An attribution usually includes the title, author, publisher, and ISBN. For example: "*Unity Development Cookbook* by Paris Buttfield-Addison, Jon Manning, and Tim Nugent (O'Reilly). Copyright 2023 Secret Lab Pty. Ltd., 978-1-098-11371-1."

If you feel your use of code examples falls outside fair use or the permission given above, feel free to contact us at *permissions@oreilly.com*.

O'Reilly Online Learning

 For more than 40 years, *O'Reilly Media* has provided technology and business training, knowledge, and insight to help companies succeed.

Our unique network of experts and innovators share their knowledge and expertise through books, articles, and our online learning platform. O'Reilly's online learning platform gives you on-demand access to live training courses, in-depth learning paths, interactive coding environments, and a vast collection of text and video from O'Reilly and 200+ other publishers. For more information, visit *https://oreilly.com*.

How to Contact Us

Please address comments and questions concerning this book to the publisher:

O'Reilly Media, Inc.
1005 Gravenstein Highway North
Sebastopol, CA 95472
800-889-8969 (in the United States or Canada)
707-829-7019 (international or local)
707-829-0104 (fax)
support@oreilly.com
https://www.oreilly.com/about/contact.html

We have a web page for this book, where we list errata, examples, and any additional information. You can access this page at *https://oreil.ly/unity-dev-cookbook*.

For news and information about our books and courses, visit *https://oreilly.com*.

Find us on LinkedIn: *https://linkedin.com/company/oreilly-media*

Follow us on Twitter: *https://twitter.com/oreillymedia*

Watch us on YouTube: *https://youtube.com/oreillymedia*

Acknowledgments

Jon thanks his mother, father, and the rest of his crazily extended family for their tremendous support.

Paris thanks his amazing mother, without whom he wouldn't be doing much of anything at all, really, let alone with enthusiasm, and his amazing wife, Mars. He couldn't do this without you both.

Tim thanks his parents and family for putting up with his rather lackluster approach to life.

We'd all like to thank our friend Rachel Roumeliotis, whose skill and advice have been invaluable in our writing over the last decade.

Thank you to our editor on this book, Michele Cronin. We so thoroughly enjoy working with you, and cannot wait to start a new book. Also huge thanks to Jeff Bleiel, our editor on the first edition of this book. You were calm, clear, enthusiastic, and wonderful to work with. We'd love to work on more books with you in the future as well!

Likewise, all the O'Reilly Media staff we've interacted with over the course of writing the book have been the absolute gurus of their fields. O'Reilly Media has a vast array of incredibly talented people on staff, on contract, and generally surrounding them. It's actually terrifying how good they are at their jobs.

A huge thank you to Tony Gray and the Apple University Consortium (AUC) for the monumental boost they gave us and others listed on this page. We wouldn't be writing this book if it weren't for them. And now you're writing books, too, Tony— sorry about that!

Thanks also to Neal Goldstein, who deserves full credit and/or blame for getting us into the whole book-writing racket.

We're thankful for the support of the goons at MacLab (who know who they are and continue to stand watch for Admiral Dolphin's inevitable apotheosis), as well as Professor Christopher Lueg, Associate Professor Leonie Ellis, and the current and former staff at the University of Tasmania for putting up with us.

Thanks also to Dave J. and his team for serving the coffee. If you ever visit Hobart, Tasmania, Australia, make sure you get a coffee at Yellow Bernard. It's the best.

Thanks also to our tech reviewers for their thoroughness and professionalism. The reviews were brilliantly helpful.

Finally, thank you very much for buying our book—we appreciate it! And if you have any feedback, please let us know. You can email us at *lab@secretlab.com.au* and find us on Twitter at @thesecretlab (*https://oreil.ly/izyYg*).

CHAPTER 1

Working in Unity

To make things in Unity, it's important to understand how Unity works and how to work with it as a piece of software. In this chapter, we'll take a tour through the interface and features of Unity, so that you'll be ready to start building things in the editor. It's a complex piece of software, and can be intimidating to new users, especially those without a background in *professional* software. It's an occasionally wild ride, but it's a fulfilling domain to create in, fusing programming with art in a unique, compelling way.

If you're brand new to Unity, we recommend reading all the recipes in this chapter, as well as in Chapter 2, before trying other recipes in this book.

This chapter also introduces you to many of the terms used in the Unity ecosystem, which will help you make sense of the rest of this book.

1.1 Getting Around in Unity

Problem

You want to learn how to navigate the Unity editor, and understand what each component does, how to use it, and how to customize it.

Solution

Unity's user interface is organized along *windows* of content. Each different view can do different things. In this recipe, we'll present some of the most important ones and talk about how to arrange the editor to suit your needs.

When you launch Unity and create a new project, you'll be taken to the editor's main window (Figure 1-1).

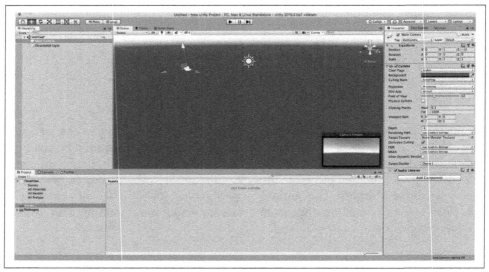

Figure 1-1. The main window of the Unity editor

 When it's first launched, Unity uses the layout that you see in Figure 1-1. However, you can resize any window by clicking and dragging its edges. You can also reposition the window by clicking and dragging its tab to somewhere else. If you drag a tab to the edge of another window, it will be placed at that side of the window. If you drag a tab onto the middle of the window, it will be added to the list of tabs at the top of the window.

There are several features that are of particular importance to anyone working in Unity. Let's take a look at each of them!

 Unity defaults to "dark mode" when you install it, but we've set it to "light mode" for better screenshots in this book. Don't be alarmed if your Unity is a different color than ours!

Toolbar

The toolbar contains controls that affect Unity as a whole (Figure 1-2). It's always at the top of the editor window and can't be moved.

Figure 1-2. The toolbar

The toolbar, from left to right, contains the following controls:

Tools palette
> This palette controls the behavior of the transform controls that appear when an object is selected. Only one mode can be selected at a time; they are:

Hand tool
> Clicking and dragging in the Scene view will move your view of the scene.

Move tool
> Objects that are selected can be moved.

Rotate tool
> Objects that are selected can be rotated around their pivot point or center.

Scale tool
> Objects that are selected can be scaled around their pivot point or center.

Rectangle tool

Objects that are selected have a rectangle drawn around them, and can be scaled and repositioned. This tool is largely used for 2D objects like sprites and user interface elements.

Transform tool

This tool combines the Move, Rotate, and Scale tools. Selected objects can be moved, rotated, and scaled.

Custom tool

Any custom tools that are defined by the code in your game will appear here.

Pivot/Center toggle

This toggle sets whether the transform controls are placed at the local pivot point of the object or in the center of the object's volume. (This can be different for certain 3D models; for example, models of human characters typically place the pivot point at the character's feet.)

Local/Global toggle

This toggle sets whether the Transform tool operates in global space or local space. For example, in local space, dragging the blue "forward" arrow of the Move tool moves an object forward based on its own orientation, while in global mode, dragging the blue "forward" arrow ignores the object's orientation.

Play button

This button starts Play mode, which enters your game. You can click the button again to end Play mode and return to editing.

 You can edit the scene while in Play mode, but any changes you make to the scene will be lost when you end the game. Don't forget to check if you're playing the game or not before doing a large amount of work!

Pause button

This button pauses the game. If you're in Play mode, the game will pause immediately. If you're not in Play mode, you can still click this button; if you then click the Play button, the game will pause immediately after the first frame.

Step button

This button advances one frame, while keeping the game paused.

To be more specific, stepping forward "one frame" means that Unity will advance the game's clock by the *fixed timestep* and then rerender the game. By default, the fixed timestep is 0.02 seconds; you can configure this in the project's Time settings (from the Edit menu, choose Project Settings → Time).

Collab menu

This menu provides controls for working with Unity Collaborate, Unity's version control service.

 Unity Collaborate is outside the scope of this book, but the Unity manual (*https://oreil.ly/9i3QP*) provides a good introduction.

Services button

This button opens the Services view, which allows you to work with Unity's web-based services like Cloud Build, Unity Analytics, and more. For more information, see Unity's Support and Services page (*https://oreil.ly/75Qto*).

Account button

This button allows you to configure your Unity account.

Layers button

With this button you can choose which layers are currently visible or selectable.

Layout button

This button allows you to save and restore a predefined layout of windows. This is useful when you have a layout that works well for tasks like animation, or level layout, and you want to switch between different tasks without having to fiddle with precise window placement.

Scene view

The Scene view allows you to view, select, and modify the objects in a scene (Figure 1-3). In the Scene view, you can left-click any object to select it; when an object is selected, you can move, rotate, or scale it by using the transform controls, depending on which tool you have selected in the toolbar (see Figure 1-4).

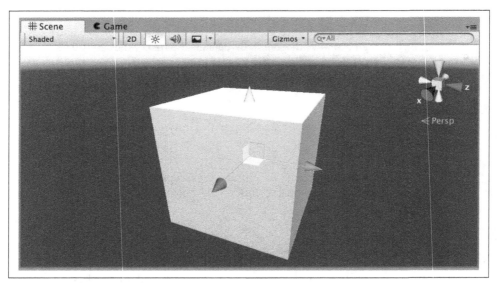

Figure 1-3. The Scene view

To use the transform controls on a selected object, click and drag the arrows (when using the Move tool), circles (the Rotate tool), or boxes (Scale tool) attached to it. Hold down the Shift key to snap the movement, rotate, and scale to a predefined increment. To move around the Scene view, select the Hand tool from the palette at the top left of the view, and click and drag. You can also hold the Alt key (Option on a Mac) to make clicking and dragging rotate the view; Alt-Control (Option-Command) and drag will pan the view around. You can use the scroll wheel on your mouse, or a two-finger gesture on a trackpad, to zoom in and out.

 You can also quickly move the Scene view to focus on the currently selected object. To do this, press the F key.

Figure 1-4 shows the Transform tool with an object selected. Here, a Camera has been selected, and the Transform tool is in Move mode. Clicking and dragging the arrows will move the selected object in that direction.

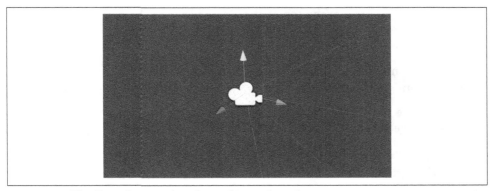

Figure 1-4. The Transform tool with an object selected

Game view

The Game view displays the view through the camera, and shows what the player would see if the game were running outside of Unity (Figure 1-5). The Game view itself isn't interactive unless the editor is in Play mode.

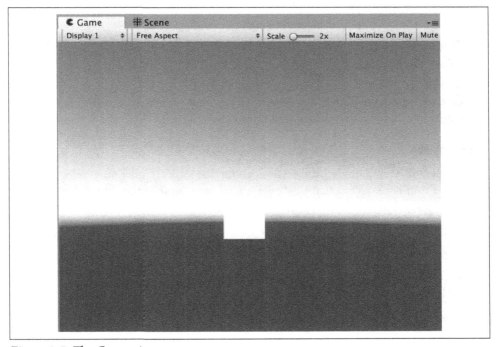

Figure 1-5. The Game view

There are a few controls at the top of the Game view that let you control how the game is presented:

Display menu
> Lets you control which display's contents to show in the view. (In Unity, a camera can be configured to send its results to the main screen, or to an external screen.)

Resolution menu
> Lets you specify an aspect ratio or fixed resolution for the game display.

Scale slider
> Lets you zoom in on the rendered view of the game.

Maximize On Play toggle
> This button, when selected, makes the Game view fill the entire editor window when the game enters Play mode.

Mute Audio toggle
> This button disables all audio playback from the game. (This is useful when you don't want the game's audio to play over the top of your music while you're working, for example.)

Stats toggle
> This button controls whether performance statistics will be displayed in an overlay panel.

Gizmos button
> Lets you control whether the *gizmos*—icons that represent certain objects in the scene, like cameras—appear in the Game view, like they do in the Scene view.

Inspector view

The Inspector view shows information about the objects currently selected (Figure 1-6). From here, you can control every *component* attached to the game object.

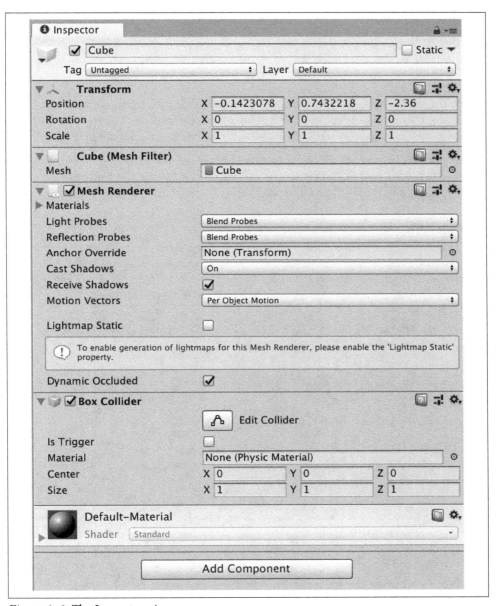

Figure 1-6. The Inspector view

Components are a huge part of how Unity works, which means we'll discuss them in Recipe 1.3, instead of here.

At the top of the Inspector, you can set the name of the currently selected object. You can also set an icon for the object by clicking the icon to the left of the object's name and choosing a symbol to use. This is useful for game objects that are invisible.

By default, the Inspector will change its contents when the current selection changes. If you don't want it to do this, you can click the Lock icon at the top-right corner of the Inspector, and it will stay on the object that it's currently displaying.

Hierarchy view

The Hierarchy view shows the list of objects in the current scene (Figure 1-7). From here, you can browse through the list of objects in your scene. If you select an item in the Hierarchy, it becomes selected in the Scene view, and vice versa. You can also drag and drop one object on another to make it a child of that second object.

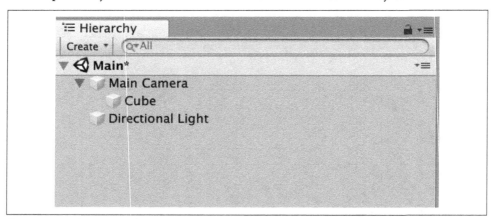

Figure 1-7. The Hierarchy view

Project view

The Project view shows the contents of the project's *Assets* folder (Figure 1-8). Any files that are in the folder will be visible here; you can also move and rename files.

When you rename a file, do it inside the Project view, and not outside of Unity. Unity tracks the additional metadata about your assets, such as import settings for textures, by creating a new file with the extension *.meta* next to each asset file. For example, an asset file called *Hero.png* would have a file called *Hero.png.meta* placed next to it. If you rename, move, or delete the asset file inside Unity, Unity will also update the *.meta* file, but if you rename, move, or delete the asset file outside of Unity, it won't know what to do, and it will have to re-create the *.meta* file from scratch (which means that any references to the file are lost, as well as any import settings).

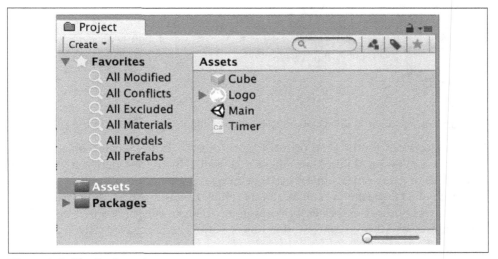

Figure 1-8. The Project view

Discussion

You can right-click the menu at the top bar of any window to close it. If you've closed a window and you want to get it back, you can usually find it in the Window menu. If you're really stuck, open the Window menu and choose Layouts → Revert Factory Settings.

1.2 Working with Game Objects

Problem

You want to create and modify game objects, which populate your game's scenes.

Solution

To create a new, empty game object, open the GameObject menu, and choose Create Empty. A new, empty game object will be added to the scene. It won't be visible in the scene, because it won't have any components that render anything. To learn more about components, see Recipe 1.3.

 You can also press Command-Shift-N (Control-Shift-N on a PC) to create a new, empty game object.

You can rename a game object by selecting it and changing its name in the Inspector.

Game objects can be the *child* of other game objects. When a game object moves, rotates, or scales, its children are affected as well. This means that you can create hierarchies of game objects that work together as a system; for example, a car could have each of its four wheels as child objects, which means that they automatically stay in the correct position as the car moves around. To make one game object the child of another, drag and drop it onto another object in the Hierarchy (see "Hierarchy view" on page 10).

You can also reorder an object by dragging and dropping it in the Hierarchy. As a shortcut, you can make an object move to the end of its siblings by pressing Command-Equals (Control-Equals on a PC), and move to the start of its siblings by pressing Command-Minus (Control-Minus on a PC).

Discussion

You can also create new game objects by dragging and dropping assets into the Scene view. For example, if you drag and drop a 3D model asset into the Scene view, Unity will create a new game object that contains the necessary components for rendering that model.

As a shortcut, you can quickly create an empty game object as a child of the currently selected object by opening the GameObject menu and choosing Create Empty Child. You can also press Option-Shift-N (Alt-Shift-N on a PC).

1.3 Working with Components

Problem

You want to add and modify components, which control the appearance and behavior of your game objects.

Solution

On its own, a game object is just an empty container. It's the components that make a game object actually do anything useful.

To get started in thinking about components, we'll create a new game object that comes with some useful components built in: we'll add a cube to the scene!

To do this, follow these steps:

1. Open the GameObject menu, and choose 3D Object → Cube. A new cube will be added to the scene (Figure 1-9).

2. Select the new cube in the Hierarchy or the Scene view. The Inspector will update to show the list of components attached to it (Figure 1-10).

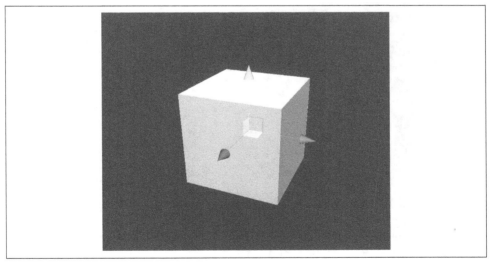

Figure 1-9. A new cube, freshly added to the scene

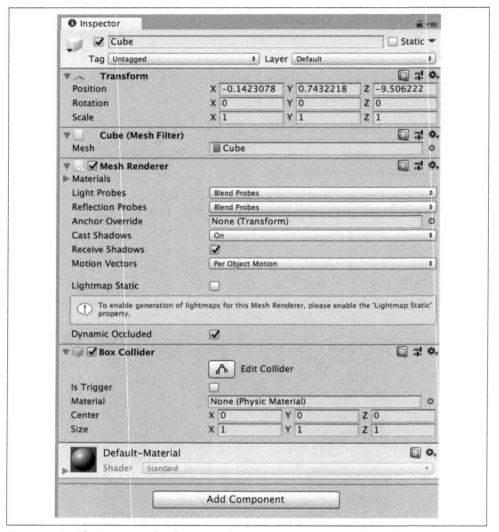

Figure 1-10. The Inspector for the new cube

Every game object has at least one component: a `Transform`. The `Transform` component stores the position, rotation, and scale of an object, and is also responsible for keeping track of the parent of an object. You can't remove the `Transform` component.

On the cube, you'll find several additional components. Each of them does something different:

`MeshFilter`
> Loads a mesh from a file on disk for the `MeshRenderer` to use. (For the cube object we're adding in this recipe, the asset is supplied by Unity; most of the game objects in your games will use assets you add to the project.)

`MeshRenderer`
> Draws the mesh on the screen, using a Material asset to determine its appearance.

`BoxCollider`
> Defines the physical shape of the object in the world.

Components let you configure how they work by exposing properties that are listed in the Inspector. For example, the `MeshFilter` component has a single property: the `Mesh` that it should be using. This is an example of an *object field*—it's a reference to another object that's part of your project. In the case of the `MeshFilter`, the field can take any `Mesh` object; these are found in the assets you add to your project. The type of object that an object field can use is determined by the component; you can't drop any other kind of object besides a `Mesh` into this field, for example.

> Object fields don't have to refer to assets—they can refer to other objects in the scene, too.

To add a component yourself, you can either use the Component menu or click the Add Component button at the bottom of the Inspector. Both of these options will let you specify what kind of component you want to add.

Discussion

You can remove a component by clicking the Gear icon at the component's top-right corner, and choosing Remove Component.

To copy a component to another game object, click the Gear icon, and choose Copy Component. Next, go to the object you want to copy the component to, and click the Gear icon on any existing component (if it doesn't have any, use the Transform tool). Click Paste Component As New, and the component you copied will be pasted.

Scripts (which we discuss in Chapter 2) are components, too, and work in the exact same way as any other component you might attach to a game object.

1.4 Working with Prefabs

Problem

You want to store a game object in a file, so that you can reuse multiple copies of it.

Solution

Normally, game objects you add to your scenes are stored entirely within the scene. If you want to define an object ahead of time, and then make multiple copies of it, you can store it as a *prefab*. A prefab is an asset that stores a game object; you can *instantiate* the prefab, which creates a copy of it in your scenes.

To make a prefab, first create the original object in the scene. For example, create a new cube by opening the GameObject menu and choosing 3D Object → Cube. The object will appear in both the scene and the Hierarchy.

Next, drag and drop the object from the Hierarchy into the Project view. A new file will be created (Figure 1-11): this is the prefab! You'll also notice that the cube's entry in the Hierarchy view has turned blue, which indicates that it's an instance of a prefab. You can now safely delete the original cube from the scene.

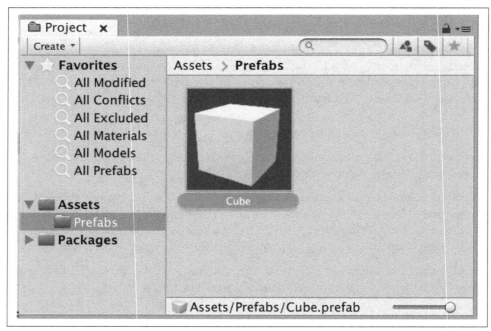

Figure 1-11. The new prefab, created from the cube

You can create an *instance* of a prefab by dragging and dropping the prefab into the scene. An instance is a copy of the game object and components stored in the prefab.

Edit a prefab by selecting the file in the Project view, clicking Open Prefab in the Inspector, and making changes to it (Figure 1-12).

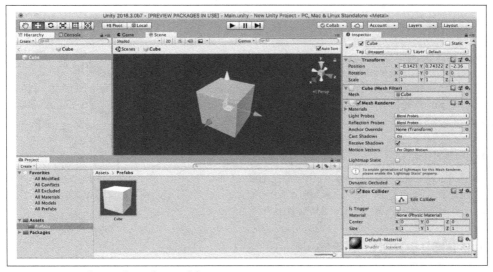

Figure 1-12. Editing the cube prefab

When you're done, click the back arrow button in the Hierarchy. All instances of the prefab across your entire project will be updated to include your changes.

Discussion

Instantiated copies of prefabs are linked to their original; if you make changes to the prefab, the changes you make apply to any instances of it. The reverse is not true by default: if you make changes to an instance, they won't apply to the original. For example, if you add an instance of the cube prefab to the scene and modify its Scale property, the changes will apply only to that instance. Additionally, the property that you change will be highlighted in bold, and with a blue line, to make it easier to see.

However, if you *do* want to apply the changes, right-click the property that you've changed, and click "Apply to Prefab." If you want to apply all of your changes, open the Overrides menu at the top of the Inspector and click Apply All.

From the Overrides menu, you can also see a summary of the changes you've made to an instance.

1.5 Working with Scenes

Problem

You want to create and edit scenes, which are the containers for your game's objects.

Solution

When you create a new project, Unity will create a new, empty scene for you. When you press Command-S (Control-S on a PC), Unity will save the scene file to disk; if this is the first time that the scene has been saved, Unity will ask you where to save it. You can create more scenes by opening the File menu and choosing New Scene. Don't forget to save your new scene to store it on disk.

Discussion

You can use scenes for a variety of purposes. For example, your main menu can be stored as a scene, as well as each of your game's levels. During gameplay, you can load new scenes via code. We'll discuss this in Recipe 9.1.

1.6 Managing Assets

Problem

You want to add files to your project and configure how Unity imports them as assets.

Solution

To add a file to your project, simply drag and drop it from the Explorer (Windows) or Finder (macOS) into the Project view. Unity will import it and make it available to your project.

 When a file is added to a Unity project, it is referred to as an *asset*.

Once Unity has imported it, you can select the file and configure *how* Unity imports it by looking at the Inspector. Different file formats have different options; for example, you can configure an image to be imported as a sprite, in which case Unity will generate an additional sprite data asset for use in the sprite system (discussed in Chapter 5), or as one of multiple different types of textures.

Discussion

Unity supports a wide variety of file formats:

3D objects
> Autodesk FBX and Collada; Unity can also import Maya, Cinema 4D, 3ds Max, Cheetah3D, Modo, LightWave, Blender, and SketchUp files, if the corresponding software is installed.

Audio
> WAV, MP3, OGG, and AIFF; Unity also supports a variety of tracker module formats—specifically, Impulse Tracker (*.it*), Scream Tracker (*.s3m*), Extended Module File Format (*.xm*), and Module File Format (*.mod*).

2D textures
> Adobe Photoshop, BMP, PNG, JPG, BMP, and TGA.

Text
> TXT and JSON.

 Unity will pick up most changes made to files in external programs, but often relies on that specific program being installed. For example, if you want to work with Blender *.blend* files as assets in Unity, then you'll need to have the Blender application installed on the same system.

1.7 Building Unity Projects

Problem

You want to configure Unity to build your game, so that you can distribute the game to players.

Solution

To build your game, open the Build Settings view by opening the File menu and choosing Build Settings (Figure 1-13).

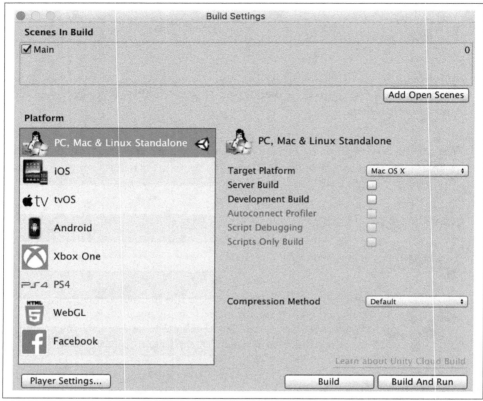

Figure 1-13. The Build Settings view

When you build your game, you specify which scenes should be included. If you haven't already saved your current scene, you should do so now by opening the File menu and choosing Save, or by pressing Command-S (Control-S on a PC). You can drag and drop the scenes you want to include into the Scenes In Build list, or you can click the Add Open Scenes button to add all scenes that you have open right now.

Next, you need to select which platform you want to build for. Unity supports a wide range of platforms, ranging from desktop PCs to mobile phones to consoles and more. Only one platform can be selected at a time; the current platform will be marked with a Unity logo next to it. To build for a different platform, select it and click the Switch Platform button.

When you're ready, click the Build button. Unity will ask you where you want to save the build; once that's done, Unity will start building.

Discussion

To build for certain platforms, you need to download the appropriate platform support module. If you don't have the necessary module, you won't be able to build; to get the module, click the platform and click the Open Download Page button. You'll be taken to the appropriate web page for downloading the module.

> Certain platforms, like consoles, require a special license; see the Unity Platform Module Installation page (*https://oreil.ly/KHvvw*) for more information.

1.8 Accessing Preferences

Problem

You want to access the settings that control Unity's behavior, both for the entire application and for your current project.

Solution

To open the per-project settings, open the Edit menu, and choose Project Settings. The Project Settings view will appear (Figure 1-14).

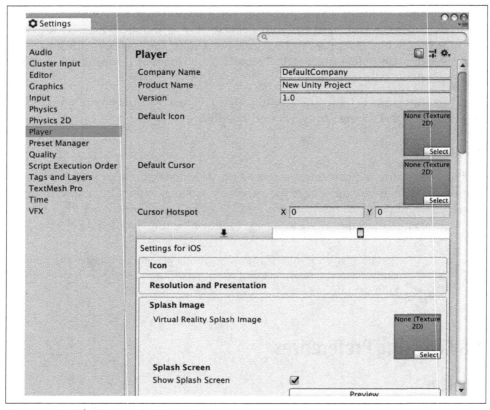

Figure 1-14. The Project Settings view

In the Project Settings view you can configure a wide range of possible settings for your game, including the maximum resolution, build name, graphical quality settings, input, and more.

For settings that affect the entire Unity application itself, access the Preferences view.

Discussion

The Preferences view (Figure 1-15) allows you to configure things like colors, hotkeys, and other settings that apply to all projects. Access these settings on a PC by opening the Edit menu and choosing Preferences; on a Mac, open the Unity menu and choose Preferences.

Figure 1-15. The Preferences view

1.9 Installing Unity Packages

Problem

You want to install a Unity package, to add extra features to the Unity engine.

Solution

You can use the Unity Package Manager to install new packages (which typically add new features).

> Packages live inside a specific project. So if you install a package, you've installed it for the project you're working with at the time, and would need to install it again for other projects.

To find the Package Manager, open the Window menu and select Package Manager. You'll be able to search for and install new packages (which are downloaded from the internet).

Discussion

Unity's Package Manager allows various components to be distributed separately, and updated separately from the engine.

 You may see the Unity Package Manager referred to as "UPM."

You'll work with a few packages in this book, and most features of Unity are distributed as packages these days. You can learn more in the Unity documentation (*https://oreil.ly/-XVoh*).

CHAPTER 2

Scripting

Creating behaviors in Unity means writing code, or scripting. Scripts in Unity are written in C# (pronounced "C sharp"). C# was originally developed by Microsoft, and has since evolved to include a full, fantastic open source implementation, which Unity makes extensive use of.

We strongly recommend that you review Chapter 1 before you work through any of the recipes in this chapter!

This book isn't going to try to give you a complete guide to programming, or a complete guide to programming in C#—that'd be a whole other book. Instead, we'll show you how to write scripts for use in Unity, using C# as the language.

There are other languages you can use to write code in Unity. For example, there are a number of bindings to other languages, and Unity supports a range of visual scripting tools that we'll touch on in other chapters, but that are beyond the scope of this book.

If you're interested in learning C# in a broader sense, we strongly recommend *C# 7.0 in a Nutshell* by Ben and Joseph Albahari (O'Reilly), as well as *Head First C#* by Andrew Stellman and Jennifer Greene (O'Reilly).

2.1 Adding a Script to an Object in a Unity Scene

Problem

You want to add scripts to your game objects, so that you can give them behavior using C# code.

Solution

Unity game objects are containers for *components*. A MonoBehaviour—named for *Mono*, the scripting runtime that Unity uses—is a script component. When a Mono Behaviour is attached to a game object, it participates in the game's update loop and gives you the opportunity to run code every frame.

 Even if you're building something other than a game, such as a simulation, the basic Unity object is currently called a game object. So we're going to stick to that terminology.

To add code to a game object, you create a new MonoBehaviour script and attach it to the game object as a component. This means that you'll need a game object to use. In a Unity scene:

1. Create a new cube by opening the GameObject menu and choosing 3D Object → Cube.
2. Use the Move tool to position the cube to somewhere in front of the camera.

Next, we'll create a new script:

1. Go to the Project tab and right-click the *Assets* folder. Choose Create → C# Script.
2. A new file will be created, and Unity will prompt you to name it. Name the file "Mover."

 Unity uses the name you provide to determine the contents of the file. It's important that the C# classes that you write have the same name as the file they're in, since Unity uses that information to save the contents of the scene. If you rename the file, be sure to rename the class that's inside it as well.

3. Double-click the script. Unity will open it in your editor: by default, Visual Studio if you're on a PC, Visual Studio for Mac if you're on a Mac, or your text editor if you're on Linux.

You can customize which program Unity uses to edit scripts by going to Unity's preferences and choosing External Tools → External Script Editor. We're particularly keen on Visual Studio Code and BBEdit on macOS.

You'll see code that looks like this:

```
using System.Collections;
using System.Collections.Generic;
using UnityEngine;

public class Mover : MonoBehaviour
{
    void Start()
    {

    }

    void Update()
    {

    }
}
```

Start is called before the first frame update, and Update is called once per frame.

4. Modify the Mover class to look like this:

```
public class Mover : MonoBehaviour
{
    public Vector3 direction = Vector3.up;

    float speed = 0.1f;

    void Update()
    {
        var movement = direction * speed;
```

```
                    this.transform.Translate(movement);
          }
     }
```

 This code, while very good for a simple demo, isn't the most effective way to move an object. To learn why, and to see a better approach, see Recipe 2.3.

This code does a few things:

- It creates a new public Vector3 variable called direction, and initializes it to the value of Vector3.up. This is a Vector3 that's equal to (0, 1, 0).

- It creates a new private float variable called speed, and initializes it to the value 0.1f.

 The f at the end of the speed value is important, because in C#, a noninteger number (like 0.1) is a double type, not a float. This means that the following line of code will cause a compiler error:

```
float speed = 0.1;
```

You need to say 0.1f instead:

```
float speed = 0.1f;
```

- It defines a new method called Update; in this method, a variable called movement is created that's set to the result of multiplying direction by speed. The object is then moved by calling the Translate method on the transform property.

Now that we've created the script, we need to attach it as a component to the game object:

1. Select the cube you added earlier.

2. Drag and drop the *Mover.cs* script onto the Inspector.

   The Inspector shows the public variables, allowing you to make changes to them. Because the default value of direction is Vector3.up, you can see that its value is equal to 0, 1, 0 (Figure 2-1).

3. Press the Play button. The object will start moving upward. Press the Play button again to stop.

4. Change one of the numbers in the `direction` variable, and press Play again. You'll see that the object moves in a different direction or at a different speed.

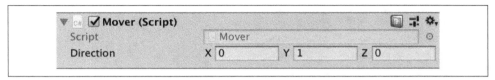

Figure 2-1. The Inspector for the `Mover` component, showing the Direction variable

Discussion

`MonoBehaviour` is a C# class. You create subclasses of it and implement certain methods that Unity calls at the appropriate times; for example, if you define an `Update` method, Unity will call it every frame, and if you define an `OnDestroy` method, Unity will call it just before the object is removed from the scene. We'll discuss the important methods in detail in Recipe 2.2.

In addition to creating a script via the editor's menus, you can also create one through the Add Component button, which you'll find at the bottom of the Inspector. To do this, click Add Component and type the name of the script you want to create. Unity will attempt to find a component by that name; it'll also offer to create a script with that name (Figure 2-2). New scripts that you create this way are placed in the top-level *Assets* folder, but you can move them elsewhere after they're created.

Variables that you mark as `public` appear in the Inspector. These variables are also accessible to other scripts in your code; if you want a variable to appear in the Inspector but don't want it to be accessible to other scripts, remove the `public` access modifier and put a `[SerializeField]` attribute above it, like so:

```
// This variable is private, but will appear in the Inspector because of the
// SerializeField attribute
[SerializeField]
float speed = 0.1f;
```

If you want a variable to be public, but *don't* want it to appear in the Inspector, use the [HideInInspector] attribute instead.

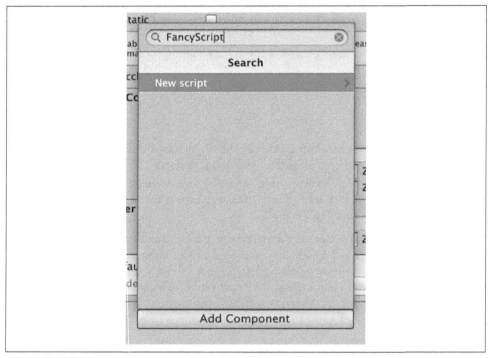

Figure 2-2. Creating a new script from the Add Component menu

2.2 Running Code at Specific Times in a Script's (or Game Object's) Life

Problem

You want to run code at specific times during the life cycle of a script.

Solution

Unity calls different methods on your MonoBehaviours at different times:

Start

> The `Start` method is called once per object for each script, on the first frame that the script is active. If the script is attached to the object when the game starts, then `Start` is called on the first frame.

Update

> The `Update` method is called once per frame for each script on each active object, before the camera renders the scene. Because it's called every frame, it's your best opportunity to do work that happens continuously, like movement.

Awake

> The `Awake` method, like the `Start` method, is called when the script becomes active. Unity guarantees that all `Awake` methods will complete before any `Start` methods begin; this means that the `Awake` method is the best time to set up references between scripts (using `GetComponent` and `FindObjectOfType`, discussed in Recipes 2.4 and 2.5), and `Start` is the best time to start accessing data from those references.

LateUpdate

> The `LateUpdate` method is called after `Update`. As with `Awake` and `Start`, Unity calls `LateUpdate` only after all scripts have had a chance to run `Update`. This gives you a chance to apply behavior, knowing that it's taking place after something else. For example, if you have a script on one object that moves it, and a script on another object that rotates it to look at the first object, you should put the code that does the movement in `Update`, and the code for the rotation in `LateUpdate`, so that you're guaranteed that the rotation code will aim at the correct location.

Discussion

In addition to these common methods, there are other methods that can be called, depending on the circumstances. For example, if a script implements the `OnDestroy` method and the object is destroyed, the `OnDestroy` method will be called. Some methods will be called only if there's a component of a specific type attached to the same game object. For example, if a script implements the method `OnBecameVisible` *and* it has a `Renderer` component attached (such as a `SpriteRenderer` or `Mesh Renderer`), the `OnBecameVisible` method will be called when the object comes into view of a camera.

These methods aren't overridden from any parent class. Unity examines the class, registers the fact that the class implements the method, and calls it directly.

As a result, it doesn't really matter if the methods are `public` or `private`; Unity will call them anyway. As a matter of coding convention, many developers make the methods `private` to prevent other classes from calling them, since only the engine should be doing this.

 You can potentially improve the performance of your frame by removing any unused `Update` methods from classes. For more information, see the Unity documentation (*https://oreil.ly/vPggZ*).

By default, Unity doesn't guarantee the order in which different scripts have their methods run. However, if you *really* want to ensure that scripts of type A have their `Update` method run before scripts of type B, you can manually configure their execution order. To do this, open the Edit menu and choose Settings, and then select Script Execution Order. From here, you can manage the execution order of certain scripts, ensuring that they're in the order that you want (Figure 2-3).

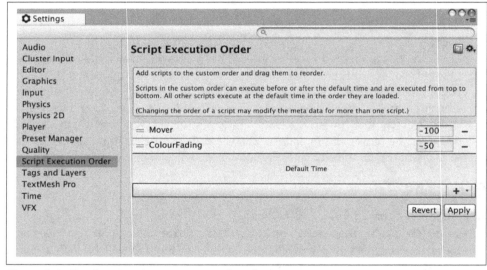

Figure 2-3. Configuring the execution order of some scripts

2.3 Creating Frame Rate–Independent Behavior

Problem

You want to ensure that processes take place over a fixed period of time, regardless of how many frames per second your project is running at (known as the frame rate).

Solution

Use the `Time` class's `deltaTime` property to access the amount of time needed to render the last frame, and incorporate this into your calculations:

```
void Update()
{
    var movement = direction * speed;

    // Multiply by delta time; movement now represents 'units per second,'
    // rather than 'units per frame'
    movement *= Time.deltaTime;

    this.transform.Translate(movement);
}
```

Discussion

Unity will attempt to run everything at the fastest possible speed, rendering as many frames per second as it can (up to the limits of the various hardware involved, including the GPU and the display). The number of frames that can be rendered each second can vary, depending on the complexity of the scene, which means that the amount of time taken for each frame can vary as well.

This means we can make a simple `Update` method in which an object is moved by a fixed amount every frame:

```
void Update()
{
    var movement = direction * speed;

    this.transform.Translate(movement);
}
```

This simple code will result in the object moving that fixed distance *more often* when the renderer is able to render more often, and *less often* when the renderer can't produce as many frames per second, because it's moving every time a frame is rendered. This results in the object moving faster and slower, because it's moving more or less distance every second.

The solution is to take into account the amount of time taken to render the last frame. This is available as `Time.deltaTime`.

 The Greek letter delta (Δ) is often used in mathematical notation to represent a change in value. *Delta time*, therefore, is the amount of additional time that's elapsed since the last frame.

When you multiply movement by Time.deltaTime, movement no longer represents a fixed distance, but rather a distance *over time*. When you provide this to the transform's Translate method, you'll find the object moving at a fixed speed, regardless of how quickly the renderer can produce new frames.

deltaTime isn't the only property available to you. If you want to find out how long the project has been running, you can access the time variable. You can also slow down and speed up time by modifying the Time.timeScale property, which is quite useful for pausing the project.

2.4 Using the Components of a Game Object

Problem

You want to make use of components attached to a game object.

Solution

Use the GetComponent method to get a component that's attached to the same game object as your script.

When you call GetComponent, you specify the type of component you're looking for as a generic parameter. For example, to get a Renderer component on the game object, you call the method GetComponent<Renderer>.

 If there's no component of the right type attached to the game object, GetComponent will return null. If you try to use this object by calling methods on it or accessing properties and fields, you'll cause a NullPointerException to be thrown, which at the very least will immediately stop your script for the frame, and at worst can cause the entire project to crash. Always check first to see if the result is null.

Once you have a reference to another component, you can make use of it. For example, if you have a MeshRenderer, you can change the color of its material over time by accessing the component via GetComponent, and then accessing its properties:

```
public class ColorFading : MonoBehaviour
{

    void Update()
    {
        var meshRenderer = GetComponent<MeshRenderer>();
```

```
    // Check to make sure that it's valid before we use it
    if (meshRenderer == null) {
        return;
    }

    var sineTime = Mathf.Sin(Time.time) + 1 / 2f;
    var color = new Color(sineTime, 0.5f, 0.5f);
    meshRenderer.material.color = color;
    }
}
```

Discussion

In addition to the GetComponent method, there are a number of related methods that access *multiple* components, access components on a parent object, or access components on a child object:

GetComponent<T>

Finds a component of type T on the current object

GetComponents<T>

Finds *all* components of type T on the current object and returns them as an array

GetComponentInChildren<T>

Finds the first component of type T on the current object, or any of its children (or any of *their* children, performing a depth-first search)

GetComponentsInChildren<T>

The same as GetComponentInChildren<T>, but finds *all* matching components and returns them as an array

GetComponentInParent<T>

Finds the first component of type T on the current object, or its parents (up to the top-level object)

GetComponentsInParent<T>

Finds the first component of type T on the current object, or its parents (up to the top-level object)

If you'll be using an object every frame, you can improve performance a little bit by calling GetComponent (or its related functions) in Awake or Start, and storing the result in a variable on the class.

For example, here is the same code from before, but with one difference—
GetComponent is called only once, in the Start method:

```
public class ColorFading : MonoBehaviour
{

    // The mesh renderer component will be stored in this after Start
    MeshRenderer meshRenderer;

    void Start()
    {
        // Get the component and cache it
        meshRenderer = GetComponent<MeshRenderer>();
    }

    void Update()
    {

        // Check to make sure that it's valid before we use it
        if (meshRenderer == null) {
            return;
        }

        // meshRenderer has already been stored, so we can just start
        // using it

        var sineTime = Mathf.Sin(Time.time) + 1 / 2f;
        var color = new Color(sineTime, 0.5f, 0.5f);
        meshRenderer.material.color = color;
    }
}
```

2.5 Finding Objects Attached to a Game Object

Problem

You want to make use of components that are attached to a game object, but you don't
know which game object has them.

Solution

Use the FindObjectOfType method to find a single component of the desired type:

```
// Find a single Mover object in the scene
var mover = FindObjectOfType<Mover>();
```

If there's more than one component of the type you specify, `FindObjectOfType` will pick one at random. The random object is typically picked in ascending order of its `InstanceID`. For example, an object `-24084` would be returned before an object `-24082`.

If you want to find *all* components of a specific type, use `FindObjectsOfType`, which returns an array of all of them:

```
// Find all Mover objects in the scene
var allMovers = FindObjectsOfType<Mover>();
```

Note that, like `GetComponent` (see Recipe 2.4), `FindObjectsOfType` will return `null` if it can't find what you're asking for. Always check your results to see if they're `null` before you try to use them.

These methods will only return objects that are currently active. They won't find any objects that are inactive.

Discussion

`FindObjectOfType` works by searching every single component on every single object in the scene. Don't call it in an `Update` method, because it incurs a significant amount of work for Unity, and you don't want to do that every frame. Instead, call the method at `Start` or `Awake`, and store the results in a variable for later use.

2.6 Singletons

Problem

You want to create a class that always has a single instance, and which other code can always access.

Solution

A *singleton* is a class that's designed to only ever have one instance. For example, things that are globally available throughout the entire game, like gameplay managers, input managers, or other utilities, are often implemented as singletons.

To create one, first create your game object, and create and attach a new script.

Next, create a `public` `static` variable on your class, using the type of the class. Then, in the `Awake` method, set that variable's value to `this`, which means that any other part of your code will be able to refer to that specific instance of that class. For example:

```
public class SimpleSingleton : MonoBehaviour
{

    // A 'static' variable is shared between all instances of the class
    public static SimpleSingleton instance;

    void Awake() {
        // When this object wakes up, it sets the instance variable to itself;
        // because the instance variable is public and static, any
        // class from any location can access it and call its methods.
        instance = this;
    }

    // An example method that any other part of the code can call, as long
    // as there's a game object in the scene that has a
    // SimpleSingleton component attached
    public void DoSomething() {
        Debug.Log("I'm the singleton! Hello!");
    }

}
```

You can access the singleton instance by using the `instance` variable on the class:

```
// Accessing the singleton and calling a method on it
SimpleSingleton.instance.DoSomething();
```

This singleton instance is accessible from anywhere in your code, and will work as long as there's a game object that has the script attached to it.

Discussion

If you have more than a couple of singleton classes, it can become tedious to have to write the `instance` variable and `Awake` methods, and duplicated code can lead to accidental bugs.

You can create a more sophisticated singleton class by using generics. The following class is designed to be subclassed, and provides an automatic implementation of the `instance` method. It also handles the problem of setting up the `instance` variable to point to the single instance—if the script is already attached to a game object in the scene, it will be found; if it doesn't exist, a new one will be created:

```
// This class is generic, which means that you can create multiple versions
// of it that vary depending on what type you specify for 'T'.
// In this case, we're also adding a type constraint, which means that 'T'
// must be a MonoBehaviour subclass.
public class Singleton<T> : MonoBehaviour where T : MonoBehaviour
{
```

```
// The instance. This property only has a getter, which means that
// other parts of the code won't be able to modify it.
public static T instance {
    get {
        // If we don't have an instance ready, get one by either
        // finding it in the scene, or creating one
        if (_instance == null) {
            _instance = FindOrCreateInstance();
        }
        return _instance;
    }
}

// This variable stores the actual instance. It's private, and can
// only be accessed through the 'instance' property above.
private static T _instance;

// Attempts to find an instance of this singleton. If one can't be
// found, a new one is created.
private static T FindOrCreateInstance() {

    // Attempt to locate an instance.
    var instance = GameObject.FindObjectOfType<T>();

    if (instance != null) {
        // We found one. Return it; it will be used as the shared instance.
        return instance;
    }

    // Script components can only exist when they're attached to a game
    // object, so to create this instance, we'll create a new game
    // object, and attach the new component.

    // Figure out what to name the singleton
    var name = typeof(T).Name + " Singleton";

    // Create the container game object with that name
    var containerGameObject = new GameObject(name);

    // Create and attach a new instance of whatever 'T' is; we'll return
    // this new instance
    var singletonComponent =
        containerGameObject.AddComponent<T>();

    return singletonComponent;
}

}
```

You can define your own new singletons by subclassing `Singleton`. Don't forget that you need to specify the name of the class twice—once when naming the class, and once as the generic parameter (the part between the angle brackets < >):

```
public class MoverManager : Singleton<MoverManager>
{
    public void ManageMovers() {
        Debug.Log("Doing some useful work!");
    }

}
```

Any class defined like this can be accessed through the `instance` variable. This property will never be `null`; if you don't set up the instance in the scene, it will be set up the very first time the `instance` variable is used:

```
MoverManager.instance.ManageMovers();
```

 Singletons can be convenient, but the architectures they lead to can be difficult to maintain. Wherever a class calls a method of another class, this creates an architectural dependency between them: you can't change or remove the method without also modifying the place from which the method was called. When a class is easily called from anywhere, it becomes easy to create a large number of calls, which means a large number of dependencies. As your code grows in complexity, it becomes more difficult to maintain. If you find yourself calling a singleton class from many different places, consider reorganizing your code to reduce the amount of dependencies.

2.7 Using Coroutines to Manage When Code Runs

Problem

You want to write some code that takes place over multiple frames.

Solution

In most applications, code is intended to run as fast as possible and finish its task immediately. However, games take place over time; it takes more than an instant for a ball to roll down a hill, and gameplay often relies on timed events.

In Unity, *coroutines* are a way to write code that takes place over time. A coroutine is a method that is able to temporarily return, or *yield*, to the rest of the system, and then resume at a later time.

 Coroutines are implemented as generators, using C#'s `yield return` syntax.

A coroutine is any method that returns an `IEnumerator`, and is started using the `StartCoroutine` method. Inside the method, you can temporarily suspend execution of the method by `yield returning` an object that represents to Unity how long you want to wait.

For example, suppose you want to write a method that does some work, pauses for one second, and then does some more work. To implement this, you'd create a new method, make it return an `IEnumerator`, and at the point where you want to wait for a second, you'd `yield return` a `WaitForSeconds` object:

```
IEnumerator LogAfterDelay() {
    Debug.Log("Back in a second!");

    yield return new WaitForSeconds(1);

    Debug.Log("I'm back!");
}
```

 You can only use `yield return` inside a method that returns an `IEnumerator`.

To start a coroutine, you use the `StartCoroutine` method. Call your coroutine method and use its return value as the parameter to `StartCoroutine`. Unity will start running the coroutine, and will ensure that it's resumed at the right time:

```
StartCoroutine(LogAfterDelay());
```

The `Start` method can also be a coroutine. All you have to do is set its return type to `IEnumerator`, and you can use `yield return` inside it:

```
IEnumerator Start()
{
    Debug.Log("Hello...");

    yield return new WaitForSeconds(1);

    Debug.Log("...world!");
}
```

Just like any other method, coroutines can receive parameters. For example, given the following method:

```
IEnumerator Countdown(int times) {
    for (int i = times; i > 0; i--) {
        Debug.LogFormat("{0}...", i);
        yield return new WaitForSeconds(1);
    }
    Debug.Log("Done counting!");
}
```

you can call this coroutine by providing parameters when starting it:

```
// Parameters for coroutines are supplied as part of the function call
StartCoroutine(Countdown(5));
```

Because coroutines yield control back to the engine, they can be used in conjunction with infinite loops:

```
IEnumerator LogEveryFiveSeconds() {

    // Enter an infinite loop, in which we wait for five seconds and then
    // do something useful
    while (true) {
        yield return new WaitForSeconds(5);
        Debug.Log("Hi!");
    }

}
```

> Be careful while using `while (true)` or other loops that never end!
> If you don't yield at some point in the loop, Unity will not be able
> to break out of it and will freeze up. You won't be able to leave Play
> mode, and you won't be able to save any unsaved changes in your
> scene. Be careful!

If you `yield return null`, Unity will wait for exactly one frame before resuming.

The following coroutine, for example, acts as a frame counter, and logs every time 100 frames are rendered:

```
IEnumerator RunEveryHundredFrames() {
    while (true) {
        // Yielding 'null' will wait one frame.
        yield return null;

        if (Time.frameCount % 100 == 0) {
            Debug.LogFormat("Frame {0}!", Time.frameCount);
        }

    }
}
```

Finally, you can exit a coroutine using `yield break`:

```
while (true) {
    yield return null;

    // Stop on frame 354
    if (Time.frameCount == 354) {
        yield break;
    }
}
```

Discussion

In this recipe, we've mostly been using `WaitForSeconds`. It's quite useful, but there are other objects you can return that wait for different amounts of time.

`WaitForEndOfFrame` waits until after all cameras have rendered, but before the frame is displayed on the screen. You can use this to, for example, capture the contents of the screen in a screenshot, knowing that all rendering is complete.

`WaitForSecondsRealtime` waits for a fixed number of seconds, just like `WaitForSeconds`. However, it ignores `Time.timeScale`.

`WaitUntil` and `WaitWhile` take a *delegate*—an inline function, or a reference to a method—that is repeatedly called every frame to see if execution should continue. The function is required to take no parameters and return a `bool` value.

`WaitWhile` stops until the function you provide returns `false`:

```
// Wait while the Y position of this object is below 5
yield return new WaitWhile(() => transform.position.y < 5);
```

`WaitUntil` stops until the function you provide *no longer* returns `false`:

```
// Wait _until_ the Y position of this object is below 5
yield return new WaitUntil(() => transform.position.y < 5);
```

2.8 Managing Objects Using an Object Pool

Problem

You have a project in which you're regularly creating and destroying objects, and you want that process to be more efficient.

Solution

Create an *object pool*: a system that allows objects to temporarily deactivate when they're no longer needed, and reactivate when asked for (as opposed to objects that destroy themselves when they're not needed, removing themselves from memory entirely).

We'll do this by creating a script that manages a queue of GameObjects and exposes a method called GetObject. When GetObject is called, it will first look in the queue to see if there are any existing objects that aren't being used and can be recycled. If there are, one will be removed from the queue and returned; if there aren't any, a new one will be created.

When an object is no longer needed, it contacts the object pool that created it, is deactivated, and is added back to the queue, ready for future reuse. At no point is the object destroyed; it's only temporarily parked for later reuse.

Implementing the system

To implement this functionality, we'll create a new script that performs this behavior. We'll also create an interface that objects can implement if they want to be notified when they enter or leave the queue; this will be optional, but it's useful for objects that need to perform setup whenever they (re)enter the scene:

1. Create a new C# script called *ObjectPool.cs*.
2. Add the following code to it:

```
public interface IObjectPoolNotifier {
    // Called when the object is being returned to the pool.
    void OnEnqueuedToPool();

    // Called when the object is leaving the pool, or has just been
    // created. If 'created' is true, the object has just been created,
    // and is not being recycled.

    // (Doing it this way means you use a single method to do the
    // object's setup, for your first time and all subsequent times.)
    void OnCreatedOrDequeuedFromPool(bool created);
}
```

3. Update the `ObjectPool` class to look like the following:

```
public class ObjectPool : MonoBehaviour
{

    // The prefab that will be instantiated.
    [SerializeField]
    private GameObject prefab;

    // The queue of objects that are not currently in use
    private Queue<GameObject> inactiveObjects = new Queue<GameObject>();

    // Gets an object from the pool. If there isn't one in the queue,
    // a new one is created.
    public GameObject GetObject() {

        // Are there any inactive objects to reuse?
        if (inactiveObjects.Count > 0) {

            // Get an object from the queue
            var dequeuedObject = inactiveObjects.Dequeue();

            // Queued objects are children of the pool, so we move them
            // back to the root
            dequeuedObject.transform.parent = null;
            dequeuedObject.SetActive(true);

            // If there are any MonoBehaviours on this object that
            // implement IObjectPoolNotifier, let them know that this
            // object just left the pool

            var notifiers = dequeuedObject
                .GetComponents<IObjectPoolNotifier>();

            foreach (var notifier in notifiers) {
                // Notify the script that it left the pool
                notifier.OnCreatedOrDequeuedFromPool(false);
            }

            // Return the object for use
            return dequeuedObject;

        } else {

            // There's nothing in the pool to reuse. Create a new object.

            var newObject = Instantiate(prefab);
```

```
            // Add the pool tag so that it's able to return to the pool
            // when done.
            var poolTag = newObject.AddComponent<PooledObject>();

            poolTag.owner = this;

            // Mark the pool tag so that it never shows up in the
            // Inspector. There's nothing configurable on it; it only
            // exists to store a reference back to the pool that
            // creates it.
            poolTag.hideFlags = HideFlags.HideInInspector;

            // Notify the object that it was created
            var notifiers = newObject
                .GetComponents<IObjectPoolNotifier>();

            foreach (var notifier in notifiers)
            {
                // Notify the script that it was just created
                notifier.OnCreatedOrDequeuedFromPool(true);
            }

            // Return the object we just created.
            return newObject;
        }
    }

    // Disables an object and returns it to the queue for later reuse.
    public void ReturnObject(GameObject gameObject)
    {
        // Find any component that we need to notify
        var notifiers = gameObject
                .GetComponents<IObjectPoolNotifier>();

        foreach (var notifier in notifiers)
        {
            // Let it know that it's returning to the pool
            notifier.OnEnqueuedToPool();
        }

        // Disable the object and make it a child of this one, so that
        // it doesn't clutter up the Hierarchy
        gameObject.SetActive(false);
        gameObject.transform.parent = this.transform;

        // Put the object into the inactive queue
        inactiveObjects.Enqueue(gameObject);

    }
}
```

This code won't compile yet, because the `PooledObject` class doesn't exist yet. We're about to add it.

In order for objects to be able to return to the pool that created them, they need to have a reference to them. To support this, we'll create a very simple script that has no logic, and stores a reference to the object pool.

Because this script doesn't really influence gameplay, there's no reason to include it in the Inspector. This is what the `hideFlags` property controls; by setting it to `HideInInspector` in the `GetObject` method, we're telling Unity to not display it. This is convenient for this use case, but be careful about using this feature, because it's easy to forget that a component exists if you can't see it. You might accidentally write a component that does some behavior that you can't understand because you don't realize that the component exists.

1. Create a new script called *PooledObject.cs*, and add the following code to it:

```
// A simple script that just exists to store a reference to an
// ObjectPool. Exists to be used by the ReturnToPool extension method.
public class PooledObject : MonoBehaviour
{
    public ObjectPool owner;
}
```

To simplify the process of returning a `GameObject` to an object pool, we'll *add* a method to `GameObject` that makes it very convenient. To do this, we add an extension method called `ReturnToPool`; once this code exists, you can call `ReturnToPool` on any `GameObject`, and it will return to the pool that created it.

2. Add the following code to *PooledObject.cs*:

```
// A class that adds a new method to the GameObject class: ReturnToPool.
public static class PooledGameObjectExtensions {

    // This method is an extension method (note the "this" parameter).
    // This means that it's a new method that's added to all instances
    // of the GameObject class; you call it like this:
    //     gameObject.ReturnToPool()

    // Returns an object to the object pool that it was created from
    public static void ReturnToPool(this GameObject gameObject) {
```

```
// Find the PooledObject component.
var pooledObject= gameObject.GetComponent<PooledObject>();

// Does it exist?
if (pooledObject == null) {
    // If it doesn't, it means that this object never came from
    // a pool.
    Debug.LogErrorFormat(gameObject,
        "Cannot return {0} to object pool, because it was not" +
                        "created from one.", gameObject);
    return;
}

// Tell the pool we came from that this object should be
// returned.
pooledObject.owner.ReturnObject(gameObject);
    }
}
```

We're now done implementing the system.

Testing it out

To test it out, we're going to create two scripts. One will make use of an object pool, and the other will exist to return itself (which really means whatever it's attached to) to the object pool after a delay. We'll start by making the object pool:

1. Create a new C# script called *ObjectPoolDemo.cs*, and add the following code:

```
// An example of using an object pool.
public class ObjectPoolDemo : MonoBehaviour
{
    // The object pool from which we'll be getting our objects
    [SerializeField]
    private ObjectPool pool;

    IEnumerator Start() {

        // Get and place an object from the pool every 0.1-0.5 seconds
        while (true) {

            // Get (or create, we don't care which) an object from pool
            var o = pool.GetObject();

            // Pick a point somewhere inside a sphere of radius 4
            var position = Random.insideUnitSphere * 4;

            // Place it
            o.transform.position = position;
```

```
            // Wait between 0.1 and 0.5 seconds and do it again
            var delay = Random.Range(0.1f, 0.5f);

            yield return new WaitForSeconds(delay);
        }
    }
}
```

This script uses an object pool to create objects and randomly place them in the scene after a short delay.

2. We'll now create the script that returns itself to the object pool after a short delay. Create a new C# script called *ReturnAfterDelay.cs,* and add the following code:

```
// An example of a script that works with an object pool. This object
// waits for one second, and then returns itself to the pool.
public class ReturnAfterDelay : MonoBehaviour, IObjectPoolNotifier
{
    // Our opportunity to do any setup we need to after we're either
    // created or removed from the pool
    public void OnCreatedOrDequeuedFromPool(bool created)
    {
        Debug.Log("Dequeued from object pool!");

        StartCoroutine(DoReturnAfterDelay());
    }

    // Called when we have been returned to the pool
    public void OnEnqueuedToPool()
    {
        Debug.Log("Enqueued to object pool!");
    }

    IEnumerator DoReturnAfterDelay() {
        // Wait for one second and then return to the pool
        yield return new WaitForSeconds(1.0f);

        // Return this object to the pool from whence it came
        gameObject.ReturnToPool();
    }

}
```

Note that this script doesn't call `Destroy`, but rather `ReturnToPool`. If it called `Destroy`, its memory would be freed.

We can now set up the scene to use these scripts. First, we'll create the object that we'll create instances of:

1. Create a new sphere by opening the GameObject menu and choosing 3D Object → Sphere.

2. Name the sphere "Pooled Object."

3. Drag the *ReturnAfterDelay.cs* script into the Inspector.

4. Drag the object into the Project tab to turn it into a prefab.

5. Delete the sphere from the scene.

Next, we'll create the object pool itself, and configure it to create and manage instances of the Pooled Object prefab:

1. Create a new, empty game object by opening the GameObject menu and choosing Create Empty.

2. Name the new object "Object Pool."

3. Select the object, and drag the *ObjectPool.cs* script into the Inspector.

4. Drag the Pooled Object prefab into its Prefab slot.

Finally, we'll create an object that asks the object pool to produce objects:

1. Create a new, empty game object by opening the GameObject menu and choosing Create Empty.

2. Name the new object "Object Pool Demo."

3. Drag the *ObjectPoolDemo.cs* script into the Inspector.

4. Drag the Object Pool object from the hierarchy into the Pool slot.

Play the game to test it out. Spheres will appear and then vanish. Initially, the Hierarchy will show new objects appearing, but after a while the number will stabilize, as there are usually enough objects in the pool to meet the demand for new objects (Figure 2-4). As objects return to the pool, they are disabled and temporarily made children of the object pool rather than being destroyed and having their memory freed.

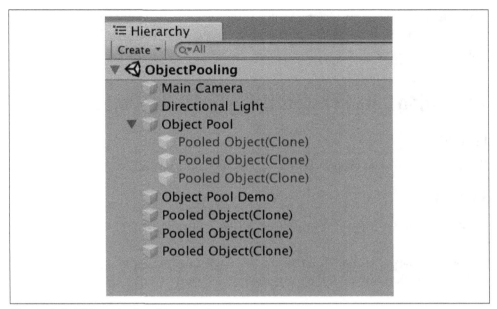

Figure 2-4. Objects in the object pool

Discussion

Instantiating a prefab means that Unity needs to allocate memory. On its own, this isn't a problem, but it turns into one when you consider the consequences of what happens when that memory is no longer needed. Unity uses a garbage collector to manage its memory, which means that any memory that is no longer being referred to by the rest of the system is periodically hunted down and freed. This process, *garbage collection*, is relatively performance intensive, and is something to avoid when you're building performance-intensive software like games. Additionally, allocating memory in the first place is not free of performance costs; it takes CPU resources to do it.

To avoid garbage collection, we should avoid allocating and freeing memory, and instead reuse memory as much as possible. An object pool, therefore, is a system for producing and managing the life cycle of objects that minimizes the need for allocating new objects. When an object is requested, the pool first checks to see if there are any objects that have already been allocated but are not currently being used in the scene. If there are, they're made active, removed from the pool of inactive objects, and returned. If—and only if—there are no inactive objects, a new object is created.

Rather than being destroyed completely via the Destroy method, objects are returned to the pool. To simplify things, this recipe adds an *extension method* on the Game Object class, which makes it as easy to return an object to the pool as it is to destroy it.

2.9 Storing Data in Assets Using ScriptableObject

Problem

You want to store data inside asset files that your scripts can access.

Solution

Create a subclass of the ScriptableObject class, and add the properties you want in there.

For example, let's create an asset that stores a color, and a script that uses that asset to set its renderer's color when the game starts. We'll start by creating the color-storing asset:

1. Create a new C# script called *ObjectColour.cs*, and add the following code to it:

```
// Create an entry in the Asset -> Create menu that makes it easy to
// create a new asset of this type
[CreateAssetMenu]

// Don't forget to change the parent class from 'MonoBehaviour' to
// 'ScriptableObject'!
public class ObjectColour : ScriptableObject
{
    public Color color;
}
```

The [CreateAssetMenu] attribute tells Unity to add a new entry in the Assets → Create menu, which lets you create a new asset file that stores an instance of the ScriptableObject subclass.

Because the object is stored on disk as an asset, it can be dragged and dropped into the Inspector of other objects across multiple scenes, just as you can with other assets, like models and textures.

 You can use any types of variables in a ScriptableObject that you can use in a MonoBehaviour subclass.

2. Open the Assets menu, and choose Create → Object Color. A new `ObjectColour` asset is created.

3. Select it, and go to the Inspector (Figure 2-5). You'll find the variables that it exposes, just as you do with `MonoBehaviours`.

4. Set the color in the Inspector.

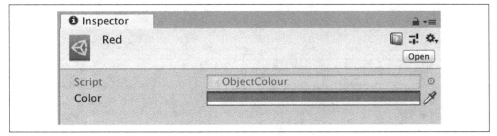

Figure 2-5. The Inspector for the scriptable `ObjectColour` asset

We'll now create a simple script that makes use of an `ObjectColour` asset. This script will take the color that's stored in the `ObjectColour` asset and use it to modify a renderer's material:

1. Create a new C# script called *SetColorOnStart.cs*, and add the following code to it:

```
public class SetColorOnStart : MonoBehaviour
{
    // The ScriptableObject that we'll draw data from
    [SerializeField] ObjectColour objectColour;

    private void Update()
    {
        // Don't try to use the ObjectColour if it hasn't been provided
        if (objectColour == null)
        {
            return;
        }

        GetComponent<Renderer>().material.color = objectColour.color;
    }
}
```

2. Create a cube by opening the GameObject menu and choosing 3D Object → Cube.

3. Drag the *SetColorOnStart.cs* script onto the cube.

4. Select the cube, and drag the `ObjectColour` asset you created earlier into the cube's Object Colour slot (Figure 2-6).

5. Run the game. The cube will change to the color stored in the asset.

Try creating multiple cubes that all use the same asset. They'll all use the same color.

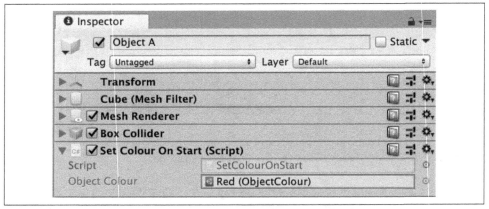

Figure 2-6. The Inspector for the object that uses the scriptable object

Discussion

You can use this technique to separate the data for an object from its logic, and reuse the data across multiple different objects in your game. This approach also makes it easier to quickly replace an entire set of data for an object—all you need to do is swap out the asset it uses.

CHAPTER 3

Input

Letting the player exert control over your game is, well, kind of important! It's a core tenet of interactive games. In this chapter, we'll look at some of the most common input requirements game developers have. Thankfully, Unity has a variety of input methods available, ranging from keyboard and mouse input to gamepad input to more sophisticated systems allowing for mouse pointer control. We'll touch on each of them here.

 You'll use both the *legacy* Input class, as well as Unity's new input system in this chapter. They both have their place in a modern Unity project.

3.1 Getting Simple Keyboard Input

Problem

You want to know when the user is pressing keys on a keyboard, with as few steps as possible.

Solution

Use the legacy Input class's GetKeyDown, GetKeyUp, and GetKey methods to find out what keys are being pressed:

```
if (Input.GetKeyDown(KeyCode.A))
{
    Debug.Log("The A key was pressed!");
}
```

```
if (Input.GetKey(KeyCode.A))
{
    Debug.Log("The A key is being held down!");
}

if (Input.GetKeyUp(KeyCode.A))
{
    Debug.Log("The A key was released!");
}

if (Input.anyKeyDown) {
    Debug.Log("A key was pressed!");
}
```

Discussion

Each of these methods responds at different times:

- GetKeyDown returns true when the key started being pressed on this frame.
- GetKeyUp returns true when the key was released on this frame.
- GetKey returns true if the key is currently being held down.

You can also use the anyKeyDown property to find out if any key at all is being pressed, which is useful for when you want to ask the player to "press any key to continue."

 The Input class is part of the legacy *Input Manager* system, which dates back to the earliest releases of Unity. Input is simple to work with and is available by default in new projects, but it has a number of limitations: it doesn't allow customizing the mapping of buttons to in-game actions, it isn't terribly easy to set up in-game actions, and you end up having to build a number of systems on top of it.

A better solution is the Unity Input System, which solves all of these problems, and is what we'll be working with for the remainder of this chapter.

3.2 Using the Unity Input System

Problem

You want to use the Unity Input System to get user input.

Solution

Install the Unity Input System from the Package Manager (Recipe 1.9) by following these steps:

1. Open the Package Manager window by choosing Window → Package Manager.

2. Change the Packages setting at the top left of the window from In Project to Unity Registry.

3. Scroll down to Input System in the list of packages, or search for Input System in the search field at the top right.

4. Select the Input System from the list, and click the Install button.

Unity will download and install the Input System package into your project. Unity may ask you if you want to update your project's settings to use the new Input System; select Yes, and it will restart the Editor.

Once the Input System has been installed, you can make use of it in your code.

For example, we could use the following to re-create what we did in Recipe 3.1, but using the Input System:

```
using UnityEngine.InputSystem;


if (Keyboard.current.aKey.wasPressedThisFrame) {
    Debug.Log($"The A key was pressed!");
}
if (Keyboard.current.aKey.isPressed) {
    Debug.Log($"The A key is being held down!");
}
if (Keyboard.current.aKey.wasReleasedThisFrame) {
    Debug.Log($"The A key was released!");
}

if (Keyboard.current.anyKey.wasPressedThisFrame) {
    Debug.Log("Some key was pressed!");
}
```

Discussion

While it's definitely possible to directly access specific buttons, like keys on the keyboard, there's a much better way to work with user input: Input Actions, which we'll cover in the next recipe.

One place where you *might* want to directly access buttons is for development purposes. For example, when you're in the early stages of development, or testing a version of your game, it can be convenient to have special *developer keys* that perform special tasks in your game, like making the player immune to damage. You typically don't expose these to the player, so there's no reason to do the extra work in setting them up as an Input Action, and instead just access the buttons directly.

3.3 Using Input Actions

Problem

You want to set up Input Actions, which map physical inputs to in-game actions.

Solution

In the Unity Input System, an *Input Action* is an in-game action that the player can perform in the game (for example, moving, jumping, turning) that's represented by one or more physical controls that the user can interact with (for example, the W key on a keyboard, or the left thumbstick on a gamepad).

Input Actions allow you to think in terms of the higher-level things that happen in your game, rather than having to think at the low level of pressing specific buttons. More importantly, because you can bind multiple controls to a single action, it makes it a lot easier to build a game that targets a variety of control schemes.

 Before following the steps in this recipe, make sure you've installed the Unity Input System in your project by following the steps in Recipe 3.2.

To demonstrate Input Actions, we'll start by creating a simple little scene that can be controlled by user input:

1. In a new empty scene, create a new cube by opening the GameObject menu and choosing 3D Object → Cube.

2. Select the newly created cube, and in the Inspector, click Add Component. Type **CubePlayer**, click "New script," and then click Create and Add.

3. Open the newly created file, *CubePlayer.cs*, and replace all of its contents with the following:

```
using UnityEngine.InputSystem;

public class CubePlayer : MonoBehaviour
{
    [SerializeField] float moveSpeed = 5;
    private Vector2 moveInput = Vector2.zero;

    public void Update() {
        var movement = new Vector3(moveInput.x, moveInput.y, 0)
            * moveSpeed
            * Time.deltaTime;
```

```
        transform.Translate(movement);
    }

    public void ChangeColour() {
        var color = Color.HSVToRGB(Random.value, 0.8f, 1f);
        GetComponent<Renderer>().material.color = color;
    }
}
```

4. Save the file, and return to Unity.

If you enter Play Mode, the cube won't do anything. We'll sort that
out next!

Now that we have a cube that's ready to respond to user input, we'll create an object
that receives user input and sends it to the cube:

1. Create a new empty game object by opening the GameObject menu and choosing
   Create Empty. Name the new object "Player Input."

2. Click the Add Component button, and choose Input → Player Input.

3. Click the picker (the circle icon) to the right of the Actions field, and choose
   DefaultInputActions.

DefaultInputActions is a predefined collection of Input Actions. One of these
predefined actions is "Move," which is bound to common movement-related controls
like the WASD keys on a keyboard, and the left thumbstick on a gamepad. We'll make
the cube move in response to that:

1. Add the following method to *CubePlayer.cs*:

```
public void OnMove(InputAction.CallbackContext context) {
    // Whenever anything happens with this action, get its current value
    // and store it.
    moveInput = context.ReadValue<Vector2>();
}
```

2. Save the file and return to Unity.

3. Next, we'll make this method get called by the input system whenever the Move
   action changes state. To begin, select the Player Input object.

4. In the Inspector for the Player Input component, set Behaviour to Invoke Unity
   Events.

5. A new section will appear at the bottom, labeled Events. Open Events → Player.

6. Click the + button attached to the Move event to add a new entry.

7. Drag and drop the Cube object into the object slot.

8. Change the function drop-down from No Function to CubePlayer → OnMove.

9. Press Play, and use the W, A, S, and D keys to move the cube around.

With this setup, the Player Input component will call the `OnMove` method on the cube's `CubePlayer` script. This method receives an `InputAction.CallbackContext` method that lets the code get information about what specific input was received. The Move action is defined as one that contains two-dimensional information (that is, left-to-right and forward-to-backward). In `OnMove`, we call `ReadValue<Vector2>` to fetch that data and store it in the `moveInput` variable. This variable is then used in `Update` to actually move the cube around.

 The reason that we do the actual movement in `Update` rather than in `OnMove` is because `OnMove` will only be called when the input *changes*. If you press the W key on the keyboard, `OnMove` will be called one time, and when you release the key, it will be called a second time. Because we want pressing W to mean *start* moving and not "move one time," we need to store information that persists across multiple frames.

If you have a gamepad, connect it to your computer, and move the left thumbstick. The cube will move. (You can use basically any recent controller available from a games store. Controllers for popular video game consoles, like the Xbox, PlayStation, or Switch, tend to give better results, since they're more commonly owned by players.)

Discussion

The default actions come with some generally useful actions already set up for *move*, *look*, and *shoot* (the three video game verbs!). If this is all your game needs, great! Otherwise, you can create your own.

Input Actions are stored in an asset in your project, so if you want to create new custom Input Actions, you'll need to create an asset to store them:

1. Select the Player Input game object, and go to the Inspector for the Player Input component attached to it.

2. Clear the Actions slot by clicking it and pressing the Backspace key.

3. Click the Create Actions button.

4. Unity will ask you where you want to save the new asset. Save it somewhere in the *Assets* folder.

Unity will open the newly created asset, and you're now looking at the list of actions.

You can also create a new Input Actions asset using the Assets → Create → Input Actions menu, but this creates a blank collection. Doing it via the Player Input component saves you having to set it all up again if all you want to do is *add* a new action to the default set.

The default actions are split into two different *input maps*: Player and UI.

Input maps represent different modes that a player can be in. For example, the default set has two: Player is for general gameplay, and UI is for interacting with the user interface. Having multiple input maps allow the game to interpret different controls to mean different actions; for example, when the input map is set to UI, the left thumbstick means "navigate the UI," rather than "move."

Let's look at the Player input map. There are three actions in it: Move, Look, and Shoot. Each action has a number of *bindings*, which are the connections to physical buttons that the player can interact with. For example, Move is bound to the left stick on a gamepad; the W, A, S, and D keys on a keyboard; the primary 2D axis of a VR controller; and the stick movement on a joystick.

Let's create a new action—it'll be a Button (i.e., we can get *is pressed* information from it), and we'll make it change the color of the cube:

1. In Actions, click the + button to create a new action. Name the new action "Change Colour."

   Note that the Action Type is set to Button. Leave it set to that. There are other kinds of actions; for example, the Move action is a Value and is configured to produce a 2D Vector for its output. (This is why `OnMove` in *PlayerCube.cs* uses `ReadValue<Vector2>`.) If Change Colour is a Button, it will fire events when the button is pressed and released.

2. The newly created action starts with a single unconfigured binding. Let's set that up. To begin, select the empty binding inside Change Colour.

3. Open the Path drop-down menu, and choose Keyboard → By Location of Key (US Layout) → C.

The Path drop-down lets you configure which specific physical control should be bound to the action. You can have as many bindings as you like; if you open the Move action, for example, you'll see a large number of bindings, each for different kinds of input devices.

The By Location of Key path allows you to specify a *location* on the keyboard. In this example, we'll set it to whatever key is at the position the C key has on a US-layout keyboard.

Keyboards and the Meaning of Keys

While keyboards were originally designed to make it possible to type text, games don't use keyboards like that for their controls. Game designers who are designing the controls for a PC game typically choose *where* on the keyboard they want the player's fingers to be, and work backward from that.

There's nothing inherently special about the letter W that means "forward," after all, but the W, A, S, and D keys happen to be laid out such that a right-handed player on a US QWERTY layout keyboard can comfortably rest their left hand over the keyboard and have easy access to a cluster of keys that happen to be a good layout for controlling forward, backward, and side-to-side movement. However, if you bound those actions to the *specific letters*, anyone *not* using that specific keyboard layout will be at a serious disadvantage. At the same time, it's fairly cumbersome to work in terms of "the third key on the second row of the keyboard, not counting the function keys."

By Location of Key works around this problem by *specifying* a key in the US layout, but *meaning* a location. When you bind the Change Colour action to the location of the C key, the action will be bound to whatever that key is on other keyboards.

It's worth noting that By Location of Key is generally best for buttons that you expect the player to use very frequently, and to develop a muscle memory for. If an action will be used less frequently, then it may make more sense to bind the action to a specific named key, and not its location, because it can make it a lot easier to locate the appropriate key by name for infrequent actions.

---

4. Set Use In Control Scheme to Keyboard & Mouse. This will make the binding active when the current control scheme is set to use these devices.

5. Next, we'll also bind the action to a button on a gamepad controller. In the actions list, click the + button for Change Colour, and choose Add Binding. A new empty binding will appear.

6. Select the new binding, and set its Path to Gamepad → Button South.

 Just about every modern game controller has four buttons on its righthand side, in a diamond shape. These are often referred to as the *face buttons*. The *South* button represents the bottom of this diamond. Different controllers refer to these buttons by different names: the south button is the X button on a PlayStation controller, the A button on an Xbox controller, and the B button on a Nintendo Switch controller. Much like how By Location of Key works for specifying the position of a control rather than the name of a control, specifying "south button" lets you refer to the position of the button on a controller.

7. Set the binding's Use In Control Scheme to Gamepad.

 If you don't have a gamepad available to use, try binding it to something else (for example, the left mouse button).

8. Click Save Asset, and close the window.

Now that we've created the new action and bound it to some controls, we'll make our cube able to respond to the action:

1. Add the following method to *CubePlayer.cs*:

```
public void OnChangeColour(InputAction.CallbackContext context) {
    // When this action is performed, change color.
    if (context.performed) {
        ChangeColour();
    }
}
```

2. Save the file, and return to Unity.

3. Select the Player Input object, and go to the Inspector for its Player Input component.

 When you created the new actions asset earlier, the Input Actions field was set to the new asset. You can change which actions asset the component is using by dragging and dropping a replacement asset into the Input Actions field.

4. Open the Events section, and choose Player → Change Colour.

5. Click the + button to add a new receiver.

6. Drag and drop the Cube object into the object field, and change the function to CubePlayer → OnChangeColour.

7. While you're here, perform the same steps you did earlier for connecting the Move action to the CubePlayer's OnMove method; the connection will have been lost when you changed which actions asset the component uses.

Enter Play Mode, and press the C key on the keyboard or the south gamepad button (or any other control you've bound to the Change Colour action). The cube will change color.

3.4 Locking and Hiding the Mouse Cursor

Problem

You want to make use of mouse movement in your game, but you don't want a cursor to be shown onscreen.

Solution

Set the Cursor.lockState property to either CursorLockMode.Locked or CursorLock Mode.Confined to prevent the mouse cursor from leaving your game, and set Cursor.visible to false to make the cursor invisible:

```
// Lock the cursor to the middle of the screen or window.
Cursor.lockState = CursorLockMode.Locked;

// Prevent the cursor from leaving the window.
Cursor.lockState = CursorLockMode.Confined;

// Don't restrict the mouse cursor at all.
Cursor.lockState = CursorLockMode.None;

// Hide the mouse cursor.
Cursor.visible = false;
```

Discussion

In the editor, you can press the Escape key to re-enable the mouse cursor and free it from cursor jail.

3.5 Responding to Mouseover and Click Events

Problem

You want to detect when users move a mouse over an object, and when they click it.

Solution

To detect this, you can use the Event System, which is capable of tracking the position of a cursor on the screen and detecting when it's over an object in the scene. To begin working with the Event System, create an object with an EventSystem component attached, via the GameObject menu:

1. Open the GameObject menu, and select UI → EventSystem. A new EventSystem object will be created.

 If you create a Canvas, you'll also create an EventSystem at the same time, because the UI system relies on the same techniques as we're using in this recipe.

2. Next, create a *raycaster* component that the Event System will use to determine what objects are under the cursor. Raycasters trace lines from the camera position through the cursor position and into the scene to detect what a ray hits. If the ray hits a collider, then the Event System dispatches events to the target object.

3. Select the main Camera object.

4. Open the Component menu, and choose Event → Physics Raycaster. (You can also add it by clicking the Add Component button at the bottom of the Inspector, and choosing Event → Physics Raycaster.)

> In this recipe, we use 3D objects by utilizing the 3D physics system. For a 2D game, the same techniques apply, but you'll add a Physics 2D Raycaster to your camera instead of a Physics Raycaster. The Physics Raycaster detects only 3D colliders, and the Physics 2D Raycaster detects only 2D colliders. If you're using both collider types in your scene, both of them can be on your camera at the same time.

5. Next, we'll write a script that detects when a cursor moves over the object that the script is attached to and changes the color of its renderer. Create a new C# script called *ObjectMouseInteraction.cs*.

6. Add the following `using` directive to the top of the class:

```
using UnityEngine.EventSystems;
```

> After creating the Event System, if you've configured your project to use the Unity Input System (see Recipe 3.2), it will warn you that you will need to update the component to one that works with the Input System. To do this, click Replace with InputSystemUIModule.

To access the classes and interfaces we need for working with the pointer, we need to access the `UnityEngine.EventSystems` namespace. Once that's done, we make our class conform to certain interfaces that mark the `MonoBehaviour` as something that needs to know about input events.

7. Delete the `ObjectMouseInteraction` class from the code, and replace it with the following code:

```
public class ObjectMouseInteraction :
    MonoBehaviour,
    IPointerEnterHandler,    // Handles mouse cursor entering object
    IPointerExitHandler,     // Handles mouse cursor exiting object
    IPointerUpHandler,       // Handles mouse button lifting up on this
                             // object
    IPointerDownHandler,     // Handles mouse button being pressed on this
                             // object
    IPointerClickHandler     // Handles when mouse is pressed and
                             // released on this object
{

}
```

By implementing these interfaces, Unity will know to contact this script when input events happen to the attached object.

In this recipe, we're using more interfaces than you'd probably use in a real situation (for example, we're handling pointer up and down *and* clicks), but it serves as a good demonstration. These aren't the only events you can register to receive method calls for; check the Unity documentation (*https://oreil.ly/deI0V*) for more.

8. Next, we'll add code that makes it simpler to modify the color of the object. Add the following variable and method to the `ObjectMouseInteraction` class:

```
Material material;

void Start() {
    material = GetComponent<Renderer>().material;
}
```

9. Finally, we'll add the methods that will be called when the cursor moves over or clicks the object. Add the following methods to the `ObjectMouseInteraction` class:

```
public void OnPointerClick(PointerEventData eventData)
{
    Debug.LogFormat("{0} clicked!", gameObject.name);
}
```

```
public void OnPointerDown(PointerEventData eventData)
{
    Debug.LogFormat("{0} pointer down!", gameObject.name);

    material.color = Color.green;

}

public void OnPointerEnter(PointerEventData eventData)
{
    Debug.LogFormat("{0} pointer enter!", gameObject.name);

    material.color = Color.yellow;
}

public void OnPointerExit(PointerEventData eventData)
{
    Debug.LogFormat("{0} pointer exit!", gameObject.name);

    material.color = Color.white;
}

public void OnPointerUp(PointerEventData eventData)
{
    Debug.LogFormat("{0} pointer up!", gameObject.name);

    material.color = Color.yellow;
}
```

We're now done with the code, and can put it to use. We'll create a cube that has this component attached; it will change its color when the mouse interacts with it:

1. Open the GameObject menu, and choose 3D Object → Cube.

2. Place the new cube somewhere in front of the camera.

3. Drag the *ObjectMouseInteraction.cs* script onto the cube.

Play the game. As the mouse moves over it or clicks it, the cube changes color.

Discussion

Remember that the camera's Physics Raycaster component can only "see" colliders. Objects without colliders won't receive these events. You can also debug the Event System by looking at the Event System object's Inspector. During play, it displays information about where the cursor is and what object currently receives a raycast (Figure 3-1).

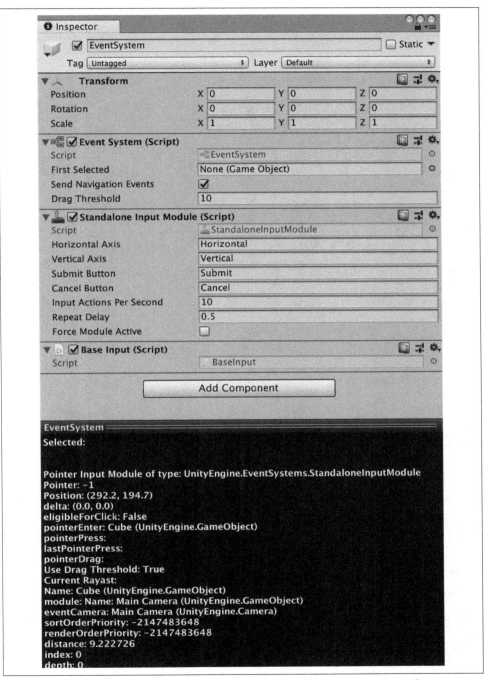

Figure 3-1. The debugging information in the Inspector of an Event System object

CHAPTER 4

Mathematics

Mathematics is an unavoidable part of using a spatial development tool like Unity. Like it or loathe it, you need to use it, acknowledge it, and even downright embrace it to get anything done. Fortunately, you can gloss over or pretend a lot of it isn't there, but it's always there, supporting you, and lurking beneath.

This chapter explores some of the most common math-related problems you'll encounter when developing using Unity.

This isn't all the math you'll need for game, or Unity, development; far from it! But it's enough math to help out, and get you started. We've done our best to structure it around the problems you might want to solve using the math, rather than the math itself.

Have you ever wondered what a vector is? Or how to use a matrix? What about a quaternion? We'll cover them here, while also touching on common math problems in Unity development, like calculating the angles and distances to something else in your Unity-based project.

Nothing in this chapter is unique or specific to development with Unity. We do cover things from a Unity-centric perspective when we talk about code, but everything here is just plain old math for spatial or game development.

Read on for just enough math for Unity development.

We can't more highly recommend Paco Nathan's *Just Enough Math* video series, also from O'Reilly. Check it out if you want to learn even more math.

4.1 Storing Coordinates of Varying Dimensions Using Vectors

Problem

Unity development involves a lot of coordinates of varying dimensions:

- One-dimensional coordinates, such as 1 or –9
- Two-dimensional coordinates, such as 8, 3 or –1, 4
- Three-dimensional coordinates, such as 3, 1, –3 or –7, 6, 1

Realistically, when you're building something in Unity, as long as you're keeping track of what you need to keep track of, it often doesn't matter how you do it. However, one common, useful way of keeping track of coordinates is vectors.

Vectors are a set of coordinates of varying dimensions. Thus, our problem here is: how do I use vectors and Unity, and what can I use them for?

Solution

To provide a solution here, we're going to have to unpack the problem a little. We admit, we wrote a deliberately broad problem statement, but that's so we can show you everything you need to know about vectors without having to have one tiny recipe for each manipulation or action you might want to make with a vector.

You'll often see quite specific meanings applied to vectors: in video games it's usually coordinates in geometry, but there's absolutely no reason you can't store anything you want in them. They're just a data structure.

First up, in Unity, you can define a `Vector2`: one with two dimensions, usually an *x* and a *y*. A `Vector2` is typically used to represent a point in 2D space in Unity.

You can define a `Vector2` with two dimensions:

```
Vector2 direction = new Vector2(0.0f, 2.0f);
```

Or use one of Unity's built-in vectors:

```
var up    = Vector2.up;    // ( 0,  1)
var down  = Vector2.down;  // ( 0, -1)
var left  = Vector2.left;  // (-1,  0)
var right = Vector2.right; // ( 1,  0)
var one   = Vector2.one;   // ( 1,  1)
var zero  = Vector2.zero;  // ( 0,  0)
```

Unity also has a type called `Vector3`, which is a vector with three dimensions. There are several predefined vectors available from the `Vector3` class:

```
Vector3 point = new Vector3(1.0f, 2f, 3.5f);

var up      = Vector3.up;      // ( 0,  1,  0)
var down    = Vector3.down;    // ( 0, -1,  0)
var left    = Vector3.left;    // (-1,  0,  0)
var right   = Vector3.right;   // ( 1,  0,  0)
var forward = Vector3.forward; // ( 0,  0,  1)
var back    = Vector3.back;    // ( 0,  0, -1)
var one     = Vector3.one;     // ( 1,  1,  1)
var zero    = Vector3.zero;    // ( 0,  0,  0)
```

 You can learn more about `Vector2` (*https://oreil.ly/tFrZH*) and `Vector3` (*https://oreil.ly/NCyb4*) in Unity's API documentation.

Every `Transform` component in Unity has local direction vectors defined, which are relative to their current rotation. For example, an object's local forward direction can be accessed as:

```
var myForward = transform.forward;
```

Naturally, you can perform basic arithmetic with vectors. Vectors can be added together:

```
var v1 = new Vector3(1f, 2f, 3f);
var v2 = new Vector3(0f, 1f, 6f);

var v3 = v1 + v2; // (1, 3, 9)
```

and subtracted from each other:

```
var v4 = v2 - v1; // (-1, -1, 3)
```

You can also get the *magnitude* of a vector. Also known as the *length* of the vector, the vector's magnitude is the straight-line distance from the origin (0, 0, 0) to the vector. The magnitude of a vector is the square root of the sums of the squares of the components. For example, the magnitude of the vector (0, 2, 0) is 2; the magnitude of the vector (0, 1, 1) is approximately 1.41 (that is, the square root of 2):

```
var forwardMagnitude = Vector3.forward.magnitude; // = 1

var vectorMagnitude =
    new Vector3(2f, 5f, 3f).magnitude; // ~= 6.16
```

 A vector whose magnitude is 1 is called a *unit vector*.

The magnitude can then be used to make other calculations. For example, to calculate the distance between two vectors, you can subtract one vector from another, and calculate the magnitude of the result:

```
var point1 = new Vector3(5f, 1f, 0f);
var point2 = new Vector3(7f, 0f, 2f);

var distance = (point2 - point1).magnitude; // = 3
```

The built-in method `Distance` performs the same calculation for you:

```
Vector3.Distance(point1, point2);
```

Calculating the magnitude of a vector requires a square root. However, there are cases where you don't need the actual value of a vector's magnitude, and just want to compare two lengths. In these cases, you can skip the square root, and work with the square of the magnitude. Doing this is a bit faster, and we care quite a lot about fast calculations…especially in game development.

To get this value, use the `sqrMagnitude` property:

```
var distanceSquared = (point2 - point1).sqrMagnitude; // = 9
```

Lots of operations work best on vectors that have a magnitude of 1. A vector with a magnitude of 1 is also called a *unit* vector, because its magnitude is a single unit (that is, one). You can take a vector and produce a new one that has the same direction but with a magnitude of 1 by dividing it by its own magnitude. This is called *normalizing* a vector:

```
var bigVector = new Vector3(4, 7, 9); // magnitude = 12.08
var unitVector =
    bigVector / bigVector.magnitude; // magnitude = 1
```

This is a common operation, so you can directly access a normalized version of a vector by using the *normalized* property:

```
var unitVector2 = bigVector.normalized;
```

Vectors can also be scaled. When you multiply a vector by a single number (a *scalar*), the result is a vector in which every component of the source is multiplied by that number:

```
var v1 = Vector3.one * 4; // = (4, 4, 4)
```

You can also perform component-wise scaling by using the `Scale` method. This method takes two vectors and produces a third vector in which each component of the first is multiplied by the corresponding component of the second—that is, given two vectors A and B, the result of `A.Scale(B)` is `(A.x * B.x, A.y * B.y, A.z * B.z)`:

```
v1.Scale(new Vector3(3f, 1f, 0f)); // = (12f, 4f, 0f)
```

You can also get the *dot product* of two vectors, which tells you the difference between the directions they are pointing.

The dot product is defined as the sum of the products of the two vectors. That is, given two three-dimensional vectors A and B, `A•B = sum(A.x * B.x, A.y * B.y, A.z * B.z)`.

You can use the dot product to determine the similarity of two vectors. The dot product between two vectors aiming in the same direction is 1:

```
var parallel = Vector3.Dot(Vector3.left, Vector3.left); // 1
```

The dot product between two vectors aiming in the opposite directions is –1:

```
var opposite = Vector3.Dot(Vector3.left, Vector3.right); // -1
```

And the dot product between two vectors at right angles to each other is 0:

```
var orthogonal = Vector3.Dot(Vector3.up, Vector3.forward); // 0
```

As a happy side effect, the dot product between two vectors is also the cosine of the angle between the two vectors. This means that, given the dot product between two vectors, you can calculate the angle between the vectors by taking its arc cosine:

```
var orthoAngle = Mathf.Acos(orthogonal);
var orthoAngleDegrees = orthoAngle * Mathf.Rad2Deg; // = 90
```

 The `Mathf.Acos` method returns a value measured in radians. To convert it to degrees, you can multiply it by the `Mathf.Rad2Deg` constant.

The dot product is a great way to tell if an object is in front of or behind another.

To tell if one object is in front of another, we first need to decide what "in front of" means. In Unity, the local *z*-axis represents the forward-facing direction, and you can access it through the `forward` property on an object's `Transform`.

We can produce a vector representing the direction from the first object to the second by subtracting the position of the second from the position of the first. We can then take the dot product of that vector against the forward direction of the first object.

We can now use what we know about the dot product to figure out if the second object is in front of the first. Recall that the dot product of two vectors aiming in the same direction is 1. If the second object is directly in front of the first, then the direction to that object will be identical, which means that the dot product of the two vectors will be 1. If it's 0, then the object is at a right angle to the forward direction. If it's –1, then it's directly behind the object, because it's in the exact opposite direction of forward:

```
var directionToOtherObject =
    someOtherObjectPosition - transform.position;
var differenceFromMyForwardDirection =
    Vector3.Dot(transform.forward, directionToOtherObject);

if (differenceFromMyForwardDirection > 0) {
    // The object is in front of us
} else if (differenceFromMyForwardDirection < 0) {
    // The object is behind us
} else {
    // The object neither before or behind us; it's at a perfect right
    // angle to our forward direction.
}
```

The cross product, a third vector orthogonal to (at right angles to) two input vectors, is also available:

```
var up = Vector3.Cross(Vector3.forward, Vector3.right);
```

 The cross product is only defined for three-dimensional vectors.

You can also get a new vector from two vectors, moving from one to the other at a certain magnitude. This is particularly useful to prevent overshooting. Here we move from (0, 0, 0) to (1, 1, 1), without moving any further than 0.5 units:

```
var moved =
    Vector3.MoveTowards(Vector3.zero, Vector3.one, 0.5f);
// = (0.3, 0.3, 0.3) (a vector that has a magnitude of 0.5)
```

Or reflect off a plane, defined by a normal:

```
var v =
    Vector3.Reflect(new Vector3(0.5f, -1f, 0f), Vector3.up);
// = (0.5, 1, 0)
```

You can also *linearly interpolate*, or *lerp*, between two input vectors, given a number between 0 and 1. If you provide 0, you'll get the first vector; if you provide 1, you'll get the second; and if you provide 0.5, you'll get somewhere right in the middle of the two:

```
var lerped = Vector3.Lerp(Vector3.zero, Vector3.one, 0.65f);
// = (0.65, 0.65, 0.65)
```

If you specify a number outside the range of 0 to 1, lerp will clamp it to between 0 and 1. You can prevent this by using LerpUnclamped:

```
var unclamped =
    Vector3.LerpUnclamped(Vector3.zero, Vector3.right, 2.0f);
// = (2, 0, 0)
```

Discussion

This is just a taste of using vectors in Unity. The mathematical operations that Unity provides for you to perform on a vector can simplify a lot of things. You can use the dot product, for example, to tell if a point is in front of or behind a player character, or to create a radar to figure out where enemies are.

Vectors also make complex operations, like scaling or rotating something, very straightforward. Instead of having to calculate each object and its relation to the others manually, you can just use vector math.

Basically, vectors let you address geometry-related issues with significantly cleaner code than you would otherwise need. They're wonderful mathematical tools in your game development toolkit!

4.2 Rotating in 3D Space

Problem

You want to rotate things in 3D space.

Solution

To rotate in 3D space, you'll need to work with *quaternions*, which are mathematical structures that are very useful for representing rotations in 3D space. A quaternion can represent a rotation around any axis by any angle.

Quaternions can be a tricky beast, since—in pure math terms—they're four-dimensional numbers. For the purposes of game development, though, all they are is a rotation, and it doesn't matter if you don't quite understand exactly *why* a quaternion works.

For example, you can use a quaternion to define a rotation that rotates around 90 degrees on the *x*-axis:

```
var rotation = Quaternion.Euler(90, 0, 0);
```

And then use this to rotate a point around the origin:

```
var input = new Vector3(0, 0, 1);

var result = rotation * input;
// = (0, -1, 0)
```

There is an identity quaternion, which represents no rotation at all:

```
var identity = Quaternion.identity;
```

You can *interpolate*—that is, blend—between two rotations using the `Slerp` method, which smoothly moves between rotations such that the change in angle is constant at every step. This is better than a linear interpolation of angles, in which the angles change at a nonconstant rate:

```
var rotationX = Quaternion.Euler(90, 0, 0);

var halfwayRotated =
    Quaternion.Slerp(identity, rotationX, 0.5f);
```

`Slerp` is short for *spherical linear interpolation*.

You can also combine quaternions. For example, to rotate something around the *y*-axis, and then around the *x*-axis, you multiply them (they're applied in the reverse order):

```
var combinedRotation =
    Quaternion.Euler(90, 0, 0) * // rotate around x
    Quaternion.Euler(0, 90, 0);  // rotate around y
```

This combination is not commutative: the order of multiplication matters! Rotating by *x* and then by *y* is not the same thing as rotating by *y* and then by *x*.

Discussion

Another method of representing rotations in 3D space is with *Euler angles*—that is, rotations around the *x*-, *y*-, and *z*-axes, stored separately. Euler angles are easy to understand, and it's common to use them when expressing rotations in code.

However, this approach is prone to a problem called *gimbal lock*, which occurs when an object is rotated such that two of its rotational axes are parallel. When this happens, the object loses a degree of freedom. This problem doesn't exist in quaternions, which can always by rotated in any direction from any other orientation.

An alternative method for avoiding gimbal lock is to use a matrix that represents a rotation (see Recipe 4.3). However, a 4×4 rotation matrix is 16 numbers, while a quaternion is just 4, which means quaternions take up less space than matrices for the same result.

4.3 Performing Transformations in 3D Space with Matrices

Problem

You want to represent an entire set of transformations—that is, movement, rotation, and scaling—in a single structure.

Solution

You can use a *matrix* to represent an entire transform. A matrix is just a grid of numbers (Equation 4-1):

```
var matrix = new Matrix4x4();
```

Equation 4-1. A 4×4 matrix

$$\begin{bmatrix} 1 & 0 & 0 & 0 \\ 0 & 1 & 0 & 0 \\ 0 & 0 & 1 & 0 \\ 5 & 0 & 0 & 1 \end{bmatrix}$$

You can set and get values at each location in the grid:

```
var m00 = matrix[0, 0];

matrix[0, 1] = 2f;
```

You can multiply a matrix with a vector to produce a new vector. Depending on the values inside the matrix, this has the result of moving, scaling, and rotating the original vector. You can also perform more complex operations, like shearing or applying perspective projections.

You can multiply two matrices together to produce a third matrix. When you multiply this new matrix with a vector, the result is the same as if you'd separately multiplied each of the original matrices with the vector in sequence.

Computer graphics, and therefore game development, typically use 4×4 matrices because they can be used to perform a wide range of common transformations.

Now we'll create a matrix that moves (translates) a vector by 5 units, on the x-axis. First, we'll define a new matrix, using four Vector4s (four-dimensional vectors):

```
var translationMatrix = new Matrix4x4(
    new Vector4(1, 0, 0, 5),
    new Vector4(0, 1, 0, 0),
    new Vector4(0, 0, 1, 0),
    new Vector4(1, 0, 0, 1)
);
```

Each of the Vector4s that we use to create a matrix represents a column, not a row.

The matrix that this code creates is shown in Equation 4-1.

When we multiply a three-dimensional vector by a matrix, we add 1 to the end of the vector, forming a four-dimensional vector. The additional component is commonly referred to as the w component.

Multiplying this matrix by a four-dimensional vector, V, gives the following result:

```
1*Vx  +  0*Vy  +  0*Vz  +  5*Vw = resultX
0*Vx  +  1*Vy  +  0*Vz  +  0*Vw = resultY
0*Vx  +  0*Vy  +  1*Vz  +  0*Vw = resultZ
0*Vx  +  0*Vy  +  0*Vz  +  1*Vw = resultW
```

For example, to multiply the point (0, 1, 2) (a `Vector3`) with this matrix:

1. We first add our `w` component:

```
Vx = 0, Vy = 1, Vz = 2, Vw = 1

1*0  +  0*1  +  0*2  +  5*1 = 5
0*0  +  1*1  +  0*2  +  0*1 = 1
0*0  +  0*1  +  1*2  +  0*1 = 2
0*0  +  0*1  +  0*2  +  1*1 = 1
```

2. Then we discard the fourth component, leaving our result. Our final result is therefore the vector (5, 1, 2).

Rather than making us do all this work ourselves, though, Unity provides a `Multiply Point` method as part of the `Matrix4x4` type:

```
var input = new Vector3(0, 1, 2);

var result = translationMatrix.MultiplyPoint(input);
// = (5, 1, 2)
```

You might be wondering why the matrix has the fourth row at all, since it just means we need to add and remove a useless fourth component to our vectors. It's there to provide for operations like perspective projections. If you're only doing transformations like translations, rotations, and scales, you can get away with only using part of the matrix, and can use `Matrix4x4`'s `MultiplyPoint4x3` function instead. It's a bit faster, but can be used only for translations, rotations, and scaling, and not for any of the other tasks.

Unity also provides helper methods to translate points using a matrix:

```
var input = new Vector3(0, 1, 2);

var translationMatrix = Matrix4x4.Translate(new Vector3(5, 1, -2));

var result = translationMatrix.MultiplyPoint(input);
// = (5, 2, 0)
```

You can also rotate a point around the origin using matrices and quaternions:

```
var rotate90DegreesAroundX = Quaternion.Euler(90, 0, 0);

var rotationMatrix = Matrix4x4.Rotate(rotate90DegreesAroundX);

var input = new Vector3(0, 0, 1);

var result = rotationMatrix.MultiplyPoint(input);
```

In this case, the point has moved from in front of the origin to below it, resulting in the point (0, –1, 0).

If your vector represents a direction, and you want to use a matrix to rotate the vector, you can use `MultiplyVector`. This method uses only the parts of the matrices that are necessary to do a rotation, so it's a bit faster:

```
result = rotationMatrix.MultiplyVector(input);
// = (0, -1, 0) - the same result.
```

You can also use a matrix scale a point away from the origin:

```
var scale2x2x2 = Matrix4x4.Scale(new Vector3(2f, 2f, 2f));

var input = new Vector3(1f, 2f, 3f);

var result = scale2x2x2.MultiplyPoint3x4(input);
// = (2, 4, 6)
```

Multiplying matrices together results in a new matrix that, when multiplied with a vector, produces the same result as if you'd multiplied the vector by each of the original matrices in order. In other words, if you think of a matrix as an instruction to modify a point, you can combine multiple matrices into a single step.

When we combine matrices like this, we call it *concatenating* the matrices.

In this example, we concatenate matrices:

```
var translation = Matrix4x4.Translate(new Vector3(5, 0, 0));
var rotation = Matrix4x4.Rotate(Quaternion.Euler(90, 0, 0));
var scale = Matrix4x4.Scale(new Vector3(1, 5, 1));

var combined = translation * rotation * scale;

var input = new Vector3(1, 1, 1);
var result = combined.MultiplyPoint(input);
Debug.Log(result);
// = (6, 1, 5)
```

As with quaternions, the order of multiplication matters! Matrix multiplication is not *commutative*, while multiplying regular numbers is. For example, 2 * 5 is the same calculation as 5 * 2: both calculations result in the number 10.

However, moving an object and then rotating it doesn't produce the same result as rotating an object and then moving it. Likewise, combining a matrix that translates a point with one that rotates a point won't have the same result if you combine them in the reverse order.

Combining matrices with multiplication will apply them in reverse order of multiplication. Given a point P, and matrices A, B, and C:

```
P * (A * B * C) == (A * (B * (C * P)))
```

you can create a combined translate-rotate-scale matrix using the `Matrix4x4.TRS` method:

```
var transformMatrix = Matrix4x4.TRS(
    new Vector3(5, 0, 0),
    Quaternion.Euler(90, 0, 0),
    new Vector3(1, 5, 1)
);
```

This new matrix will scale, rotate, and then translate any point you apply it to.

You can also get a matrix that converts a point in the component's position in local space to world space, which means taking the local position and applying the local translation, rotation, and scaling from this object as well as those of all its parents:

```
var localToWorld = this.transform.localToWorldMatrix;
```

You can also get the matrix that does the reverse—that is, it converts from world space to local space:

```
var worldToLocal = this.transform.worldToLocalMatrix;
```

Phew. That's a lot of things you can do with matrices!

Discussion

Internally, Unity uses matrices to represent transforms. For simplicity, you spend most of your time directly accessing the position, rotation, and scale. However, knowing how things work under the hood is always a good thing.

4.4 Working with Angles

Problem

You want to work with the angles between vectors.

Solution

In Unity, most rotations that are represented as Euler angles are given as degrees.

We can rotate things using degrees, using the `Transform` class's `Rotate` method:

```
// Rotate 90 degrees - one quarter circle - around the X axis
transform.Rotate(90, 0, 0);
```

 There are 360 *degrees* in a circle; there are 2π *radians* in a circle. They're just different units of measurements for angles.

Degrees are much more familiar to most people, but radians are often easier to calculate with. This is why parts of Unity, particularly those related to math, expect radians. There are 2π radians in a circle:

```
// The sine of pi radians (one half-circle) is zero
Mathf.Sin(Mathf.PI);  // = 0
```

You can convert from radians to degrees, and back again, like so:

```
// Converting 90 degrees to radians
var radians = 90 * Mathf.Deg2Rad; // ~= 1.57 (π / 2)

// Converting 2π radians to degrees
var degrees = 2 * Mathf.PI * Mathf.Rad2Deg; // = 360
```

Discussion

The dot product of two unit vectors is equal to the *cosine* of the angle between them. If you have the cosine of a degree, you can get the original degree by taking the *arc cosine* of it. This means that you can find the angle between two vectors like this:

```
var angle = Mathf.Acos(Vector3.Dot(Vector3.up, Vector3.left));
```

The result of this is π radians; if you want to show it to the user, you should convert it to degrees first. There are 2π radians in a circle, while there are 360 degrees in a circle; as a result, to convert a number from radians to degrees, you multiply it by 180/π. For example, π/2 radians in degrees = (π/2) * (180/π) = 90. Converting from degrees to radians works in reverse: you multiply it by π/180. For example, 45 degrees in radians is 45 * (π/180) = π/4.

You can simplify this in your code by using the `Mathf.Deg2Rad` and `Mathf.Rad2Deg` constants. If you multiply an angle expressed in radians by `Mathf.Rad2Deg`, you'll get the result in degrees; if you multiply an angle expressed in degrees by `Mathf.Deg2Rad`, you'll get the result in radians.

4.5 Finding the Distance to a Target

Problem

You want to check to see if an object is within a certain range of another.

Solution

You'll need to create and add a script to the object that needs to know when the other object is in range of it:

1. Create a new C# script called *RangeChecker.cs*, and add the following code to it:

```csharp
public class RangeChecker : MonoBehaviour {

    // The object we want to check the distance to
    [SerializeField] Transform target;

    // If the target is within this many units of us, it's in range
    [SerializeField] float range = 5;

    // Remembers if the target was in range on the previous frame.
    private bool targetWasInRange = false;

    void Update () {

        // Calculate the distance between the objects
        var distance = (target.position - transform.position).magnitude;

        if (distance <= range && targetWasInRange == false) {
            // If the object is now in range, and wasn't before, log it
            Debug.LogFormat("Target {0} entered range!", target.name);

            // Remember that it's in range for next frame
            targetWasInRange = true;

        } else if (distance > range && targetWasInRange == true) {
            // If the object is not in range, but was before, log it
            Debug.LogFormat("Target {0} exited range!", target.name);

            // Remember that it's no longer in range for next frame
            targetWasInRange = false;
        }

    }
}
```

2. Attach this script to any object, and attach any other object to the script's Target field, and the script will detect when the target enters and exits the specified range.

Discussion

If you combine this recipe with Recipe 4.6, you can pretty easily put together a behavior in which an object can only "see" nearby objects that are in front of it. A more sophisticated version of this script can be seen in Recipe 10.1.

4.6 Finding the Angle to a Target

Problem

You want to find the angle between two objects.

Solution

You'll need to create and add a script to the object that needs to know the angle between it and another object:

1. Create a new C# script called *AngleChecker.cs*, and add the following code to it:

```
public class AngleChecker : MonoBehaviour {

    // The object we want to find the angle to
    [SerializeField] Transform target;

    void Update () {

        // Get the normalized direction to the target
        var directionToTarget =
            (target.position - transform.position).normalized;

        // Take the dot product between that direction and our forward
        // direction
        var dotProduct = Vector3.Dot(transform.forward,
                                     directionToTarget);

        // Get the angle
        var angle = Mathf.Acos(dotProduct);
```

```
// Log the angle, limiting it to 1 decimal place
Debug.LogFormat(
    "The angle between my forward direction and {0} is {1:F1}°",
    target.name, angle * Mathf.Rad2Deg
);

    }
}
```

2. Attach this script to any object, and attach any other object to the script's Target field, and the script will log the angle, in degrees, between the object's forward direction and the target object.

Discussion

The concept of "angle between two objects" depends on you choosing at least one direction. You can't get the angle between two points in space, because there's an infinite number of possible angles between them. Instead, you need to pick a direction relative to the first object, and compare that with the direction to the second.

CHAPTER 5

2D Graphics

Unity is often best known for its 3D features, but it's just as capable for working with 2D graphics. In this chapter, we'll look at what you'll need to know to put together a game designed for a flat perspective.

None of the concepts covered in this chapter are restricted to 2D projects, we're just approaching them from a 2D perspective. Recipes in this chapter revolve around concepts related to 2D graphics, such as sprites, and collisions between sprites, particle effects, and sprite sorting.

5.1 Importing Images as Sprites

Problem

You want to import 2D image files into your project as texture assets, and use them as sprites.

 Sprites are 2D graphical objects. The term *sprite* is effectively used as shorthand for any 2D graphical object. To learn more about the etymology of the term, check out the Wikipedia article on sprites (*https://oreil.ly/d3Sl-*).

Solution

To import images as sprites:

1. Drag and drop the images into your project.
2. Select the images and set the Texture Type to Sprite (2D and UI) (Figure 5-1).
3. Click Apply.
4. You can now use this image as a sprite.

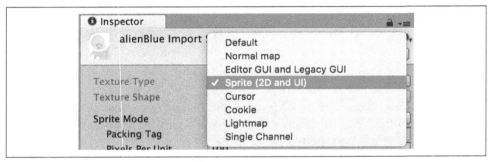

Figure 5-1. Setting the texture type for a sprite

Discussion

If your project was created with Unity's 2D template, incoming sprites will automatically be set up this way. Otherwise, images are imported as textures, for use in materials for 3D models.

You can change your project to behave this way by going to Edit → Project Settings → Editor and setting Default Behavior Mode to 2D (Figure 5-2). This makes all new textures default to sprites. It will also make any new scenes you create have a different set of initial objects—they won't have a light or skybox.

Figure 5-2. Setting the default mode for a project to 2D

5.2 Adding a Sprite to the Scene

Problem

You want to add a sprite to the scene.

Solution

To add a sprite to a scene:

1. First, ensure that your image is configured to be a sprite (Figure 5-1).
2. Drag and drop it into your scene.

When you do, Unity will create a game object for you with the name of the sprite, add a SpriteRenderer component to it, and make the SpriteRenderer display the sprite.

Discussion

The Pixels Per Unit value controls the relationship between the size of the source image, in pixels, and the size of the sprite in the scene. If a sprite is 1 pixel per unit, then each pixel will be 1 unit in width and height; if a sprite is 100 pixels per unit, then each pixel will be 1/100 of a unit in width and height.

5.3 Creating a Sprite Animation

Problem

You want to create a sprite that runs an animation.

Solution

Select the images that you want to play as part of an animation, and drag them into the scene.

Unity will do the following for you:

1. Create a new animator controller asset and save it next to the image assets you dragged in.
2. Create a new animation clip and ask you where to save it. The animation clip will be configured to update the sprite over time. The animation clip will also loop.

3. Add the animation clip as a state in the animator controller.

4. Create a new game object that has an `Animator` and a `SpriteRenderer` component.

You can test the animation by playing the game.

Discussion

If you already have an object set up with an `Animator`, you can attach new animation states to it. We discuss how to do this in detail in Chapter 8; the only difference between 3D animations, which that chapter covers, and 2D animations is that the animation clips modify the sprite renderer's Sprite field, rather than the positions of 3D transforms.

5.4 Creating a Sprite with 2D Physics

Problem

You want to add physics to your sprites that work in two dimensions.

Solution

To create a sprite with 2D physics:

1. Add a game object with a sprite renderer to your scene.

2. Select the game object and click Add Component.

3. Select Physics 2D → Rigidbody 2D, or type **Rigidbody 2D** into the search field and select it.

Much like regular `Rigidbody` objects, which work in three dimensions, `Rigidbody2D` objects define the mass and position of a physical object and respond to physical forces. However, they don't define a shape on their own. To add a shape, you need to add a collider.

Discussion

As with regular colliders, you should not have more than one 2D collider on an object. If you want a more complex shape, either use a polygon collider or create child game objects that have a different collider. The child objects don't need to have their own rigidbody.

You can edit polygon colliders after they've been added. To do this, select the object that has the polygon collider component attached and click the Edit Collider button. You can now reposition the points of the polygon by dragging them around, add new points by clicking and dragging the lines between the points, and remove a point by holding the Control key and clicking a point.

5.5 Customizing Sprite Collision Shapes

Problem

You want to customize the physical outline of a sprite.

Solution

To customize sprite collision shapes:

1. Select the sprite you want to configure, and ensure that Generate Physics Shape is turned on (Figure 5-3).

2. Click the Sprite Editor button. The Sprite Editor window will appear.

3. In the drop-down list at the top-left corner, select Custom Physics Shape.

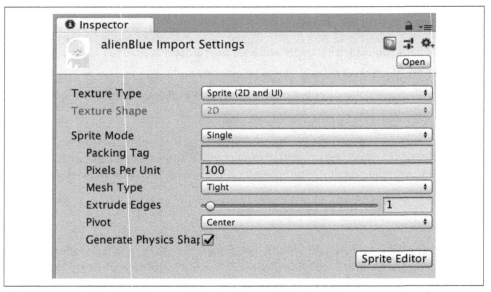

Figure 5-3. Enabling the Generate Physics Shape option in the import settings for a sprite texture

You can now begin defining the shape of the sprite (Figure 5-4):

1. Click and drag to add a new path to the shape.
2. Click the points of a path to move them.
3. Click and drag between two points to insert a new point between them. (You can also hover over the line, and click to add new points!)
4. Click a point and press Command-Delete (Control-Delete on a PC) to delete it.
5. When you're done, click Apply.

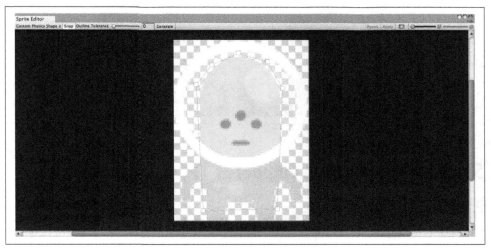

Figure 5-4. Creating the shape for a sprite

Discussion

The physics outline is used as the default shape when you add a polygon collider to an object that has a sprite renderer (Figure 5-5). If a sprite doesn't have a physics outline set up in it, Unity generates one for you using the transparent regions of the sprite. Unity will generally try to create a very close outline, which means that the default shape is often more complex than it needs to be. When you customize the physical outline of a sprite, you can provide a simpler shape for the physics system to use.

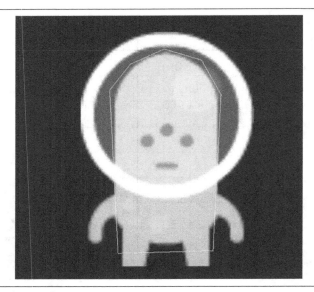

Figure 5-5. The physics shape in use

5.6 Using a Composite Collider

Problem

You want to combine multiple 2D colliders into a single collider for efficiency. Composite colliders work by grouping the colliders of their child game objects.

Solution

To create a composite collider:

1. Create your game objects that have the individual colliders. These can be any type of 2D collider, such as a box, polygon, or circle.

2. Create an empty game object, and make it the parent of the objects with colliders.

3. Next, add a `CompositeCollider2D` component to the parent.

4. Finally, select the child game objects and select the Used By Composite checkbox (Figure 5-6). When you select the parent object, its collider shape will be defined by combining the shapes of its children.

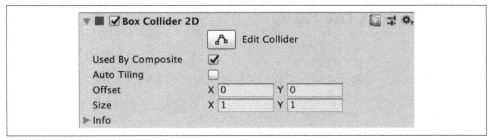

Figure 5-6. Enabling the Used By Composite option on a collider

Discussion

Composite colliders can be more efficient and also prevent problems caused by two colliders that are right next to each other. When two flat colliders are next to each other, an object sliding over them can "trip" over the point where they meet because of precision problems that affect most physics engines. This problem is solved by removing the corner completely.

Figure 5-7 shows an example of this. The top object does not use a composite collider, and contains three box colliders in a row, with the lines between them visible. The bottom object also has three box colliders in a row, but is configured to be part of a composite collider. The lines between them are gone, and the final collider is one large rectangular shape with no corners.

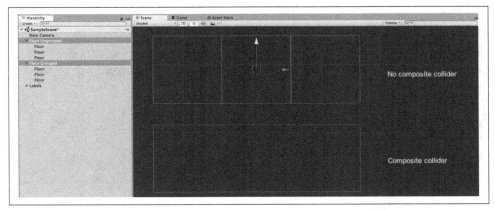

Figure 5-7. Two groups of colliders: with and without composite collider

5.7 Using the Sprite Packer

Problem

You want to pack multiple sprites into a single texture to save on wasted space.

Solution

To use the sprite packer:

1. Create a new Sprite Atlas by opening the Assets menu and choosing Create → Sprite Atlas.
2. Drag the sprites you want to be grouped together into the Objects for Packing list. You can drag folders as well.

Discussion

A *texture atlas* is a single texture that contains multiple images. When the game is built, Unity collects all of the sprites in the atlas and builds a single texture image that packs them all together; during gameplay, when a sprite renderer needs to display its sprite, the subsection of the atlas that contains the necessary data is used.

Texture atlasing can lead to better performance. If multiple sprite renderers are using sprites that are stored in the same atlas, they can be drawn at the same time. Additionally, the packing process trims the edges from a sprite, which reduces the amount of memory needed to store the final image.

You don't need to do anything to use an atlas, besides creating the atlas itself. Sprite renderers will automatically use an atlas texture if the sprite they need to draw is stored inside one.

5.8 Applying Forces to 2D Objects

Problem

You want to apply a physical force to a 2D object.

Solution

You can apply forces to a 2D object through a script, using the `Rigidbody2D` class's `AddForce` method.

The following script demonstrates how to use player input to apply forces to an object:

```
public class AlienForce : MonoBehaviour {

    // The amount of force to apply.
    [SerializeField] float verticalForce = 1000;
    [SerializeField] float sidewaysForce = 1000;

    // A cached reference to the Rigidbody2D on this object.
    Rigidbody2D body;

    // On game start, get the reference to the rigid body and cache it.
    void Start() {
        body = GetComponent<Rigidbody2D>();
    }

    // You will get smoother movement if you apply physical forces in
    // FixedUpdate, because it's called a fixed number of times per second,
    // with a fixed simulation timestep, which means more stable simulation
    void FixedUpdate () {
        // Get user input, and scale it by the amount of force we want to
        // apply
        var vertical = Input.GetAxis("Vertical") * verticalForce;
        var horizontal = Input.GetAxis("Horizontal") * sidewaysForce;

        // Generate a force vector from these inputs, scaled by time
        var force =
            new Vector2(horizontal, vertical) * Time.deltaTime;

        // Add the force to the sprite
        body.AddForce(force);
    }
}
```

 It's not especially practical for such a small example, but input would typically be collected in Update, rather than FixedUpdate as we did here. FixedUpdate can run more than once per render frame, which can mean you end up with extra input!

Discussion

Unlike Rigidbody components, which operate in three dimensions, Rigidbody2D components operate only in two dimensions. This means that all the forces you apply are Vector2D, rather than Vector3D. Additionally, because there's only one degree of rotational freedom, you can apply rotation only on one axis.

In addition to applying forces with code, you can also use a `ConstantForce2D` component (Figure 5-8). These components, as their name suggests, continuously apply a force on an object. They're good for objects and effects where you know that something needs to move around, but you don't really need to have control over it.

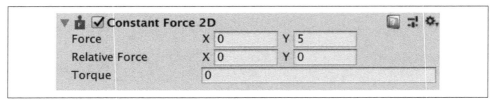

Figure 5-8. A `ConstantForce2D` component

5.9 Creating a Conveyor Belt

Problem

You want to create an object that pushes around any object that touches it. For example, you want to create a conveyor belt.

Solution

Surface effectors apply forces that push bodies along the edges of the effector. To create a conveyer belt:

1. Create a new game object, and add a `BoxCollider2D` component to it. Name it "Conveyor Belt."

2. Turn on the Used By Effector setting (Figure 5-9).

3. Add a `SurfaceEffector2D` component by clicking the Add Component button and choosing Physics 2D → Surface Effector 2D (Figure 5-10).

4. Place above it any object with a `Rigidbody2D` and a `Collider2D` attached.

5. Run the game. The object will fall onto the effector and be pushed by it.

 If the Speed value is a positive number, objects will be pushed to the right; if it's a negative number, objects will be pushed to the left. The Speed Variation value lets you add random variation to the speed applied to the objects.

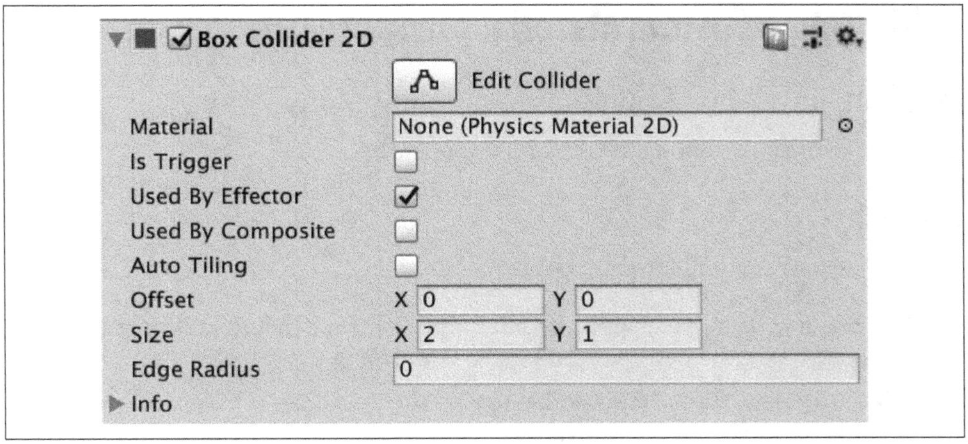

Figure 5-9. Enabling the Used By Effector option on a collider

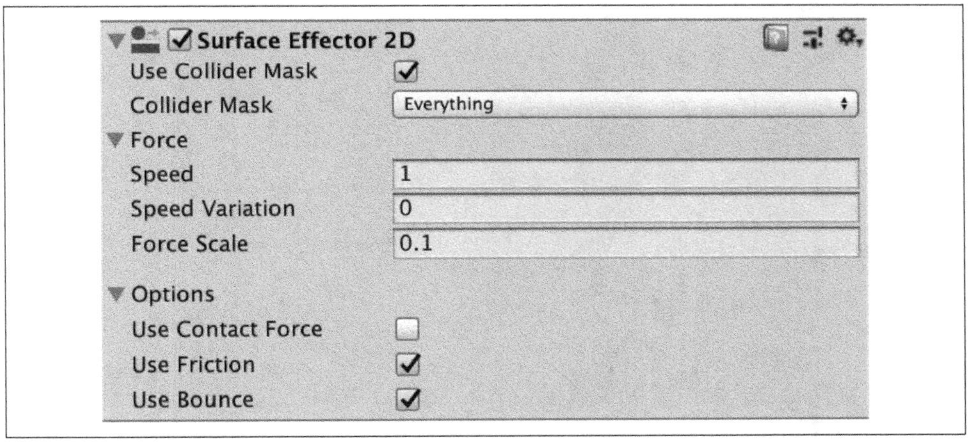

Figure 5-10. The settings of a SurfaceEffector2D component

Discussion

Effectors work with colliders to apply forces to objects. When an object that has a Rigidbody2D collides with a Collider2D that has an effector, the effector applies forces to it based on the effector's type and settings. (If the effector's Collider2D component is marked as a trigger, forces are applied to objects within the bounds.)

There are multiple effectors in Unity's 2D physics engine. For example, point effectors can attract and repel objects from a single point in space, buoyancy effectors apply an upward force that mimics buoyancy, and platform effectors create forces that enable one-way movement through objects.

5.10 Using a Custom Material for Sprites

Problem

You want to use a custom material to draw your sprites.

Solution

To use a custom material for your sprites:

1. Create a new material asset by opening the Assets menu and choosing Create → Material. Name the new material "Sprite Diffuse."

2. Select the new sprite, and at the top of the Inspector, change the shader to Sprites → Diffuse (Figure 5-11).

3. Select any game object in your scene that has a sprite renderer, and drag your Sprite Diffuse material into its Material slot. It will now respond to lighting (Figure 5-12).

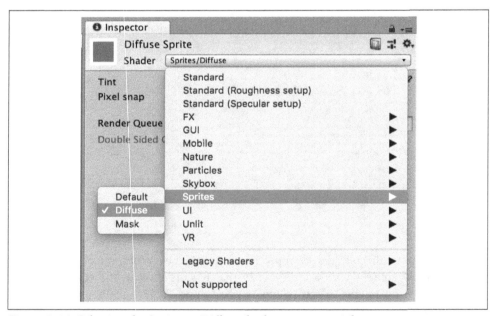

Figure 5-11. Selecting the Sprites → Diffuse shader on a material

Figure 5-12. A sprite using the Diffuse shader

Discussion

The default shader ignores lights—the color of the texture is what's used onscreen (as opposed to being shaded by the environment).

> If you plan on lighting your sprites, you should design your sprites to be very bright. Unless the sprite is hit straight-on by bright light, it will be darker than it appears in the texture.

5.11 Managing Sprite Sorting

Problem

You want to ensure that an object is drawn in front of or behind another object.

Solution

To manage sprite sorting:

1. Select the sprite renderer for which you want to control the draw order.

2. Change the Order in Layer value. Sprite renderers are drawn in decreasing order of this number within a sorting layer; bigger numbers are drawn in front of smaller numbers.

Discussion

The Order in Layer setting controls the drawing order of a sprite within its sorting layer. And there's always at least one sorting layer, called Default, which can't be removed.

To create sorting layers, open the Edit menu, and choose Project Settings → Tags & Layers. Create your sorting layer, and rearrange their order (Figure 5-13).

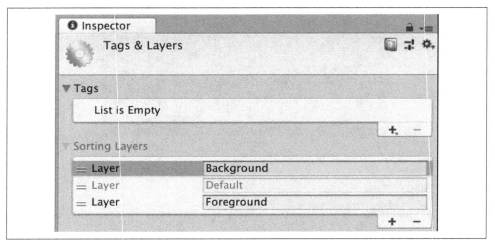

Figure 5-13. Creating and configuring sorting layers

Use sorting layers to ensure that large sprite collections are drawn above or below other collections. For example, you might create one sorting layer called Background and another called Characters; objects on the Background sorting layer are always drawn behind objects on the Characters layer, regardless of their Order in Layer property.

You can select a sorting layer for a sprite renderer by changing its Sorting Layer property in the Inspector (Figure 5-14).

Sorting layers have a similar name to Layers, but they're a different thing. Two objects can be on different sorting layers while being on the same layer.

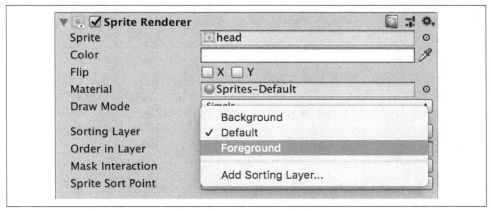

Figure 5-14. Selecting a sorting layer for a sprite renderer

5.12 Using Sorting Groups

Problem

You want to use a sorting group to ensure that a collection of sprites are drawn together.

Solution

Use a sorting group to manage the sorting order of sprites:

1. Create an empty game object. Name it "Sprite Group."

2. Add a `SortingGroup` component to it.

3. Move any sprite renderers that you want to stay in sorted order so they're children of this object.

The sprites will now stay in that order, regardless of any other objects that might be in the same screen area.

Discussion

Sorting groups ensure that all members of that group are drawn together, and that no other objects can be drawn between them.

For example, Figures 5-15 and 5-16 both show two characters, each of which is composed of a number of other sprites. These sprites have their sort order configured so that, for example, the head is drawn on top of the body, and one of the arms is drawn behind the body. In Figure 5-15, the two characters have a sorting group on their parent object, while in Figure 5-16, they don't. This results in the various body parts incorrectly overlapping the other character's.

Figure 5-15. Two groups of sprites, each with a sorting group attached to its parent

Figure 5-16. The same two groups of sprites, with the sorting group disabled

5.13 Creating a 2.5D Scene

Problem

You want to create a scene that has a blend of 2D and 3D elements.

Solution

To create a 2.5D scene:

1. Select your camera and change its Projection mode to Perspective.
2. Select your background objects and move them farther away from the camera.

When the camera moves from side to side, objects farther from the camera will move "slower," just as 3D objects (and real-life objects) do, which creates a sense of depth.

Note that when you're using a perspective camera, you're more prone to encountering sorting issues, especially when your sprites aren't directly facing the camera. Use sorting groups to ensure that 2D objects are sorted correctly.

Discussion

There are lots of different styles of "2.5." For example, you can use multiple flat planes and get a parallax effect, which means that your art assets are still flat, painted sprites, but the player gets an impression of them existing in a deeper environment. Many games use this technique; for example, a game that we helped on, *Night in the Woods*, is made almost entirely out of flat sprites, but some of them are farther from the camera. Because the camera's Projection mode is set to Perspective, distant objects move slower, which reinforces a feeling of distance.

Another technique is to combine 2D sprites with a 3D background. For example, in *Ducktales: Remastered* (Capcom), all the characters are 2D sprites, but they're moving around in 3D environments. This works particularly well for platformers, because it highlights the vertical walls that you can't move through, and creates a much more dynamic environment when the camera is allowed to move up and down, which exposes multiple views of the background.

CHAPTER 6

3D Graphics

Unity has become increasingly well-known for the visual quality of its rendering engine, and a huge part of that is due to the flexibility it offers artists. In this chapter, we'll take a close look at materials, shaders, and lighting, and how you can build your own effects that suit the unique look of your game.

 We strongly recommend also reviewing the recipes in Chapter 5 for more complete coverage of graphics topics.

6.1 Creating a Simple Material

Problem

You want to customize the appearance of the surface of a 3D object by creating a material.

Solution

In this recipe, we'll customize a simple shape, though the steps apply to most other meshes you'll end up using in your game:

1. Create a new sphere by opening the GameObject menu and choosing 3D Object → Sphere.

2. Open the Assets menu, and choose Create → Material. Name it whatever you like.

3. Select the new material, and configure its colors (Figure 6-1).

4. Drag and drop the material onto the sphere.

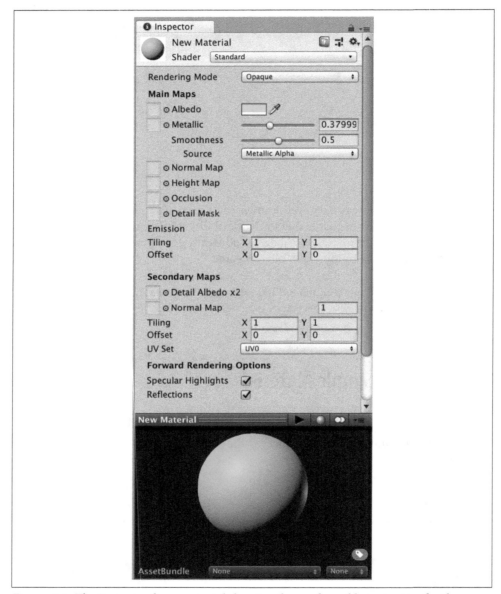

Figure 6-1. The Inspector for a material showing the configurable properties for the default Standard shader

Discussion

Materials are essential to controlling the appearance of objects in your scene. Materials work by combining a *shader*, which is a program that computes the final color of each pixel that makes up an object, with *properties*, which are inputs delivered to the shader that are combined with per-pixel information.

Most of the time, you'll likely end up using the Standard shader, which is a physically based rendering (PBR) shader that's extremely configurable. You can specify a wide variety of properties, including albedo (base) color, normal map, emissiveness, smoothness, and metalness. Try playing with the various properties and see what happens to your object's material.

The Standard shader isn't the only shader out there; we'll explore a few more of them in this chapter, and we'll also make our own.

6.2 Controlling a Material's Property Through a Script

Problem

You want to change a property of a material during gameplay, such as its color.

Solution

When you have access to a `MeshRenderer` or `SpriteRenderer`, or any other type of renderer, you can access the material from it and modify its properties. For example:

```
public class ChangeMaterialColor : MonoBehaviour {

    // The colors we're fading between
    [SerializeField] Color fromColor = Color.white;
    [SerializeField] Color toColor = Color.green;

    // The speed with which we're fading
    [SerializeField] float speed = 1f;

    // A cached reference to the renderer (The 'new' keyword makes the
    // compiler not warn us about the fact that we're overriding an
    // existing property that we inherit from MonoBehaviour; this property
    // is deprecated, so we aren't using it and it's okay to override it)
    new Renderer renderer;
```

```
private void Start()
{
    renderer = GetComponent<Renderer>();
}

private void Update()
{
    // Convert time to a number that smoothly moves between -1 and 1
    float t = Mathf.Sin(Time.time * speed);

    // Convert this to one that moves from 0 to 2
    t += 1;

    // Divide it by 2 to make it move from 0 to 1;
    t /= 2;

    // Interpolate between the two colors
    var newColor = Color.Lerp(fromColor, toColor, t);

    // Apply the new color
    renderer.material.color = newColor;
}

}
```

Discussion

There are two ways you can access the material used by a renderer: the material property and the sharedMaterial property.

The first time you access the renderer's material property, Unity creates a copy of the material that the renderer is currently using, tells the renderer to use this new copy, and returns it. This is because if multiple renderers all use the same material file, you likely don't want to change all of them when you change one of them.

If you *do* want to change every user of a material, you can use the sharedMaterial property. Accessing and modifying this property modifies the underlying material asset, which means that all renderers that use this asset will adopt the changes.

Modifying the `sharedMaterial` property modifies the asset on disk. Changes you apply to `sharedMaterial` during gameplay stay around, even after you leave Play mode, and there's no undo.

Materials have ways to directly access common properties, like `color` or `main Texture`. If you know the name of a property on a shader that you want to modify, you can change it directly through the material's `SetColor`, `SetFloat`, `SetInt`, and related methods. For the full list of available methods, see the documentation for the `Material` class (*https://oreil.ly/oi_VB*).

6.3 Creating an Unlit Material

Problem

You want to create a material that is a solid color and doesn't participate in lighting.

Solution

To create an unlit material:

1. Open the Assets menu, and choose Create → Material.
2. Set the shader to Unlit → Color.
3. Apply the shader to an object, noticing that it ignores any lighting conditions and just shows as a flat color (Figure 6-2).

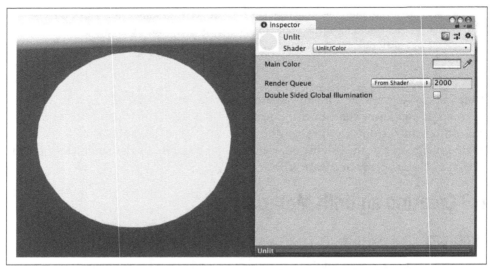

Figure 6-2. The Inspector for a material that uses the Unlit → Color shader

Discussion

When a material uses an Unlit shader, it doesn't participate in the lighting system. It won't be shaded based on nearby light sources, and instead uses only a flat color. This can be great for when you're not going for an accurate, photorealistic look.

6.4 Setting Up a Material Using Textures

Problem

You want to use textures to control the appearance of a material.

Solution

Most slots in a material can take a texture instead of a flat color. Generally, most modern materials use multiple textures to define their surface appearance; in addition to the albedo, they also use textures to define normals, roughness, ambient occlusion, and more.

For example, the seven maps shown in Figure 6-3—albedo, metallic, roughness, normal map, height map, occlusion, and a detail mask—are used in the material shown in Figure 6-4.

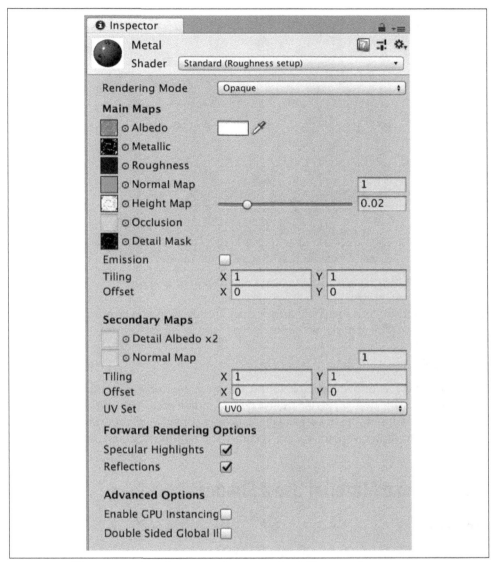

Figure 6-3. The material configuration for a scratched, blue metal texture

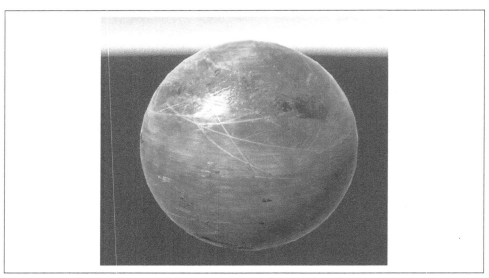

Figure 6-4. The metal material from Figure 6-3, displayed in the scene

To attach a texture to a material, simply drag and drop the texture from the Project tab into the slot. The material will immediately start using the texture.

Discussion

If you don't have your own textures to use, there are a number of good, free sites that offer textures with usable licenses. For example, ambientCG (*https://ambientcg.com*) offers high-resolution textures available under a Creative Commons Zero (CC0) license, which allows you to use its textures for commercial and noncommercial purposes.

6.5 Making a Material Use a Shader

Problem

You want to control which shader a material uses.

Solution

There are two ways you can do this.

The first option is to create a new material by opening the Assets menu, and then choosing Create → Material. Next, select your shader from the drop-down menu at the top of the Inspector.

Alternatively, if you have a shader asset that you've created (such as by following the steps in Recipe 6.10), select the shader in the Projects tab and create the material. The material will use the shader you have selected.

Discussion

Material assets combine a shader with configuration data to achieve a specific material effect. When you select a shader from the drop-down menu, Unity reads the shader and determines what information it needs—what textures, colors, and other values it uses to compute the color for each pixel of an object that the material is applied to.

You can use the built-in shaders that come with Unity, or you can produce your own. We discuss creating shaders using the Shader Graph tool in several recipes in this chapter (for example, Recipes 6.10, 6.11, and 6.12).

6.6 Setting Up a Bloom Effect Using Post-Processing with the Built-In Render Pipeline

Problem

You want to configure a camera so that post-processing effects can be applied to it.

 This recipe applies to the Built-In Render Pipeline, and not to the Universal Render Pipeline.

Solution

First, ensure that you've got the post-processing stack installed for your project:

1. Open the Window menu, and choose Package Manager.
2. Click the All tab.
3. Locate the Post-processing package, and click the Install button (Figure 6-5).

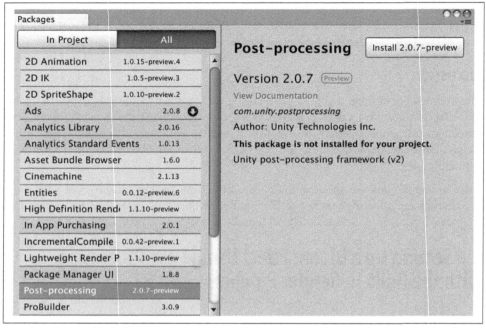

Figure 6-5. Installing the Post-processing package

Next, we'll set up the post-processing volume. This controls what post-processing effects are in place, and what their settings are:

1. Create a new, empty game object. Name it "Post Process Volume."

2. Add a new Post-Processing Volume component to it.

3. Turn on the Is Global setting. The effect will apply to the camera no matter where it is.

4. At the top-right corner of the Inspector, change the Layer to PostProcessing (Figure 6-6).

Figure 6-6. The Inspector for a post-processing volume game object

Now we'll set up the profile that determines what post-processing effects to apply. We'll set up this profile to apply a bloom effect:

1. Click the New button next to the Profile field. A new post-processing profile asset will be created. Select it.

2. In the Inspector, click Add Effect and choose Unity → Bloom. A new bloom effect will be added.

3. Click the All button to mark that you'd like to override all settings from their defaults. Set the Intensity to 5, and the Threshold to 1.1 (Figure 6-7).

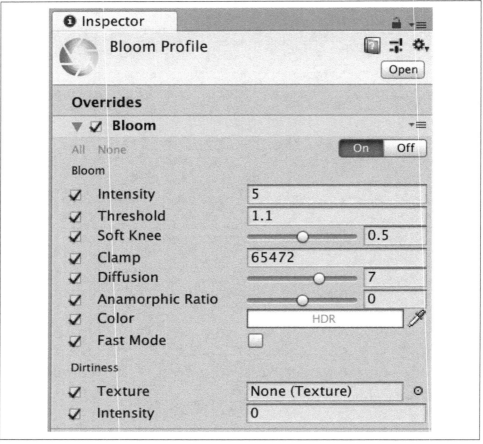

Figure 6-7. The Inspector for the post-processing profile, with a bloom effect added and configured

Next, we'll set up the camera:

1. Select the camera you want to apply post-processing effects to (typically, your main camera).

2. Add a new Post Process Layer component to it.

3. Set the Layer property to PostProcessing (Figure 6-8).

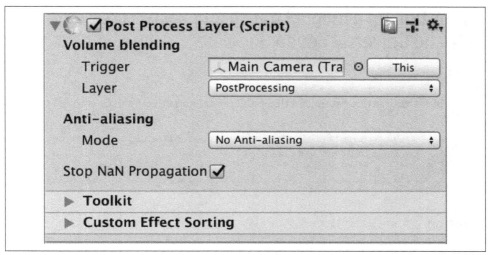

Figure 6-8. Configuring a Post Process Layer component to use the PostProcessing object layer

A bloom effect appears: bright parts of the screen will appear brighter by "bleeding" out to nearby parts of the screen.

Discussion

A *post-processing effect* is a visual effect performed on the final or near-final image that the renderer has produced. It works by taking the rendered image, putting it on a rectangle, and then running a shader on it; the shaded result is then displayed on the screen or sent to the next post-processing effect.

There are many different post-processing effects; for example, you can adjust the color curves of the final image, apply tints, modify the exposure of the scene, apply depth-of-field blur, or add a vignette. Play around with the various effects and see what unique effects you can achieve!

You can have multiple post-processing volumes in your scene. If they have a trigger collider on them, and the Post Process Layer's trigger (usually the camera, though you can make it be any transform) is within the bounds of the collider, that volume's settings will apply. This allows you to create setups where, for example, the camera can enter a haunted house and apply post-processing effects that modify the color and tone of the scene only while the camera is in the building.

6.7 Setting Up a Bloom Effect Using Post-Processing with the Universal Render Pipeline

Problem

You want to configure a camera so that post-processing effects can be applied to it.

 This recipe applies to the Universal Render Pipeline, and not to the Built-In Render Pipeline.

Solution

To set up a bloom effect using post-processing with the Universal Render Pipeline:

1. Create a new Global Volume by opening the GameObject menu and choosing Volume → Global Volume.
2. Select the newly created Volume, and find the Profile field. Click New to create a new post-processing profile.
3. Click the Add Override button, and in the menu that appears, choose Post Processing → Bloom.
4. Click All, and increase the Intensity setting to 1.
5. In the Hierarchy pane, select the Camera.
6. In the Camera's Inspector, find the Post Processing setting, and turn it on.

You can now see the bloom effect in the Game View.

Discussion

When you use the Universal Render Pipeline, post-processing is set up in a similar, but slightly different, way to the built-in pipeline. You don't need to download and install any additional packages; post-processing is already included. You still need to create a volume that defines which post-processing effects should apply, but it's a different kind of object. You don't need to set up any layers, but you do need to turn on post-processing on the camera itself.

The available post-processing effects are similar to the effects available in the Built-In Pipeline, but have slightly different ways to configure them. Not every effect available in Built-In is available in Universal, and vice versa. That said, they're a lot more similar than they are different.

6.8 Using High-Dynamic-Range Colors

Problem

You want to use high-dynamic-range (HDR) colors in your scene for more realistic effects.

Solution

First, for HDR rendering to be visible, you'll need to enable HDR mode on the camera. A quick way to demonstrate the usefulness of HDR rendering is to combine it with a bloom post-processing effect:

1. Select your camera, and turn on the HDR setting.

2. Select your scene's directional light, and increase its intensity to 5 (Figure 6-9).

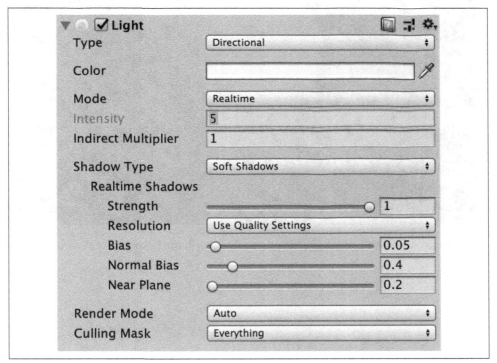

Figure 6-9. Configuring a light to use an intensity above 1

The bright reflection of the light will appear much brighter than the parts of the object that aren't facing the light (see Figures 6-10 and 6-11). Figure 6-11 shows the same shot as Figure 6-10, but with the bloom effect enabled. The light appears to be much brighter, because it seems to "leak" out.

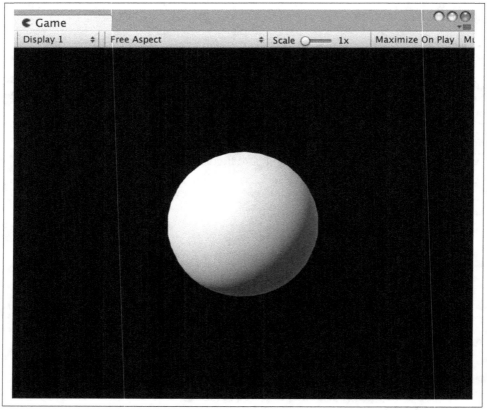

Figure 6-10. An object being lit by directional light, with the bloom effect disabled

Figure 6-11. The same shot as Figure 6-10, but with the bloom effect enabled

Discussion

HDR rendering is different from low-dynamic-range (LDR) rendering. LDR clamps the value of each color channel (red, green, and blue) to between 0 and 1, while HDR can go above or below. This means that a much wider range of exposure levels can be accomplished, and allows for greater flexibility when processing the image before it's displayed.

The display that the player sees the game through has a limited color range, which means that an HDR image must be clamped, through a process known as *tone mapping*. Tone mapping involves deciding what the top and bottom of the range of colors will be; any color level below the bottom will appear black, and any color level above the top will appear white. Because bright light scatters in camera lenses and in the lens of the human eye, we can simulate these "overbright" colors by blurring them—in other words, the bloom effect. This is why we set the threshold of the bloom effect to 1.1, so that only overbright pixels have the bloom effect on them.

6.9 Setting Up a Project to Use a Scriptable Render Pipeline

Problem

You want to use Unity's Scriptable Render Pipelines (SRPs), which allow for more advanced rendering techniques and editor features.

Solution

In this example, and in the following recipes, we'll be using the Universal Render Pipeline (URP):

1. Open the Unity Hub, and click New Project. Locate the 3D (URP) template (Figure 6-12).

2. You may need to download the template before you can use it. Click "Download template," and wait for the template to finish downloading.

3. Name the project, and click Create Project.

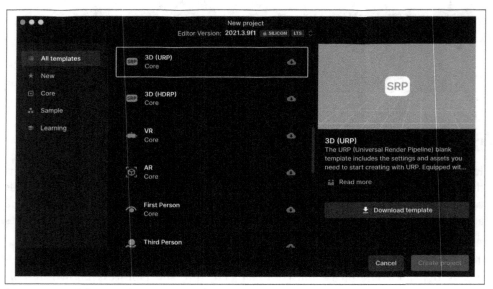

Figure 6-12. Selecting the URP template

Discussion

In Unity, it's possible to customize how the graphics system renders its frames. The Scriptable Render Pipeline system gives graphics programmers fine-grained control over what rendering features the engine should and should not enable, which allows them to meet very specific performance and visual quality targets.

However, we aren't all graphics programmers. To that end, Unity also provides two predefined pipeline setups: the High-Definition Render Pipeline (HDRP) and the URP. The HDRP supports advanced graphical techniques, but requires quite recent hardware (such as on modern PCs and recent consoles). The URP can run on just about anything and achieve good performance (for example, low-end PCs, mobile devices, and older consoles), but limits what graphical features are supported.

 In this chapter, we'll specifically be focusing on the Universal Render Pipeline.

Materials and shaders designed for one render pipeline won't work for other pipelines, because they rely on features provided by the render pipeline they were designed for. If you try to use a material designed for the Built-In Render Pipeline in a project using the Universal Render Pipeline, for example, it will render a bright, solid purple color that indicates an error.

In addition to creating a new project that's already using an SRP, you can also adapt an existing project to do it:

1. Open the Window menu, and choose Package Manager.
2. In the drop-down menu at the top left of the window, choose Unity Registry.
3. Select the Universal RP package from the package list, and click Install. Unity will download and install the package into your project.
4. Open the Assets menu, and choose Create → Rendering → URP Asset (with Universal Renderer). A new pipeline asset will be created; this asset contains the rendering settings used for your project, along with a Renderer.
5. Open the Project Settings window by opening the Edit menu and choosing Project Settings.
6. Select the Graphics settings.
7. Drag the Universal Pipeline Asset you created into the Scriptable Render Pipeline Settings slot.

Note that when you start using an SRP, you'll need to modify your materials to use shaders that are designed for the new pipeline. To do this, select your Materials in the Project tab, open the Edit menu, and choose Rendering → Materials → Convert Selected Built-In Materials to URP Materials.

6.10 Creating a Shader Using the Shader Graph

Problem

You want to use Unity's Shader Graph tool to create new shaders, with which you can create your own custom materials.

Solution

Create a new shader by opening the Assets menu and choosing Create → Shader → URP → Lit Shader Graph. Name the new shader.

You'll see a new shader graph with a single node (Figure 6-13). Click Save Asset, and your shader is ready for use in a material.

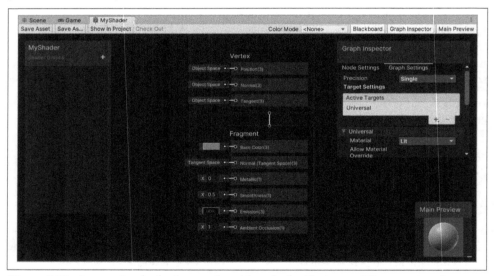

Figure 6-13. A very simple shader graph, with only the Vertex and Fragment nodes

Discussion

The Shader Graph is a visual tool for building shaders. Shaders are normally written in a language called ShaderLab, which describes the behavior of the shader to Unity, and also includes the specific instructions on *how* to perform the shading using a second language, Cg.

The ShaderLab approach is extremely powerful, but can be difficult to work with for a few reasons. First, it requires learning at least one new language; second, shader code can be difficult to debug; and third, it's challenging to get an idea of how the effect is being visually built up as you create it.

The Shader Graph tool takes a different approach. Rather than writing code, you connect nodes that generate or modify data. The final result is sent to the output node, which performs any final lighting necessary before applying the fragment color to the surface.

 Under the hood, all shaders are the same. The Shader Graph feature takes your nodes and produces ShaderLab and Cg source code, which is then compiled and sent to the GPU like any other shader. The only difference is the process by which you author them.

6.11 Creating a Glowing Effect Using the Shader Graph

Problem

You want to create a shader that makes the edges of an object glow.

Solution

To create a glowing effect, we first need to think about what we want to happen. The "edges" of the object should glow; however, the position of the "edges" varies depending on where the camera is. Additionally, the glow effect should smoothly fade out as it moves away from the edge.

One way to do this is to assume that any part of the object that's facing the camera is not an edge, any part of an object that's facing at a right angle to the camera is an edge, and anything that's in between is smoothly interpolated between the two extremes. If we combine that with a color, we'll have a nice-looking effect.

Happily for us, there's a built-in node that handles this edge effect for us, called the Fresnel Effect node.

Follow these steps to create your effect:

1. Create a new Lit Shader Graph asset (see Recipe 6.10). Name the new asset "Glowing," and open it.
2. Open the Create Node menu by either right-clicking in empty space or pressing the space bar.

3. Locate the Fresnel Effect node. You can do this by either typing the name or finding it in Math → Vector → Fresnel Effect.

The Fresnel Effect node creates a white glow. We can tint it by multiplying it with a color:

1. Create a new Color node (again, either by searching for it or by finding it in Input → Basic → Color). Set it to the color you want.

2. Create a Multiply node (Math → Basic → Multiply).

3. Click and drag from the Out slot of the Color node into one of the inputs of the Multiply node.

4. Click and drag from the Out slot of the Fresnel Effect into the other input of the Multiply node.

5. Connect the Out slot of the Multiply node into the Emission slot of the Fragment node. When you're done, the shader graph should look like Figure 6-14.

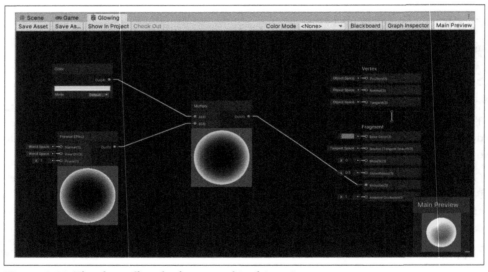

Figure 6-14. The glow effect shader created in this recipe

Finally, create a new Material that uses this shader by following these steps:

1. Save the shader by clicking the Save Asset button at the top of the Shader Editor.

2. In the Project pane, right-click the Shader, and choose Create → Material. Name the new material something useful, like "Glowing."

3. The material is now ready to be applied to an object, such as by dragging and dropping it onto an object.

Discussion

The Fresnel (pronounced "fray-nell") effect, which this shader exploits, is the observation that the amount of light reflected off a surface varies depending on the angle of the surface to the viewer. When the angle is shallow—which is the case when the direction that the surface is facing approaches a direction perpendicular to the camera—then more reflection can be seen. In this shader, we simply take the value of how "reflective" the surface would be at any given point, and instead of actually using it for reflectance, we send the value to the Emission slot. It's not physically realistic, but the effect can be quite pleasing.

If you set an HDR color by setting the Color property's Mode to HDR, and combine it with a camera set up with the Glow post-processing effect (see Recipe 6.6), the glow will appear more realistically bright (Figure 6-15), because very bright objects tend to have a blooming effect when they interact with a lens (both in a camera and in the human eye).

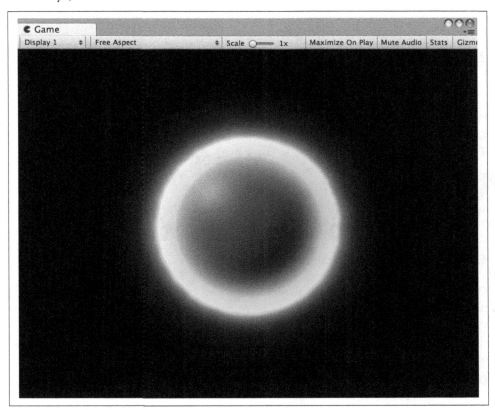

Figure 6-15. The glow effect, applied to an object in the scene

6.12 Exposing Properties from a Shader Graph

Problem

You want to expose a property from your shader graph, so that you can modify materials that use the shader without having to create and use a whole new shader.

Solution

To define a property, you first need to create it by using the Blackboard pane. The Blackboard lists all properties associated with a shader:

1. If it isn't already open, open the Blackboard by clicking the Blackboard button at the top right of the Shader editor.

2. Click the + button at the top right of the Blackboard pane in your shader (Figure 6-16).

3. Select the type of property you want to create. A new property will be created; you can drag it out into the shader graph, and it will appear as a node.

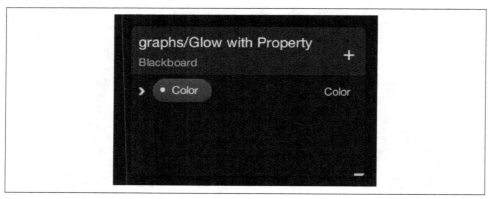

Figure 6-16. The Blackboard pane in a scene graph

Once a property node is in your shader graph, you can connect it to any other node's input and use it like any other value. The only difference is that the property will be controllable from a material.

Discussion

Properties appear in the Inspector for any material that uses this shader. They're the main way that you can customize the appearance of your materials; without properties, all the values used by your shader would be fixed and not editable.

 You can rename any property by double-clicking it in the Blackboard pane.

You can also right-click any existing Input node in your shader graph and convert it to a property node (Figure 6-17). This makes it easier to build your shader, because you can start with fixed values and then decide later that you want to expose them as properties.

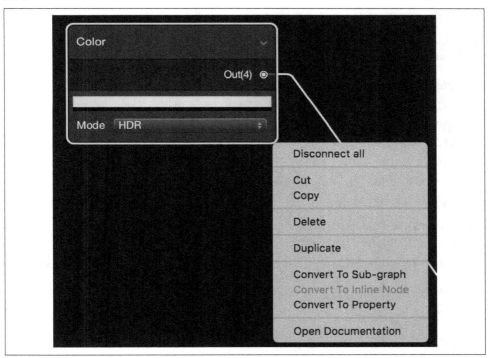

Figure 6-17. Converting an Input node into a property

6.13 Animating a Shader over Time

Problem

You want to create a shader that automatically animates over time. For example, you want to create a glowing effect that fades in and out.

Solution

Use a Time node, which exposes various representations of the amount of time that has elapsed since the game started:

1. Start with the Glow shader that you created in Figure 6-10.
2. Add a Time node (Input → Basic → Time).

The Time node exposes a Sine Time output, which is the current time, in seconds, run through the Sine function (which produces a sine wave that goes from –1 to 1).

To create a fading effect that goes from 0.2 to 1 (that is, a slight glow to a full glow), we'll use a Remap node:

1. Add a Remap node (Math → Range → Remap).
2. Set its In Min Max values to –1 and 1. (This is the range of values that it's expecting to receive.)
3. Set its Out Min Max values to 0.2 and 1. (This is the range of values that it will emit.)
4. Connect the Sine Time output from the Time node to its In port.
5. Create a new Multiply node.
6. Connect the Remap node and the original Multiply node (the one that multiplies the Color and the Fresnel effect) into the new Multiply node.
7. Connect the new Multiply node into the Emission slot of the Fragment node.

When you're done, the graph should look like Figure 6-18.

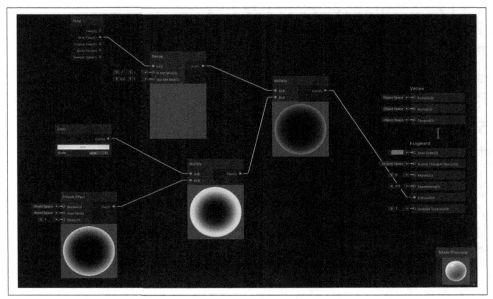

Figure 6-18. The completed shader graph, which animates over time

When you play the game, the glow will fade in and out over time.

Discussion

In this shader, the Remap node is necessary because the Sine Time node produces numbers ranging from –1 to 1, while the Emission value is expecting values of 0 or higher. It's *possible* to provide negative numbers, but it looks extremely bad. To fix this, Remap can adjust the values so that they fall between 0 and 1 instead.

For this shader, we also took the artistic license of setting the minimum to 0.2 instead of 0, because we felt that having no glow at all looked strange. One of the most useful features of the Shader Graph tool is the ability to tweak and tune your shaders until you get the result you're looking for, so don't be afraid to experiment.

6.14 Controlling the Speed of an Animated Shader

Problem

You have an animated shader that uses the Time node to change values over time, and you want to make it happen faster or slower.

Solution

To control the speed of an animated shader:

1. Use a Time node as in Figure 6-18.

2. Create a new Multiply node.

3. Connect both the Time node's Time output—not the Sine Time, or any of the others—and a `Float` input or a property to the Multiply node. Set the `Float` to be more than 1 if you want it to go faster, less than 1 if you want it to go slower, and less than 0 if you want it to go in reverse.

4. Connect the output of the Multiply node to a new Sine node (Math → Trigonometry → Sine).

5. Use the output of your Sine node as you would in any other animation.

Discussion

In the Shader Graph tool, a `Vector1` property is the same thing as a floating-point number—it's a vector that has just one component, which is the same thing as a plain number.

In this shader, we multiply the time—which is the number of seconds since the game started—by a constant value, and then take the sine of it. The Time node provides a Sine Time output, but we can't use it for the same purpose—if we multiplied that by a constant, it wouldn't oscillate faster, but would instead span a wider range. This is illustrated in Figure 6-19, in which the dashed line, the sine of time ($y = \sin(t)$), oscillates at a normal range and rate; the solid line, the sine of 2x time ($y = \sin(2t)$), oscillates at a normal range but at double the rate; and the dotted line, 2x the sine of time ($y = 2 * \sin(t)$), oscillates at a wide range and at a normal rate.

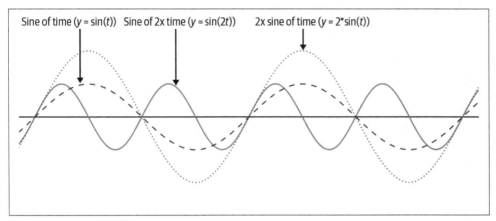

Figure 6-19. Oscillation ranges and rates

6.15 Using a Subgraph to Reuse Graph Components

Problem

You want to simplify your shader graphs by reusing common patterns of nodes.

Solution

Use a *subgraph*, which is a collection of nodes that you can store in a file and reuse in other graphs. Subgraphs appear as a single "node" in your graphs.

To create a subgraph, follow these steps:

1. Open the Assets menu, and choose Create → Shader Graph → Sub Graph.

2. Open the Graph Inspector by clicking the Graph Inspector button at the top right of the Shader Graph window.

3. Add outputs to the Output node by clicking the + button and creating new outputs.

4. Construct your nodes just as if you were making a shader. The difference is that, rather than the output being sent to a Fragment node to perform lighting calculations, the result will be exposed as outputs of the node when the subgraph is embedded in another shader. When you drag and drop the output of a node onto a slot, the slot will take on the type of the incoming value.

To use the subgraph, save it, open a shader that you want to use it in, and press the space bar to open the Node menu. Type the name of your subgraph, and it will appear as a new node.

Discussion

It's very easy for a node-based system to become overly complicated, and subgraphs are essential for keeping things organized.

Subgraphs can have properties, just like other shaders. Any properties that you create will appear as inputs to the subgraph.

For example, Figure 6-20 shows a subgraph that generates a solid color that fades between black and white, with a speed that's configurable via a property. Figure 6-21 shows the subgraph in use within another shader. The subgraph node is at the lower left; as it has a Speed property, that value appears as input to the node.

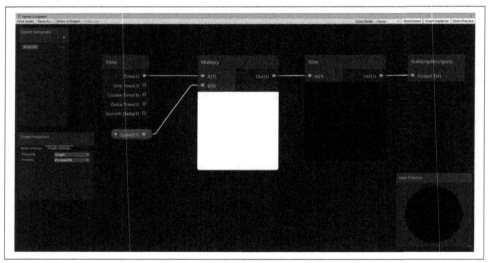

Figure 6-20. A subgraph that generates a solid color fading between black and white

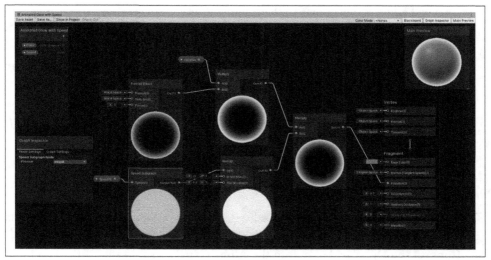

Figure 6-21. The subgraph in use within another shader

6.16 Implementing a Dissolve Effect Using a Shader Graph

Problem

You want to create an effect in which parts of the object gradually disappear. You want the edges of the effect to glow.

Solution

Follow these steps to construct a shader in the Shader Graph tool that achieves this effect:

1. Create a new Lit URP shader graph by following the instructions in Recipe 6.10. Name the new shader graph "Dissolve."

2. Open the Graph Inspector, and go to the Graph Settings tab. Scroll down to Surface Type, and change it from Opaque to Transparent. Next, turn on Alpha Clipping.

This will add two new ports to the Fragment node, called Alpha and Alpha Clip Threshold. When the Alpha value of a fragment is below Alpha Clip Threshold, the fragment will not be rendered.

3. Create three properties (see Recipe 6.12): a `Color` called Edge Color, a `Float` called Dissolve Amount, and a `Float` called Edge Thickness. Drag all three properties out into the graph, so that each has its own node.

4. Select the Dissolve Amount property, and in the Node Settings tab of the Graph Inspector, set its Default value to 0.5.

5. Select the Edge Thickness property, and set its Default value to 0.05.

6. Select the Edge Color property, and set its Default value to a bright blue with an alpha value of 100.

7. Create a Simple Noise node (Procedural → Noise → Simple Noise). Connect its Out slot to the Alpha slot of the Fragment node, and set its Scale to 50.

8. Connect the Dissolve Amount to the Alpha Clip Threshold slot of the Fragment node.

When you increase the Dissolve Amount value, parts of the object will disappear.

The next steps create the glowing edge effect:

1. Create an Add node (Math → Basic → Add).
2. Connect the Edge Thickness and Dissolve Amount properties to it.
3. Create a Step node (Math → Round → Step).
4. Connect the Simple Noise's Out slot to the Step's Edge input.
5. Connect the Add node's Out slot to the Step's In input.

If you were to connect the Step's out slot to the Fragment node's Emission input, you'd see a white edge around the dissolved parts of the object. To provide control over the color, we'll multiply this edge with a color:

1. Create a new Multiply node.
2. Connect its output to the Emission slot of the Fragment node, and the Step and Edge Color properties to its input.

Your dissolve shader is now complete; the finished graph should look something like Figure 6-22.

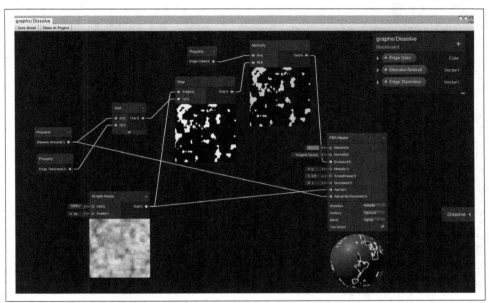

Figure 6-22. The shader graph for the dissolve effect

You can now create a new material that uses this shader; as you change the Dissolve Amount value from 0 to 1, the object will slowly dissolve (Figure 6-23).

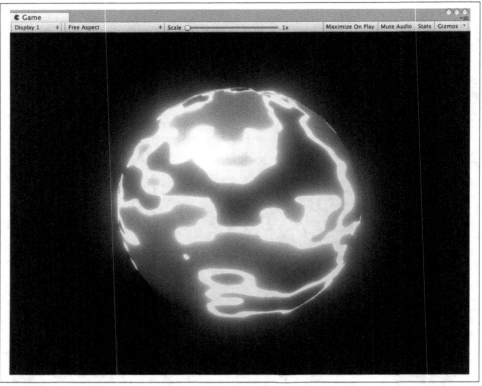

Figure 6-23. The image dissolving; we've also set up the camera to use a bloom effect

Discussion

A shader's Surface mode can be either Opaque or Transparent. When the shader is in Transparent mode, the Alpha value it receives is used to control the opacity of the surface; when it's in Opaque mode, all pixels that are drawn are fully opaque.

This doesn't mean that Alpha is ignored, however. In this shader, we use the Alpha Clip Threshold value in conjunction with the Alpha value to determine which parts of the surface are not rendered at all. Any pixel whose Alpha value is below the Alpha Clip Threshold is completely discarded and not drawn at all. Because the Alpha value varies depending on the Simple Noise node, different parts of the object have an Alpha value above or below the threshold. By varying the Alpha Clip Threshold, you can make more or less of the object appear.

The Simple Noise node generates a smoothly varying two-dimensional noise pattern. If you modify the scale of the node, you'll get more or less detail in the result, which means finer or coarser pieces. Try it and see!

Finally, to create the outline effect, we first add the Edge Thickness property to the dissolve amount, which advances the border of the dissolve effect slightly. We then use the Step node to create an image that draws a line of the specified thickness around the edge of the border, and we multiply it by the Edge Color property. This is then used as the Emission property on the Fragment node, creating a glowing edge around the dissolved area.

If you set up your camera to use a bloom post-processing effect (see Recipe 6.6), and make the Edge Color an HDR color by setting its mode to HDR, you can get a nice-looking glow on your dissolve effect.

You can tune the effect by modifying the Edge Thickness and Color properties.

A fire-like effect is pretty easy to achieve if you use an orange color.

6.17 Using Baked Lighting and Real-Time Lighting

Problem

You want to use Unity's baked lighting system, which lets you create high-quality shadows and reflected light.

Solution

Unity will automatically calculate a baked lighting solution for your scene if there's at least one object that's marked as contributing to the scene's *global illumination* (GI) data. To do this, follow these steps:

1. Select the object (or objects) that you want to be lightmapped.
2. At the top-right corner of the Inspector, click the drop-down menu, and choose Contribute GI.

Unity's lightmapper will begin calculating the baked lighting in the scene. This might take some time, depending on the complexity of your scene.

Objects that contribute to global illumination aren't allowed to move, because if they do, the lighting won't adjust to account for it. If an object needs to be able to both move around and act like it's receiving light from static objects, you'll need to use light probes; see Recipe 6.20.

Discussion

Baked lighting is the process of calculating ahead of time how light bounces around an environment. Unlike real-time lighting, which has to work as quickly as possible, baked lighting has the luxury of taking as much time as it needs to—often minutes or hours. Because it has this extra time, it's able to perform path-tracing of virtual photons as they leave the light sources in your scene and bounce around the level. As these calculations are performed, textures are generated that store the amount of light that the various parts of the objects are receiving; at runtime, these textures are used to simulate the lighting.

Baked lighting tends to look better than real-time lighting (see Figure 6-24 for an example), but it's less flexible. Because the texture is generated before gameplay and takes significant time to create, it can't be modified during gameplay. If an object that casts a baked shadow moves, the shadow won't move with it.

In Figure 6-24, we see the cube on the left is real-time lit, and the cube on the right uses baked lighting. Notice how the shadow of the cube on the right is more realistic; it's sharper near the base of the cube and blurrier further away, while the real-time-lit cube's shadow has the same fuzziness at all points around the edge.

There are multiple Static modes besides Contribute GI. If you know that an object will never move—perhaps it's fixed scenery in the level—you can click the Static checkbox at the top right of the Inspector, and *all* static modes are enabled at once. This means that Unity can enable additional optimizations, including the ability to render multiple objects that share a material at the same time, in a single batch.

Figure 6-24. Real-time lighting versus baked lighting

6.18 Using Baked Emission Sources

Problem

You want to create objects that emit light in a scene with baked lighting. For example, you want to create a lamp in the scene.

Solution

Create a material that has an emissive color. Set the intensity of the emissive HDR color to 1 or more. Apply this material to an object that is set to Contribute GI. When the lightmap calculates the lighting, light from the emissive object will illuminate other static objects. In Figure 6-25, the only light in the scene comes from the emissive object in the center. A bloom effect on the camera completes the effect of a bright object.

Figure 6-25. Emissive lighting

Discussion

In addition to casting nice shadows and creating appealing light bounces, you can introduce lighting into your scene with emissive objects, as long as they're static. Don't forget, though, that the light is "fake"—it won't affect objects that don't contribute to global illumination. If you want real-time objects to respond to this baked light, you'll need to use light probes (see Recipe 6.20), or add real-time lights that affect only real-time-lit objects (see Recipe 6.22).

6.19 Making Static Objects Cast Shadows on Dynamic Objects

Problem

You have an object that is static (that is, it contributes to global illumination), and you want it to cast shadows onto objects that do not contribute to GI (that is, they are *dynamic*). For an example, see Figure 6-26, in which three cubes and spheres are resting on a brick surface. At left, a static cube casts a high-quality shadow that doesn't affect the sphere. In the middle, a real-time cube casts a shadow that is less high-quality but affects the sphere. At right, a static cube and a cube of the same shape and size that is set to render only shadows are in the same location, so the shadow is high quality and some shadowing is still applied to the sphere.

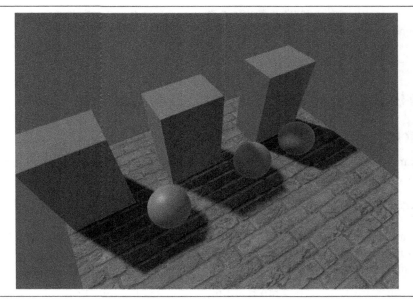

Figure 6-26. Three cubes casting shadows

Solution

To make static objects cast shadows on dynamic objects:

1. Select the mesh that you want to cast real-time shadows from, and duplicate it. Make sure it's the same size, shape, and position as the original. (Consider making it a child of the original object.)

2. Turn off Contribute GI so that it casts real-time shadows.

3. Remove every component except the `MeshRenderer`.

4. Set the `MeshRenderer`'s Cast Shadows property to Shadows Only. This means that it won't appear in the scene, but it will cast shadows onto other objects.

Discussion

Another solution is to use light probes. Place light probes in areas both inside the shadowed region and outside; this will darken objects that pass into the shadowed area, though you won't see the edges of the shadow (it will just darken uniformly). It doesn't look as good, but it's cheaper to render.

The alternative is to design your scene layouts so that static objects don't cast shadows onto a real-time object in the first place.

6.20 Using Light Probes to Influence Lighting

Problem

You want to use light probes, so that real-time objects are lit by light bouncing off objects with baked lighting.

Solution

Create a light probe group by opening the GameObject menu and choosing Light → Light Probe Group. This creates a group of probes; you can select each individual probe and reposition it.

Light probes are affected by both real-time and baked lighting. Real-time objects will use nearby light probes to calculate how they should be lit. In Figure 6-27, there are no real-time lights in the scene; instead, light probes near the light source capture how light affects objects at each point, and the cylinder is using that information to light itself. Figure 6-28 shows the light probes set up here.

Figure 6-27. A real-time cylinder, lit by a baked emissive object

Figure 6-28. The light probes used in Figure 6-27

Discussion

Objects that don't contribute to global illumination can't receive baked light, because the light doesn't really "exist" during gameplay—instead, the light is written onto textures, and the static objects read from the texture to simulate light falling on them. This means that a real-time-lit object can look out of place with its surroundings, because absent any lighting information, it will be lit only by the global environment (such as the skybox, or ambient light sources). To solve this, you *could* create a real-time light for every baked light, or set every light to be Mixed (meaning it effectively functions as a baked light *and* a real-time light), but that can be a performance hit—especially when you have lots of lights, and you're rendering on a low-powered device that can't use deferred rendering (a rendering technique that significantly reduces the cost of multiple lights).

 We don't cover deferred rendering in this book, but you can learn more in the Unity documentation (*https://oreil.ly/0tgMy*).

Light probes are a solution to this problem and allow your real-time-lit objects to approximate the lighting conditions they would have experienced had the lighting been baked. A light probe does this by measuring the amount of baked light that passes through a given point during the baking process and storing it; during gameplay, your real-time-lit object samples from a collection of lighting probes, and renders itself as though there were lights nearby.

For the most effective results, place your light probes in areas where you expect real-time objects to be, and near areas where there are sudden changes in light intensity.

6.21 Using Reflection Probes

Problem

You want to use reflection probes, so that reflective materials look more realistic and reflect the scene around them.

Solution

Creating a reflection probe doesn't take many steps, and can lead to some great improvements in your shiny and reflective objects, since they'll be able to reflect the world around them:

1. First, create a reflection probe by opening the GameObject menu and choosing Light → Reflection Probe.
2. Next, place your probe somewhere in the center of the area for which you'd like to have reflections.

You can create multiple reflection probes. If you do, nearby reflective objects will blend between them.

To test the probe, create a shiny, metallic sphere by following these steps:

1. Create a new sphere by opening the GameObject menu and choosing 3D Object → Sphere.
2. Place the sphere somewhere near your reflection probe (or move the reflection probe somewhere near the sphere).
3. Create a new material by opening the Assets menu and then choosing Create → Material.
4. Name the new material "Shiny metal."

5. Drag the material onto the sphere you added.

6. Select the material, and increase the Smoothness value to about 0.8. As you do, the sphere will get shiny and reflect nearby objects by sampling the view seen by the reflection probe. Figure 6-29 shows a shiny metal sphere, reflecting the room around it. Its reflections come from a reflection probe near it (not pictured). We've added a little texture as well, for a nicer appearance.

Figure 6-29. A shiny metal sphere, reflecting the room around it

Discussion

In real-time rendering, accurate reflections are challenging. In the real world, reflections occur when light evenly bounces off a smooth surface, which means that an in-focus image can be achieved. This means that reflections are easy in ray-tracing renderers, because they trace the path taken by light as it bounces around a scene. However, most real-time renderers don't trace rays, mostly because of the amount of computational power required. Instead, they perform approximations: rather than bouncing a virtual photon off an object, they divide it into polygons, calculate the positions of the polygon's points relative to the camera position, and determine the locations of the pixels that that polygon overlaps. Then, the renderer solves the rendering equation, which is one of several simplified approximations for determining the color and brightness of a point, given information about its location, material, and nearby light sources.

All this is to say that reflections are challenging to compute, and for real-time performance on commodity hardware, are usually faked. There are several ways to fake a reflection. One method, popularized by games in the late 1990s like *Deus Ex*, uses the innovative approach of making bathroom mirrors and shiny floors semitransparent, creating a duplicated flipped copy of the room on the other side, and performing some trickery to ensure that all objects in the "reflected" copy of the world are in the same location as the "real" world. In Figure 6-30, the polished stone floor appears reflective, but it's actually semitransparent, and there's another, duplicated, upside-down version of the same room underneath. This works well enough, but can be difficult to do convincingly, and it's easy for small mistakes to be very obvious—famously, the main character's hands in *Deus Ex* were never in the same position as his reflection's. Additionally, because the reflected versions of the rooms actually existed, it limited the level designer's flexibility—you couldn't have a room with a shiny stone floor above another room, for example.

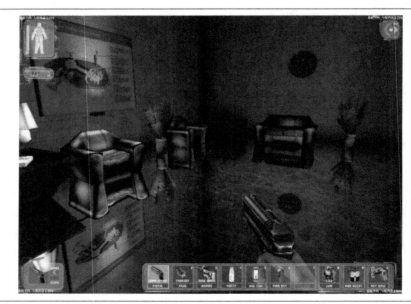

Figure 6-30. Reflections in Deus Ex *(Ion Storm Austin/Eidos Interactive)*

A more accurate approach would be to render the scene twice—once for the main view, and once flipped from the other side of the reflective surface (as done in *Uncharted 4*; see Figure 6-31). This is better, since it avoids the problems of duplicated geometry, but it also has the rather nasty side effect of rendering the same scene twice for every frame that the mirror is in view. This means that scenes that feature a mirror need to be very carefully constructed to minimize the performance hit.

Figure 6-31. Mirror reflections in Uncharted 4: A Thief's End *(Naughty Dog/Sony Interactive Entertainment)*

However, not every reflection in a game is a mirror. Sometimes, all you need is a glossy surface, or a wet floor, or vague reflections from a piece of glass that is otherwise meant to be looked through, not at. In this case, the reflected details don't need to be exact, because surface roughness means that a clear image wouldn't be clear anyway.

This means that the reflection could be generated ahead of time, and possibly from a different location. All that needs to be done is to render a snapshot, in all directions, from a single point. As long as the point at which the snapshot is taken is reasonably close to the object doing the reflecting, it'll look fine. If the reflections do need to be changed, you can change the Update mode on the reflection probe to do real-time updates as well, at a performance cost.

 The cost of rendering a scene multiple times is also why games designed for virtual reality need to be more careful with their performance. When rendering for a VR headset, each eye needs to see a different view on the scene, which means that the entire scene needs to be rendered separately for each eye.

6.22 Faking a Dynamic Emissive Object

Problem

You have a real-time object that has an emissive color, and you want it to illuminate other objects.

Solution

Fake it. Create a real-time light, and add it as a child. Make it the same color as your emissive light, and, if you place it right, the player won't realize that the emissive light isn't what's lighting up other objects. Figure 6-32 shows an object with the glow effect, with a point light inside it that's illuminating both the static walls and the real-time object next to it. Figure 6-33 shows same object with the light disabled. The effect is much less convincing.

Figure 6-32. An object with the glow effect, with a point light inside it

Figure 6-33. The same object with the light disabled

Discussion

Remember, all of computer graphics that aren't trying to physically simulate light bouncing around are just utter fakery. To the player, there's no difference between an object that's actually correct and an object that just *looks* correct.

6.23 Rendering to a Texture

Problem

You want to render a camera's view to a texture and use that texture in the scene.

Solution

Render textures can be created as assets. They don't contain anything useful when your game's not playing, but you can use the fact that they're assets as a convenient way to ensure that your components are making use of the correct textures.

Once you have a render texture, you can configure a camera to render to it (cameras that render to a render texture don't render to the screen):

1. Create a new render texture by opening the Assets menu and choosing Create → Render Texture.

2. Name the new render texture whatever you like.

3. Create a new camera by opening the GameObject menu and choosing Camera.

4. Name the new camera "Render Texture Camera," to help tell the difference between it and the main scene camera.

5. Drag the render texture asset onto the Render Texture Camera's Target Texture slot.

The Render Texture Camera will now render to the texture, and not to the screen; the texture can now be used like any other. For example, you can use this texture as part of a material; any renderer that uses this material will draw the view from the Render Texture Camera. To achieve this effect, follow these steps:

1. Create a new material by opening the Assets menu and then choosing Create → Material.

2. Name the new material whatever you like.

3. Select the material.

4. Drag the render texture asset that you created earlier onto the material's Albedo slot.

Finally, we'll create a game object to render the material:

1. Create a new quad to render the material on by opening the GameObject menu and choosing 3D Object → Quad.

2. Drag the material onto the quad you just created.

The quad will display the view seen by the camera (see Figures 6-34 and 6-35). Try moving the Render Texture Camera around to see it change.

Figure 6-34. The camera set up to render to a texture

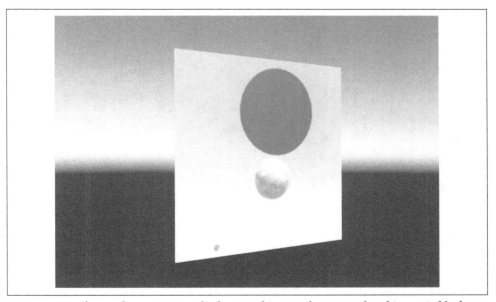

Figure 6-35. The render texture applied to an object in the scene; the objects visible from the camera are drawn onto the surface of the object

Discussion

The default resolution for render textures is 256×256, but you can change it by selecting the asset and modifying its size in the Inspector.

Don't forget that render textures consume memory—the larger the texture, the more memory it will take up.

CHAPTER 7

3D Physics and Character Control

Physics is a crucial component of many video games. Whether your game is 2D or 3D, or something in between, you'll be relying on some manner of physical force simulation at some point.

One of the most interesting things about physical simulation is that you get quite a bit of interesting gameplay opportunities for free. Human beings exist in a physical, three-dimensional world, and it's very easy for a player to relate to your game when the game has "mechanics" that they interact with every day.

To that end, we'll spend this chapter looking at ways to build gameplay systems that allow for character control in a physically simulated 3D environment, with a particular focus on first-person controls.

Unity has two physics systems: one designed for 2D physics, which we discuss in Chapter 5, and one designed for 3D physics. This chapter is about the 3D physics system.

7.1 Running Code a Specific Number of Times per Second

Problem

You want to write code that runs a fixed number of times per second.

Solution

Put the code in the FixedUpdate method of your scripts.

Discussion

In your scripts, the `Update` method is called every frame, which makes it ideal for almost everything that needs to be updated regularly.

`Update` isn't called at a regular pace; it depends on how long it takes to render each frame. If the scene gets more complex, the number of `Update` calls per second will change.

By comparison, `FixedUpdate` *is* called a fixed number of times per second. This makes it ideal for physics simulation, which behaves better when the rate of time passing between physics simulation updates remains the same.

> This doesn't mean that the same amount of real-world time will elapse between `FixedUpdate` calls; Unity just guarantees that the same *number* of `FixedUpdate` calls will happen per second.

If you want to update something at the same rate as physics, put the code in `Fixed Update`. If objects that interact with physics objects aren't updated at the same rate as physics objects, you can get odd jittering behaviors, and it doesn't feel good.

7.2 Allowing the Player to Look Around Using the Mouse

Problem

In a first-person-style game, you want to be able to control the direction in which the player is looking by using the mouse.

Solution

Allowing the player to control a first-person view using their mouse is traditionally referred to as *mouselook*.

> Mouselook is sometimes called *freelook*, as it doesn't have to be tied explicitly to mouse control: it can apply to control with a D-pad, a joystick, an analogue stick, or similar.

Implementing mouselook involves rotating two separate objects: the body and the head. The body rotates around the *y*-axis (also known as the "yaw" axis—the line that goes from down to up), while the head rotates around the *x*-axis (the line that goes from left to right). In a first-person game, the camera is attached to the head, like this:

1. Create a new, empty game object. Name it "Player."

2. Locate the main Camera object. If you don't have one, open the GameObject menu and choose Camera.

3. Drag the Camera object into the Player object, and rename it "Head."

4. Position the Head object where you want the head to be. For best results, don't modify any component of the position other than the *y*-component; the others should be at 0. This means that the camera will be directly above the center of the body.

5. Create a new C# script called *MouseLook.cs*, with the following code:

```csharp
// Implements mouselook. Horizontal mouse movement rotates the body
// around the y-axis, while vertical mouse movement rotates the head
// around the x-axis.
public class MouseLook : MonoBehaviour
{

    // The speed at which we turn. In other words, mouse sensitivity.
    [SerializeField] float turnSpeed = 90f;

    // How far up the head can tilt, measured in angles from dead-
    // level. Must be higher than headLowerAngleLimit.
    [SerializeField] float headUpperAngleLimit = 85f;

    // How far down the head can tilt, measured in angles from dead-
    // level. Must be lower than headLowerAngleLimit.
    [SerializeField] float headLowerAngleLimit = -80f;

    // Our current rotation from our start, in degrees
    float yaw = 0f;
    float pitch = 0f;

    // Stores the orientations of the head and body when the game
    // started. We'll derive new orientations by combining these
    // with our yaw and pitch.
    Quaternion bodyStartOrientation;
    Quaternion headStartOrientation;

    // A reference to the head object—the object to rotate up and down.
    // (The body is the current object, so we don't need a variable to
    // store a reference to it.) Not exposed in the interface; instead,
    // we'll figure out what to use by looking for a Camera child object
    // at game start.
    Transform head;

    // When the game starts, perform initial setup.
    void Start()
    {
```

```csharp
        // Find our head object
        head = GetComponentInChildren<Camera>().transform;

        // Cache the orientation of the body and head
        bodyStartOrientation = transform.localRotation;
        headStartOrientation = head.transform.localRotation;

        // Lock and hide the cursor
        Cursor.lockState = CursorLockMode.Locked;
        Cursor.visible = false;
    }

    // Every time physics updates, update our movement. (We do this in
    // FixedUpdate to keep pace with physically simulated objects. If
    // you won't be interacting with physics objects, you can do
    // this in Update instead.)
    void FixedUpdate()
    {

        // Read the current horizontal movement, and scale it based on
        // the amount of time that's elapsed and the movement speed.
        var horizontal = Input.GetAxis("Mouse X")
                            * Time.deltaTime * turnSpeed;

        // Same for vertical.
        var vertical = Input.GetAxis("Mouse Y")
                            * Time.deltaTime * turnSpeed;

        // Update our yaw and pitch values.
        yaw += horizontal;
        pitch += vertical;

        // Clamp pitch so that we can't look directly down or up.
        pitch =
            Mathf.Clamp(pitch, headLowerAngleLimit, headUpperAngleLimit);

        // Compute a rotation for the body by rotating around the y-axis
        // by the number of yaw degrees, and for the head around the
        // x-axis by the number of pitch degrees.
        var bodyRotation = Quaternion.AngleAxis(yaw, Vector3.up);
        var headRotation = Quaternion.AngleAxis(pitch, Vector3.right);

        // Create new rotations for the body and head by combining them
        // with their start rotations.
        transform.localRotation = bodyRotation * bodyStartOrientation;
        head.localRotation = headRotation * headStartOrientation;
    }
}
```

6. Attach a `MouseLook` component to the body.

7. Play the game. Moving the mouse will rotate the body and the head.

Discussion

By separating the head and body rotation, this approach to orienting the player's perspective avoids the problem of "rolling" the view—something that can happen if an object pitches down and then "yaws" to the side, which produces an orientation that's rotated around the forward axis.

 If you prefer your mouselook to be inverted, simply multiply the `Input.GetAxis("Mouse Y")` value by –1.

7.3 Controlling a 3D Character

Problem

You want to control a character in 3D space.

Solution

You'll typically want to start with mouselook first, since without the ability to turn, you'll only be able to move forward, backward, and side to side. We'll assume that you've followed the steps in Recipe 7.2.

Once you've implemented mouselook, we'll add some features:

1. Add a `CharacterController` component to your Player object.

2. Move the Head object to the top of the `CharacterController`.

3. Create a new C# script called *Movement.cs*, and add the following code to it:

```csharp
// Implements character controller movement.
public class Movement : MonoBehaviour {

    // The speed at which we can move, in units per second.
    [SerializeField] float moveSpeed = 6;

    // The height of a jump, in units.
    [SerializeField] float jumpHeight = 2;

    // The rate at which our vertical speed will be reduced, in units
    // per second.
    [SerializeField] float gravity = 20;
```

```csharp
    // The degree to which we can control our movement while in midair.
    [Range(0, 10), SerializeField] float airControl = 5;

    // Our current movement direction. If we're on the ground, we have
    // direct control over it, but if we're in the air, we only have
    // partial control over it.
    Vector3 moveDirection = Vector3.zero;

    // A cached reference to the character controller, which we'll be
    // using often.
    CharacterController controller;

    void Start()
    {
        controller = GetComponent<CharacterController>();
    }

    // We do our movement logic in FixedUpdate so that our movement
    // can happen at the same pace as physics updates. If it didn't,
    // we'd see jitter when we interact with physics objects that can
    // move around.
    void FixedUpdate () {

        // The input vector describes the user's desired local-space
        // movement; if we're on the ground, this will immediately
        // become our movement, but if we're in the air, we'll
        // interpolate between our current movement and this vector, to
        // simulate momentum.
        var input = new Vector3(
            Input.GetAxis("Horizontal"),
            0,
            Input.GetAxis("Vertical")
        );

        // Multiply this movement by our desired movement speed
        input *= moveSpeed;

        // The controller's Move method uses world-space directions, so
        // we need to convert this direction to world space
        input = transform.TransformDirection(input);

        // Is the controller's bottommost point touching the ground?
        if (controller.isGrounded)
        {
            // Figure out how much movement we want to apply in local
            // space.
            moveDirection = input;

            // Is the user pressing the jump button right now?
```

```
if (Input.GetButton("Jump"))
{
    // Calculate the amount of upward speed we need,
    // considering that we add moveDirection.y to our height
    // every frame, and we reduce moveDirection.y by gravity
    // every frame.
    moveDirection.y = Mathf.Sqrt(2 * gravity * jumpHeight);
} else {
    // We're on the ground, but not jumping. Set our
    // downward movement to 0 (otherwise, because we're
    // continuously reducing our y-movement, if we walk off
    // a ledge, we'd suddenly have a huge amount of
    // downward momentum).
    moveDirection.y = 0;
}
} else {
    // Slowly bring our movement toward the user's desired
    // input, but preserve our current y-direction (so that the
    // arc of the jump is preserved)
    input.y = moveDirection.y;
    moveDirection = Vector3.Lerp(moveDirection, input,
                                 airControl * Time.deltaTime);
}

// Bring our movement down by applying gravity over time
moveDirection.y -= gravity * Time.deltaTime;

// Move the controller. The controller will refuse to move into
// other colliders, which means that we won't clip through the
// ground or other colliders. (However, this doesn't stop other
// colliders from moving into us. For that, we'd need to detect
// when we're overlapping another collider, and move away from
// them. We'll cover this in another recipe!)
controller.Move(moveDirection * Time.deltaTime);
}
}
```

4. Attach a `Movement` component to your `Player` object.

5. Play the game. Pressing the arrow keys or the W, A, S, and D keys will move the player around (unless you've customized your input system). You can also jump by pressing the space bar.

Discussion

It's certainly possible to implement a completely physically correct control setup for your game, in which the player is simulated as a rigidbody and moves around by having forces applied to that body. However, for the best-feeling control in your game, it's better to manage the player's movement using your own code, rather than doing it in physics. This is because it's very challenging to create a control scheme that responds to player input in a way that feels responsive and pleasant.

Some of the games with the best-feeling controls have extremely unrealistic physics, and even games that claim realism aren't physically realistic. Every game in the *Mario* series of platform games has extremely unrealistic physics, but that doesn't matter when the goal is enjoyable gameplay. Modern action-adventure games like the *Tomb Raider* series also feature physically implausible movement. It doesn't matter; what matters is the interaction between the player and your game's controls. To that end, directly controlling the player's speed and inertia, rather than having the physics system handle it for you, gives you the control you need over the player's experience.

 A great resource on the topic of how a game feels to control is *Game Feel: A Game Designer's Guide to Virtual Sensation* by Steve Swink (CRC Press).

The setup presented in this recipe will be used in several other recipes in this chapter, since it's a good foundation.

7.4 Interacting with Switches and Objects

Problem

You want players to be able to aim a first-person controller at objects in the world, and press a *use* key. Certain objects should react to being interacted with in this way.

 This recipe assumes that you've set up your player by following Recipes 7.2 and 7.3.

Solution

Interacting with objects requires firing invisible rays out of the camera to detect what you're looking at. The rays will stop at the first collider they see that's within range; we need to ensure that we never hit the `CharacterCollider`:

1. Open the Edit menu, and choose Project Settings → Tags & Layers.
2. Set one of the blank user Layers to "Player."
3. Select your Player object—the one that contains the `CharacterController`.

---

4. Open the Layers menu at the top-right corner of the Inspector, and choose Player. When prompted to set the layer of the child objects as well, click "Yes, change children."

5. Create a new C# script called *Interactable.cs*. Add the following code to it:

```
// Implements being interacted with by an Interacting component.
// Requires a collider, because Interacting objects find their targets
// by casting rays that hit colliders.
[RequireComponent(typeof(Collider))]
public class Interactable : MonoBehaviour {

    public void Interact(GameObject fromObject) {
        Debug.LogFormat("I've been interacted with by {0}!", fromObject);
    }
}
```

6. Attach this component to the object you want to interact with. The object must have a collider of some kind.

7. Create a new C# script called *Interacting.cs*. Add the following code to it:

```
// Implements interacting with Interactable objects
public class Interacting : MonoBehaviour {

    // The key to press to interact with an object.
    [SerializeField] KeyCode interactionKey = KeyCode.E;

    // The range at which we can interact with objects.
    [SerializeField] float interactingRange = 2;

    void Update () {

        // Did the user just press the interaction key?
        if (Input.GetKeyDown(interactionKey)) {

            // Then attempt to interact.
            AttemptInteraction();
        }
    }

    void AttemptInteraction() {

        // Create a ray from the current position and forward direction
        var ray = new Ray(transform.position, transform.forward);

        // Store information about the hit in this variable
        RaycastHit hit;

        // Create a layer mask that represents every layer except the
        // players
```

```
var everythingExceptPlayers =
    ~(1 << LayerMask.NameToLayer("Player"));

// Combine this layer mask with the one that raycasts usually
// use; this has the effect of removing the player layer from
// the list of layers to raycast against
var layerMask = Physics.DefaultRaycastLayers
                        & everythingExceptPlayers;

// Perform the raycast out, hitting only objects that are on
// layers described by the layer mask we just assembled
if (Physics.Raycast(ray, out hit, interactingRange,
                     layerMask)) {

    // Try to get the Interactable component on the object
    // we hit
    var interactable = hit.collider
                        .GetComponent<Interactable>();

    // Does it exist?
    if (interactable != null) {

        // Signal that it was interacted with.
        interactable.Interact(this.gameObject);
    }
}

    }
}
```

8. Attach this component to your Head object. Play the game; when you look at a nearby object that has the `Interactable` component and press the interaction key, the `Interactable` component will log that it's been interacted with.

You can now build upon this to create interactive behaviors, like making objects appear when an in-game button is used.

Discussion

Each game object in Unity can be assigned to a *layer*, which groups them together. Layers are used in a few different parts of Unity; for example, a camera can be configured to render objects that are only on a certain layer.

Layers can also be used to control the physics system. In this case, we use layers to ensure that the raycast never hits a player, which would cause problems.

7.5 Picking Up and Putting Down Objects

Problem

You want to be able to pull objects toward you, and if they're close enough, pick them up. You want to be able to throw objects you're holding.

 This recipe assumes that you've set up your player by following Recipes 7.2 and 7.3. You'll also need to set up the Player layer, as per Recipe 7.4.

Solution

To pull, grab, hold, and throw objects, we'll first create a new C# script called *Grabbing.cs*, and add the following code to it:

```csharp
// Implements pulling, grabbing, holding, and throwing.
// A rigidbody is required because we need one to connect our
// grabbing joint to
[RequireComponent(typeof(Rigidbody))]
public class Grabbing : MonoBehaviour {

    // The range from this object at which an object can be picked up.
    [SerializeField] float grabbingRange = 3;

    // The range from this object at which an object can be pulled
    // toward us.
    [SerializeField] float pullingRange = 20;

    // The location at which objects that are picked up will be placed.
    [SerializeField] Transform holdPoint = null;

    // The key to press to pick up or drop an object
    [SerializeField] KeyCode grabKey = KeyCode.E;

    // The key to press to throw an object
    [SerializeField] KeyCode throwKey = KeyCode.Mouse0;

    // The amount of force to apply on a thrown object
    [SerializeField] float throwForce = 100f;

    // The amount of force to apply on objects that we're pulling toward
    // us. Don't forget that objects we're pulling will have friction
    // working against us, so the value might need to be higher than
    // you think.
    [SerializeField] float pullForce = 50f;

    // If the grab joint encounters this much force, break it.
```

```
[SerializeField] float grabBreakingForce = 100f;

// If the grab joint encounters this much torque, break it.
[SerializeField] float grabBreakingTorque = 100f;

// The joint that holds our grabber object. Null if we're not
// holding anything.
FixedJoint grabJoint;

// The rigidbody that we're holding. Null if we're not holding
// anything.
Rigidbody grabbedRigidbody;

private void Awake()
{
    // Do some quick validity checks when we start up

    if (holdPoint == null) {
        Debug.LogError("Grab hold point must not be null!");
    }

    if (holdPoint.IsChildOf(transform) == false) {
        Debug.LogError(
            "Grab hold point must be a child of this object"
            );
    }

    var playerCollider = GetComponentInParent<Collider>();

    playerCollider.gameObject.layer = LayerMask
                            .NameToLayer("Player");
}

private void Update()
{
    // Is the user holding the grab key, and we're not
    // holding something?
    if (Input.GetKey(grabKey) && grabJoint == null) {

        // Attempt to perform a pull or a grab
        AttemptPull();

    }
    // Did the user just press the grab key, and we're holding
    // something?
    else if (Input.GetKeyDown(grabKey) && grabJoint != null) {
        Drop();
    }
    // Does the user want to throw the held object, and we're
    // holding something?
    else if (Input.GetKeyDown(throwKey) && grabJoint != null) {
        // Now apply the throw force
```

```
        Throw ();
    }

}

// Throws a held object
void Throw()
{
    // Can't throw if we're not holding anything!
    if (grabbedRigidbody == null) {
        return;
    }

    // Keep a reference to the body we were holding, because Drop
    // will reset it
    var thrownBody = grabbedRigidbody;

    // Calculate the force to apply
    var force = transform.forward * throwForce;

    // And apply it
    thrownBody.AddForce(force);

    // We need to drop what we're holding before we can throw it
    Drop();

}

// Attempts to pull or pick up the object directly ahead of this
// object. When this script is attached to a camera, it will try to
// get the object directly in the middle of the camera's view. (You
// may want to add a reticle to the GUI to help the player know
// where the precise center of the screen is.)
private void AttemptPull()
{
    // Perform a raycast. If we hit something that has a rigidbody
    // and is not kinematic, pick it up.

    // Create a ray that goes from our current position, and goes
    // out along our current direction.
    var ray = new Ray(transform.position, transform.forward);

    // Create a variable to store the results of what we hit.
    RaycastHit hit;

    // Create a layer mask that represents every layer except the
    // players'
    var everythingExceptPlayers =
        ~(1 << LayerMask.NameToLayer("Player"));

    // Combine this layer mask with the one that raycasts usually
    // use; this has the effect of removing the Player layer from
```

```
// the list of layers to raycast against
var layerMask = Physics.DefaultRaycastLayers
                        & everythingExceptPlayers;

// Perform a raycast that uses this layer mask to ignore the
// players. We use our pulling range because it's the longest;
// if the object is actually within our (shorter) grabbing
// range, we'll grab it instead of pulling it.
var hitSomething =
    Physics.Raycast(ray, out hit, pullingRange, layerMask);

if (hitSomething == false)
{
    // Our raycast hit nothing within the pulling range.
    return;
}

// We hit something! Is it something we can pick up?
grabbedRigidbody = hit.rigidbody;

if (grabbedRigidbody == null || grabbedRigidbody.isKinematic)
{
    // We can't pick this up; it either has no rigidbody, or
    // it's kinematic.
    return;
}

// We now have an object that's within our pulling range.

// Is the object within the grabbing range, too?
if (hit.distance < grabbingRange) {

    // We can pick it up.

    // Move the body to our grab position.
    grabbedRigidbody.transform.position = holdPoint.position;

    // Create a joint that will hold this in place, and
    // configure it
    grabJoint = gameObject.AddComponent<FixedJoint>();
    grabJoint.connectedBody = grabbedRigidbody;
    grabJoint.breakForce = grabBreakingForce;
    grabJoint.breakTorque = grabBreakingTorque;

    // Ensure that this grabbed object doesn't collide with
    // this collider, or any collider in our parent, which
    // could cause problems
    foreach (var myCollider in
            GetComponentsInParent<Collider>())
    {
        Physics.IgnoreCollision(myCollider, hit.collider, true);
    }
```

```
    } else {
        // It's not in grabbing range, but it is in pulling range.
        // Pull it toward us, until it's in grabbing range.

        var pull = -transform.forward * this.pullForce;

        grabbedRigidbody.AddForce(pull);

    }

}

// Drops the object
private void Drop()
{

    if (grabJoint != null)
    {
        Destroy(grabJoint);
    }

    // Bail out if the object we were holding isn't there anymore
    if (grabbedRigidbody == null)
    {
        return;
    }

    // Re-enable collisions between this object and our collider(s)
    foreach (var myCollider in GetComponentsInParent<Collider>())
    {
        Physics.IgnoreCollision(
            myCollider,
            grabbedRigidbody.GetComponent<Collider>(),
            false);
    }

    grabbedRigidbody = null;
}

// Draw the location of the hold point
private void OnDrawGizmos()
{
    if (holdPoint == null) {
        return;
    }
    Gizmos.color = Color.magenta;
    Gizmos.DrawSphere(holdPoint.position, 0.2f);
}

// Called when a joint that's attached to the game object this
// component is on has broken.
private void OnJointBreak(float breakForce)
```

```
        {
            // When our joint breaks, call Drop to ensure that we clean up
            // after ourselves.
            Drop();
        }
    }
}
```

Next, we'll set up the Player objects to use this *Grabbing.cs* script:

1. Attach this component to the Head object.

2. Create a new child object of the Head object. Name it "Grab Point." This will be the location that objects will be held at, relative to the player's head.

3. Set the position of the Grab Point object to a position slightly lower than the Head object, and a short distance in front of it. A position of (0, –0.25, 1.25) can work well.

4. Select the Head object again, and set the Grabbing component's Hold Point field to the Grab Point object you just created.

5. Turn on the Is Kinematic option on the Head object's Rigidbody component.

Now we'll create a cube that we can grab:

1. Create a new cube by opening the GameObject menu and choosing 3D Object → Cube.

2. Set its scale to (0.25, 0.25, 0.25).

3. Add a Rigidbody component to the cube.

When you play the game, you will be able to pull the cube toward you by pressing the E key. When it's in range, you will grab it. Press the left mouse button to throw the object you're holding.

Discussion

This is a system that's very similar to the *gravity gun*, featured prominently in the second half of *Half-Life 2* (Valve Corporation).

There are a few things you might want to try, once you've got it working in your scene:

- Experiment with directly setting the velocity of thrown objects.
- Experiment with different pulling and grabbing ranges.
- Experiment with only being able to pick up objects below a certain mass (so that, for example, you can't pick up a massive rock).

You can find the mass of an object by first getting its `Rigidbody` component, and then accessing its `mass` property.

7.6 Detecting When an Object Is Touching Another Object

Problem

You want to detect when two physical objects are touching.

Solution

Add the `OnCollisionEnter`, `OnCollisionExit`, and `OnCollisionStay` methods to your scripts:

```
private void OnCollisionEnter(Collision collision)
{
    Debug.LogFormat("Object {0} started touching {1}!",
                    collision.gameObject.name, this.name);
}

private void OnCollisionExit(Collision collision)
{
    Debug.LogFormat("Object {0} stopped touching {1}!",
                    collision.gameObject.name, this.name);
}

private void OnCollisionStay(Collision collision)
{
    Debug.LogFormat("Object {0} remained touching {1}!",
                    collision.gameObject.name, this.name);
}
```

Discussion

These methods are called for any game object that has a `Collider` and a `Rigidbody` component:

OnCollisionEnter
   Called when the object begins touching another

OnCollisionExit
   Called when the object stops touching another

OnCollisionStay
   Called on every frame that the two objects remain touching

All three of these methods receive a `Collision` parameter, which stores information about the collision, including the speed at which the collision hit, and the point in the world at which the objects are making contact.

 Collisions will be detected only when at least one of the two colliding objects has a *nonkinematic* rigidbody. A kinematic rigidbody is one that applies forces to other objects, but does not respond to forces itself. For example, a floating platform that doesn't respond to gravity could be set up using a kinematic body. To make a body kinematic, check the Is Kinematic box in the Inspector (see Figure 7-1).

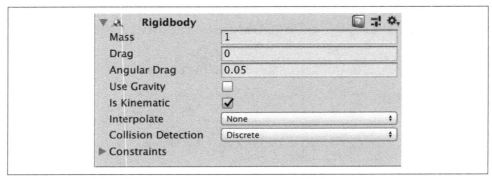

Figure 7-1. Enabling the Is Kinematic option on a rigidbody

7.7 Detecting When an Object Is in a Trigger Area

Problem

You want to detect when an object has entered a collider that's marked as a trigger.

Solution

Add the `OnTriggerEnter`, `OnTriggerExit`, and `OnTriggerStay` methods to your scripts:

```
private void OnTriggerEnter(Collider other)
{
    Debug.LogFormat("Object {0} entered trigger {1}!",
                    other.name, this.name);
}

private void OnTriggerExit(Collider other)
{
    Debug.LogFormat("Object {0} exited trigger {1}!",
```

```
                              other.name, this.name);
    }

    private void OnTriggerStay(Collider other)
    {
        Debug.LogFormat("Object {0} remained in trigger {1}!",
                              other.name, this.name);
    }
```

Discussion

When a collider is marked as a trigger, selecting the Is Trigger checkbox on its Inspector makes it behave differently in the scene. Trigger colliders do not collide with other objects; instead, they permit anything to pass through them. Because they don't collide, they don't generate the OnCollision messages discussed in Recipe 7.6. Instead, they generate OnTrigger messages.

The OnTrigger messages work similarly to the OnCollision messages, in that On TriggerEnter, OnTriggerExit, and OnTriggerStay are called when an object enters, leaves, and remains inside a trigger collider.

One significant difference between the two groups of methods is that the OnTrigger methods receive a Collider as their parameter, not a Collision. This is because there is no collision to report; the only useful information is the identity of the other collider.

 Trigger events are sent only if at least one of the colliders involved also has a rigidbody attached.

7.8 Implementing Moving Platforms

Problem

You want objects to move from point to point.

Solution

To make an object move from point to point, you need three things: a list of points in space to move between, the index of the current point that the object is moving toward, and code that moves the object toward the current point, cycling to the next point when it gets close enough:

1. Create a new C# script called *MovingPlatform.cs*, and add the following code to it:

```csharp
// Moves an object at a fixed speed through a series of points.
public class MovingPlatform : MonoBehaviour {

    // The positions that the platform will move through, stored in local
    // position.
    [SerializeField] Vector3[] points = {};

    // The speed at which it will move between them.
    [SerializeField] float speed = 10f;

    // The index into the 'points' array; this is the point we're trying
    // to move toward
    int nextPoint = 0;

    // Where the platform was when the game started
    Vector3 startPosition;

    // How fast this platform is currently moving, in units per second
    public Vector3 velocity { get; private set; }

    // Use this for initialization
    void Start () {
        if (points == null || points.Length < 2) {
            Debug.LogError("Platform needs 2 or more points to work.");
            return;
        }

        // All of our movement points are defined relative to where we
        // are when the game starts, so record that (since
        // transform.position will change over time)
        startPosition = transform.position;

        // Start our cycle at our first point
        transform.position = currentPoint;
    }

    // Returns the point that we're currently moving toward.
    Vector3 currentPoint {
        get {
            // If we have no points, return our current position
            if (points == null || points.Length == 0) {
                return transform.position;
            }
            // Return the point we're trying to get to
            return points[nextPoint] + startPosition;
        }
    }
}
```

```csharp
// Update every time physics updates
void FixedUpdate () {

    // Move toward the target at a fixed speed
    var newPosition = Vector3.MoveTowards(
        transform.position, currentPoint, speed * Time.deltaTime);

    // Have we reached the target?
    if (Vector3.Distance(newPosition, currentPoint) < 0.001) {
        // Snap to the target point
        newPosition = currentPoint;

        // Move to the next target, wrapping around to the start if
        // necessary
        nextPoint += 1;
        nextPoint %= points.Length;
    }

    // Calculate our current velocity in units per second
    velocity =
        (newPosition - transform.position) / Time.deltaTime;

    // Update to our new location
    transform.position = newPosition;

}


// Draw the path that the platform will follow
private void OnDrawGizmosSelected()
{
    if (points == null || points.Length < 2) {
        return;
    }

    // Our points are stored in local space, so we need to offset
    // them to know where they are in world space.
    Vector3 offsetPosition = transform.position;

    // If we're playing, our transform is moving, so we need to use
    // the cached start position to figure out where our points
    // are in world space.
    if (Application.isPlaying) {
        offsetPosition = startPosition;
    }

    Gizmos.color = Color.blue;

    // Loop over all the points
    for (int p = 0; p < points.Length; p++) {
```

```
                    // Get this point and the next one, wrapping around to the
                    // first
                    var p1 = points[p];
                    var p2 = points[(p + 1) % points.Length];

                    // Draw the point
                    Gizmos.DrawSphere(offsetPosition + p1, 0.1f);

                    // Draw the line between the points
                    Gizmos.DrawLine(offsetPosition + p1, offsetPosition + p2);
                }
            }
        }
```

2. Create a new cube, and add a `MovingPlatform` to it.

3. Add as many points to it as you'd like. They'll be displayed in the Scene view.

4. Play the game. The object will move to each of the points, in a circuit.

Discussion

Without additional code, the platform will move through the player. This is because the platform doesn't know where the player is, and the player doesn't know where the platform is. Without a mechanism for detecting these overlapping objects, you'll end up with objects moving through each other. This is something that's fixed in Recipe 7.9.

Note also that the movement code takes place in the `FixedUpdate` method. This is done to ensure that platform movement happens at the same rate as all other movement in the scene, including the movement of rigidbodies and the player's character controller.

 The code in this recipe stores the velocity of the platform; this isn't directly used by this recipe, but it's used in Recipe 7.9.

7.9 Implementing Platform Riding

Problem

You want your character controller to be able to stand on a moving platform, as implemented in Recipe 7.8. You also want the character controller to be pushed out of the way if a moving platform moves into it sideways.

Solution

This recipe builds upon the steps in Recipe 7.8, used to create a moving platform. If you haven't already followed that recipe, you should do that first.

We'll be adding a new script that will be attached to the player, and adds support for letting the player move with any platform they're touching. So, if they're standing on a platform, they'll be carried by it, and if a platform is pushing against them from any other direction than up, they'll be moved away:

1. Create a new C# script called *PlatformRiding.cs*, and add the following code to it:

```
// Implements platform riding (standing on a moving platform means we'll
// move with the platform), and pushing (if an object moves into us, it
// will push us away)
[RequireComponent(typeof(CharacterController))]
public class PlatformRiding : MonoBehaviour {

    // The CharacterController on this object.
    CharacterController controller;

    private void Start()
    {
        // We'll be checking our character controller a lot. Cache a
        // reference to it.
        controller = GetComponent<CharacterController>();
    }

    // Every time physics updates, check to see if our collider is
    // overlapping something, and if it is, push ourselves out of it.
    private void FixedUpdate()
    {
        // First, we'll handle pushing the character collider out of the
        // way if another object moves into it.

        // A character collider's physical shape is a capsule. We need
        // to ask the physics system if this capsule is overlapping
        // anything else; to do this, we need to figure out the values
        // that define this capsule.

        // You can think of a capsule as a cylinder with two spheres
        // on either end, where the spheres have the same radius as the
        // the cylinder. This means that a capsule can be defined by
        // three values: the locations of the centers of the two spheres,
        // and the radius.

        // Given that a character collider exposes its total height
        // (including spheres!) and the radius, we can use this
        // to figure out the location of the two capsule points
        // in world space.
```

```
// The center of the sphere at the top of the controller's
// capsule
var capsulePoint1 = transform.position + new Vector3(
    0, (controller.height / 2) - controller.radius, 0);

// The center of the sphere at the bottom of the controller's
// capsule
var capsulePoint2 = transform.position - new Vector3(
    0, (controller.height / 2) + controller.radius, 0);

// The list of colliders we may be overlapping. We're unlikely
// to overlap more than 10 colliders, so make the list that
// long. (Adjust this if you're encountering lots of overlaps.)
Collider[] overlappingColliders = new Collider[10];

// Figure out which colliders we're overlapping. We pass in the
// overlappingColliders array, and when this function returns,
// the array will be filled with references to other colliders.
// The function returns the number of colliders that overlap
// the capsule.
var overlapCount = Physics.OverlapCapsuleNonAlloc(
    capsulePoint1, capsulePoint2,  // the centers of the spheres
    controller.radius,  // the radius of the spheres
    overlappingColliders);

// (Note: we _could_ have used OverlapCapsule, which returns a
// brand-new array, but that requires the function to allocate
// the memory for it on the heap. Because we don't use this
// array after this function ends, the array would turn into
// garbage. More garbage means the garbage collector will run
// more often, which means performance hitches. By creating our
// array locally, we ensure it's stored on the stack; data on
// the stack doesn't get turned into garbage when it goes away,
// but it can't stay around after this function returns,
// which is fine for this case.)

// For each item we were told the capsule overlaps...
for (int i = 0; i < overlapCount; i++) {

    // Get the collider the capsule overlaps
    var overlappingCollider = overlappingColliders[i];

    // If this collider is our controller, ignore it
    if (overlappingCollider == controller)  {
        continue;
    }

    // We need to compute how much movement we need to perform
    // to not overlap this collider.
```

```
// First, define some variables to store the direction and
// distance.
Vector3 direction;
float distance;

// Next, provide information about both our collider and the
// other one. Our direction and distance variables will be
// filled with data.
Physics.ComputePenetration(
    controller,  // our collider
    transform.position, // its position
    transform.rotation, // its orientation
    overlappingCollider, // the other collider
    overlappingCollider.transform.position,  // its position
    overlappingCollider.transform.rotation,  // its
                                             // orientation
    out direction, // will hold the direction we should
                   // move in
    out distance   // will contain the distance we should
                   // move by
);

// Don't get pushed vertically; that's what 1. gravity and
// 2. moving platforms are for.
direction.y = 0;

// Update our position to move out of the way.
transform.position += direction * distance;

}

// Next, we'll handle standing on a moving platform.

// Cast a ray down to our feet. If it hit a MovingPlatform,
// inherit its velocity.

// (We don't need to worry about avoiding the character
// controller here, because the raycast starts inside the
// controller, so it won't hit it.)

var ray = new Ray(transform.position, Vector3.down);
RaycastHit hit;

// The maximum distance we want to look for.
float maxDistance = (controller.height / 2f) + 0.1f;

// Cast the ray. Did it hit anything?
if (Physics.Raycast(ray, out hit, maxDistance)) {
```

```
            // It did!

            // Did it have a MovingPlatform component?
            var platform = hit.collider.gameObject
                            .GetComponent<MovingPlatform>();

            if (platform != null) {
                // If it did, update our position based on the
                // platform's current velocity.
                transform.position +=
                    platform.velocity * Time.deltaTime;
            }
        }
    }
}
```

2. Add a `PlatformRiding` component to the player character—that is, the object that has your `CharacterCollider`.

3. Play the game, and jump onto an object that has a `MovingPlatform` component. Your character will be carried with the platform. Additionally, if you get off the platform and then stand in its way, you will be pushed by the platform as it moves into you.

Discussion

This recipe performs two different tests to see if the `CharacterCollider` needs to be moved:

1. First, it calculates the size of the capsule that the `CharacterCollider` occupies, and then asks Unity's physics system to check to see what colliders also occupy this space. If a platform is pushing into the character, the two colliders will be intersecting, albeit by a small amount.

   If the colliders *are* intersecting, then we ask the physics system to compute the `depenetration vector`. This is the amount of movement that it would take to move the player so that the two objects aren't overlapping. It's then a simple matter of moving the player by that vector, which means that it moves "out" of the platform; the net result is that the player is pushed away from the platform.

2. Next, it performs a raycast from the center of the `CharacterCollider` down to a short distance below the bottom of the collider. If this raycast hits a `Collider` that has a `MovingPlatform` attached to it, the player is moved in the same way as the platform: by multiplying the platform's current velocity by delta time.

   Note that because this code is run in the `FixedUpdate` method (which means that it's done at the same rate as all other physics updates), we don't use

---

`Time.deltaTime`, but rather `Time.fixedDeltaTime`—the amount of time that has elapsed since the last call to `FixedUpdate`.

It's important to note that because the player is being moved manually, there's no momentum being imparted. If you're on a platform that's moving up quickly and suddenly stops, you won't be flung into the air due to inertia.

7.10 Responding to Being Pushed by Objects

Problem

You want your character collider to be able to push rigidbodies around.

Solution

If a character collider is being moved manually, which is the case in the recipes in this chapter, the physics engine won't automatically apply *pushing* forces to other objects that the player moves into, even if the object is movable and no matter its mass. Instead, the character collider will notice the overlap and refuse to move into it, which creates the feeling of the object being huge, heavy, and immovable.

To implement pushing, then, we need to manually apply forces, or directly set the velocity. In this recipe, we'll implement a script that allows for both options:

1. Create a new C# script called *Pushing.cs*. Add the following code to it:

```
// Implements pushing rigidbodies from a character collider.
public class Pushing : MonoBehaviour {

    // Defines the possible types of pushing we can apply.
    public enum PushMode
    {
        // Don't allow any pushing
        NoPushing,

        // Push by directly setting the velocity of things we hit
        DirectlySetVelocity,

        // Push by applying a physical force to the impact point
        ApplyForces
    }

    // The type of pushing we've selected.
    [SerializeField] PushMode pushMode = PushMode.DirectlySetVelocity;

    // The amount of force to apply, when push mode is set to
    // ApplyForces.
```

```csharp
[SerializeField] float pushPower = 5;

// Called when a character collider on the object that this script
// is attached to touches any other collider.
private void OnControllerColliderHit(ControllerColliderHit hit)
{
    // Immediately exit if pushing is disabled
    if (pushMode == PushMode.NoPushing)
    {
        return;
    }

    // Get the rigidbody attached to the collider we hit
    var hitRigidbody = hit.rigidbody;

    // Is this rigidbody something we can push?
    if (hitRigidbody == null || hitRigidbody.isKinematic == true)
    {
        // Either it doesn't have a rigidbody, or the rigidbody
        // is kinematic (that is, it doesn't respond to
        // external forces).

        // Since we're going to apply a force to it, we should
        // respect its settings.
        return;
    }

    // Get a reference to the controller that hit the object, since
    // we'll  be making references to it often.
    CharacterController controller = hit.controller;

    // Calculate the world position of the lowest point on the
    // controller.
    var footPosition = controller.transform.position.y
                            - controller.center.y
                            - controller.height / 2;

    // If the thing we've hit is underneath us, then we don't want
    // to push it; it would make it impossible for us to walk on
    // top of it, because it would be "pushed."
    if (hit.point.y <= footPosition ) {
        return;
    }

    // Apply the push, based on our setting.
    switch (pushMode)
    {
        case PushMode.DirectlySetVelocity:
            // Directly apply the velocity. Less realistic, but can
            // feel better.
```

```
                    hitRigidbody.velocity = controller.velocity;
                    break;
                case PushMode.ApplyForces:
                    // Calculate how much push force to apply
                    Vector3 force = controller.velocity * pushPower;

                    // Apply this force to the object we're pushing
                    hitRigidbody.AddForceAtPosition(force, hit.point);
                    break;
            }
        }

    }
```

2. Add a `Pushing` component to the object in your scene that has a `Character Controller` attached to it.

3. Add a cube to the scene, and add a `Rigidbody` component to it.

4. Play the game, and run into the cube. It will be pushed by the impact. Try the script in both the `DirectlySetVelocity` and `ApplyForces` modes, and see the difference in how it feels to play.

Discussion

When a game object that has a `CharacterCollider` component attached touches a `Collider`, scripts on that game object that implement the `OnControllerColliderHit` method are notified. This method receives a `ControllerColliderHit` parameter, which contains information about the "collision." It's not a real collision, because there might not be a rigidbody involved, but similar information can be accessed about the event.

CHAPTER 8

Animation and Movement

The name of this chapter could mean a lot of different things, but it's primarily concerned with understanding what an animation is and how it behaves, and applying that knowledge to the Unity animation system. Almost anything can be animated in Unity.

 We strongly recommend that, for a more complete understanding of movement and animation, and how they relate to graphics in Unity, you read this chapter in concert with Chapters 5, 6, and 7.

Unity has an incredibly powerful animation system that's overkill for a lot of simple games, but because it's so powerful, flexible, and pervasive within Unity, it's very easy to animate all sorts of things. The animation system can animate everything from objects to parameters to characters, and anything in between. It even supports animations that were created outside Unity!

 If you consult the Unity documentation for the Unity animation system, you may notice that it's referred to occasionally as "Mecanim." This is its old name, and is no longer used. But "Mecanim" and the "Unity animation system" are effectively interchangeable terms.

The workflow for animating in Unity revolves around *animation clips*, which describe the position, rotation, and other properties of an object over time.

Each animation clip is effectively a recording of the different parameters you'd like each property being animated to be, over time.

8.1 Animating an Object

Problem

You want to give something a single animation.

Solution

Quick, single animations are all over the place in video games, and learning to give a single object a simple animation is a great way to begin to understand Unity's animation system. We're going to create a cube, and give it a simple bounce animation:

1. Create a new cube by opening the GameObject menu, and choosing 3D Object → Cube.

2. Create a new animator controller asset by opening the Assets menu and choosing Create → Animator Controller.

3. Add an Animator component to the cube, either by using the Component menu (Component → Miscellaneous → Animator) or by dragging and dropping the animator controller asset onto the cube in the hierarchy.

4. Open the Animator tab by opening the Window menu and choosing Animator.

You'll often find that you don't need to use any code to animate things in Unity!

5. Create a new animation asset by opening the Assets menu and choosing Create → Animation. Name the new asset "Bounce."

6. Drag the Bounce animation into the Animator component. This will create a new animation state that uses the Bounce animation. Because it's the first state, it will be marked as the default state (that is, when the game starts, the animator controller will start in the Bounce state). The graph will now look like Figure 8-1.

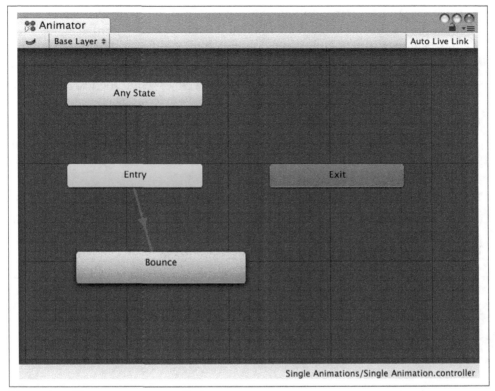

Figure 8-1. The animator controller's states

Next, we'll set up the animation itself. We'll make the animation bounce up and down by animating its local position on the *y*-axis:

1. Open the Animation pane by opening the Window menu and choosing Animation.

    The Animation pane is different from the Animator pane!

2. Select the cube. In the Animation pane, ensure that the Bounce animation is selected in the drop-down menu at the top.

3. Click the Add Property button. Choose Transform → Position.

4. Click the Add Keyframe button, which is the small button that contains a diamond shape. This will record the fact that the cube is at this position at this point in the animation.

5. Move to the 1-second position in the animation by either clicking and dragging in the top bar of the Animation pane, or by typing **60** into the text field at the top-left corner of the Animation pane. Click Add Keyframe again.

6. Move to halfway between the first and second keyframes.

7. Click the Record button, which is the red dot to the right of the Preview button. Unity will enter Record mode, which means any change you make to the object will create a new keyframe.

8. Move the cube up in the scene. A new keyframe will be created.

   The Animation pane should now look like Figure 8-2. This style of presenting an animation is called a *dopesheet*.

9. Click the Record button again to disable Record mode.

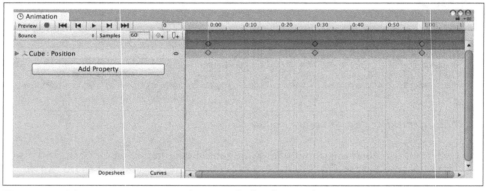

Figure 8-2. The Animation pane, showing the keyframes for an animation

We can now test the animation:

1. Click the Play button in the Animation pane, and the cube will move up and down. This gives you a good way to preview what the animation will look like.

2. Play the game, and the animation will play as soon as the game starts.

Discussion

One of the most important components of the animation system is the animator controller. The animator controller lets you control which animation clip(s) are currently playing, structured into a flowchart-style diagram of when and how each animation clip should play.

The animator controller is a state machine. Learn more about state machines and animation in the Unity manual (*https://oreil.ly/BApAA*).

You use an animator controller even when you have only one or two clips, as with the cube we just animated, since it makes it easier to manage and control how the animations behave. Each node in an animator controller can represent a specific animation, or another nested animator controller. The different behaviors you can create using this system offer near-infinite possibilities!

The specific animation clip(s) that the animator controller manages can either be imported—for example, from a motion capture system or from animations created by an artist in another piece of software (e.g., Maya)—or created within Unity, as we did here.

Inside an animation clip, there are any number of properties that can be animated—such as position, color, rotation, and scale—and that can have an animation curve. The animation curve dictates how the property behaves over time. An example of the Curves pane is shown in Figure 8-3.

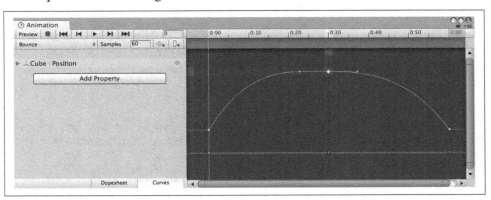

Figure 8-3. The Curves pane

Other recipes in this chapter unpack the way the animation system works a little more, and Unity's documentation (*https://oreil.ly/-NOKr*) is reasonably comprehensive.

8.2 Basic Character Movement

Problem

You want to make a character play different animations based on its speed. You want that animation to control character movement.

 In this recipe, and in many other recipes in this chapter, we'll be using the free motion-capture animations released by Unity, which are available online (*https://oreil.ly/biu3k*). This package also contains a simple human character that we'll use for demonstrating the animations.

Solution

First, we'll create a ground for a character to walk on:

1. Create a new cube by opening the GameObject menu and choosing 3D Object → Cube.

2. Set the scale of the cube to (20, 1, 20). This makes it wide and flat.

 If you like, add a textured material to the cube (see Recipe 6.1). It won't affect your animation's behavior, but it can make it easier to visually tell that a character is moving around.

To discuss how we can animate a character, we'll now need a character! So, let's start by adding the character to the scene and setting up a simple animator controller:

1. Download and import the Raw Mocap Data package (*https://oreil.ly/biu3k*).

 For a reminder on importing and managing assets, refer to Chapter 1.

2. Locate the DefaultAvatar model, and add it to your scene (see Figure 8-4).

3. Create a new animator controller, and add it to the DefaultAvatar.

Figure 8-4. The DefaultAvatar model

Next, we'll add the default state for the character, which will be an idle animation:

1. Locate the `Idle_Neutral_1` animation by searching for it in the Project tab. You'll find two items with this name: the animation itself and the file that the animation was imported from. Drag the animation into the animator controller (it has a gray icon with a play symbol in the middle of it, as seen in Figure 8-5).

2. Play the game. The character will play its idle animation.

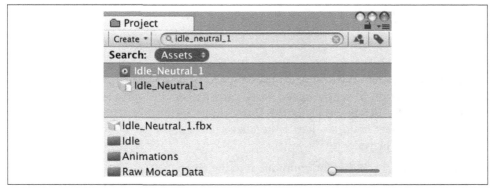

Figure 8-5. Locating the `Idle_Neutral_1` animation

Next, we'll create a parameter on the controller, which will control which animation state the character is in:

1. Open the Parameters tab, and click the + button. Choose Float. A new parameter will be added.

2. Name the new parameter "Speed."

We'll now make a new script that controls the animator controller's Speed parameter:

1. Create a new C# script called *CharacterMovement.cs*, and add the following code to it:

```
// Allows the control
public class CharacterMovement : MonoBehaviour {

    // The animator whose parameters we are controlling
    Animator animator;

    [SerializeField] float speed = 1f;

    // Use this for initialization
    void Start () {
        animator = GetComponent<Animator>();
    }

    void Update () {

        animator.SetFloat("Speed",
            Input.GetAxis("Vertical") * speed);

    }
}
```

This creates a new `Animator`, exposes a speed field to the Inspector, and uses the `Update` function to set the speed based on whether the "Vertical" input axis (see Chapter 3 for details on using the Unity Input System) is being used. In simple terms: this sets it up so that if the character is asked to go forward, the right animation is played.

2. Add a `CharacterMovement` component to the character.

Next, we'll add another animation state to the character and set up transitions between them:

1. Select the character, and go to the Animator pane.

2. Locate the `Run_Impulse` animation, and drag it into the `Animator`. A new state will be created.

3. Right-click the `Idle_Neutral_1` state, and choose Make Transition. Click the `Run_Impulse` state. A new line will be created that connects them.

We now need to configure this transition so that it applies when the Speed parameter is above a certain threshold:

1. Select the line, and go to the Conditions list at the bottom of the Inspector.
2. Click the + button, and a new condition will be added. There's only one parameter in the controller, so it will automatically be selected. Make sure that the mode is set to Greater, and set the value to 0.1. This means that this transition will apply when the Speed parameter is greater than 0.1.
3. Turn off the Has Exit Time setting. This means that this transition can apply at any time, and doesn't need to wait for the current animation to complete.

When you're done, the Inspector should look like Figure 8-6.

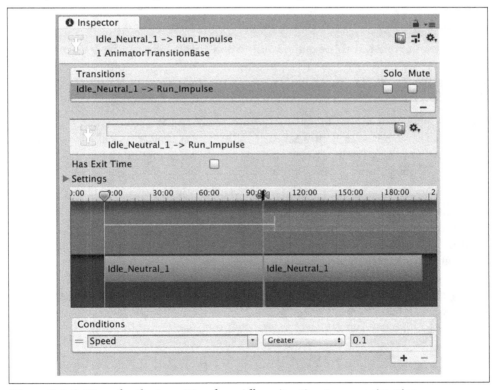

Figure 8-6. Settings for the transition from idle animation to run animation

We'll now set up the transition that happens when the speed drops below 0.1:

1. Right-click the `Run_Impulse` state, and choose Make Transition. Click the `Idle_Neutral_1` state.

2. Select the new transition you just created, and set it up the same way as the previous one. This time, however, set the mode of the condition to be Less, rather than Greater. This will make the transition happen when the speed drops below 0.1.

3. Play the game. Hold down the up arrow key or the W key, and the character will start walking forward.

Discussion

The Speed parameter that we used here is called an *animation parameter*. There can only be four types of animation parameters: integers, floats, Booleans, or triggers. A trigger is a Boolean, except it automatically returns to a `false` state in the frame after being set to `true` (making it ideal for one-off triggers like `jump` or `died`).

As we demonstrated in this example, animation parameters can be set from scripts. In this case we used `SetFloat` to access the Speed parameter from our script. You'll often find yourself modifying animation parameters from scripts to account for things like user input (as we did here) or collisions in the game world.

You may have noticed that the character moved around the scene when it animated, even though we never explicitly asked it to. This isn't magic: it's called *root motion*, and it involves the animation itself moving the object being animated. This guarantees that the object moves at the right speed.

In older animation systems, a technique sometimes called *treadmill motion* was used, where the animation played, the object being animated would always stay at its origin, and you'd use scripting to move the object around in the correct speed and manner. Root motion eliminates the headache of having to do this, since the animation itself can control how far the object needs to move.

 Root motion can be a little hard to get your head around, but it's really just the result of several interoperating components. You can learn more about root motion in the Unity manual (*https://oreil.ly/M4fGX*).

8.3 Inverse Kinematics

Problem

You want to use inverse kinematics to make a character's arm or foot reach toward a point in space.

Solution

To demonstrate this, we'll set up the scene to include a character that plays an idle animation. The inverse kinematics animations will be overlaid on the idle animation.

 This recipe makes use of the Raw Mocap Data package and floor, used in Recipe 8.2.

To use inverse kinematics:

1. Add a floor to the scene, following the same steps as in Recipe 8.2.

2. Add the DefaultAvatar object to your scene. Rename it "IK Character" (short for *inverse kinematics*, which we'll explain in a moment).

3. Open the Assets menu, and choose Create → Animator Controller. Name the new asset "IK Movement."

4. Select the IK Character, and drag the IK Movement controller that you just created into the `Animator` component's Controller slot.

5. With the IK Character still selected, go to the Animator tab by opening the Window menu and choosing Animation → Animator.

6. Locate the `Idle_Neutral_1` animation clip that you imported, and drag and drop it into the `Animator`.

7. Test your character by pressing the Play button. The character will stand, performing an idle animation.

We're now ready to add inverse kinematics to the animation setup. First, we need to enable IK on the current layer:

1. Open your animator controller, and go to the Layers tab.

2. Click the Gear icon on the base layer.

3. Turn on IK Pass. The layer list should now look like Figure 8-7.

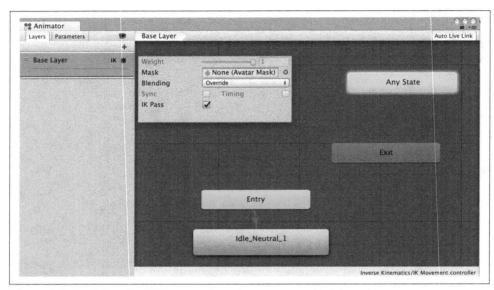

Figure 8-7. Enabling the IK Pass on the animator controller's base layer

Next, we'll create a script that tells the animator controller what to reach for, and what to reach with:

1. Create a new C# script called *IKReach.cs*, and add the following code to it:

```
// Updates the positions and weights used for a specified IK goal.
// The Animator attached to the object this script is on must have a
// layer that has an IK pass enabled. Otherwise, OnAnimatorIK won't
// be called.
[RequireComponent(typeof(Animator))]
public class IKReach : MonoBehaviour {

    // The object we're reaching toward.
    [SerializeField] Transform target = null;

    // An IK goal is a foot or hand that's reaching to a target.
    [SerializeField] AvatarIKGoal goal = AvatarIKGoal.RightHand;
```

```csharp
    // The strength with which we're reaching our goal toward the
    // target. 0 = don't reach at all; 1 = the goal must be at the same
    // point as the target, if it's within range.
    [Range(0, 1)]
    [SerializeField] float weight = 0.5f;

    // The animator that's controlling the positions.
    Animator animator;

    // Cache the reference to the animator on start.
    private void Start()
    {
        animator = GetComponent<Animator>();
    }

    // Called every time the animator is about to apply inverse
    // kinematics, which will bend the various joints to try to reach
    // the goals toward their targets. This is our opportunity to
    // provide it with updated information.
    private void OnAnimatorIK(int layerIndex)
    {
        // Set the position that the goal is trying to reach.
        animator.SetIKPosition(goal, target.position);

        // Set the weight for the goal.
        animator.SetIKPositionWeight(goal, weight);
    }
}
```

This script lets us define an object that will be reached toward, as well as the piece of the model that is doing the reaching, and performs the animation needed to consistently move the model appropriately toward the target object.

2. Add an IKReach component to the character.

3. Create a sphere in the scene, and scale it down until it's about the size of a tennis ball. Place it near the character (Figure 8-8).

4. Make the IKReach component's Target field refer to the sphere you just added.

Play the game. The character will reach toward the target. When you move the target around in the Scene view, the character's pose will change.

Figure 8-8. The scene setup for this recipe: the avatar, with a sphere placed within reach

Discussion

Kinematics refers to the movement of points and objects. Traditional animation in video games starts at a parent (joint), and then flows outward to the remainder of the connected elements, through the joints. This is called *forward kinematics*.

Inverse kinematics is the opposite: you want the outermost element to be in a specific place, so what needs to be done to align the entire system there? This is useful in video games when you want a character to correctly stand on the floor, navigate stairs and ramps, or hold or touch objects that might move around the world.

Unity's animation system supports inverse kinematics for any humanoid character that's correctly configured for the system.

 Inverse kinematics can be very complicated if you're implementing it from scratch. Unity's animation system abstracts away many of the details. Learn more about how it works in the Unity manual (*https://oreil.ly/tQ0ZC*).

Inverse kinematics is a valuable technique for building characters that can interact realistically with their world. It's not useful solely for humanoids (though it is built for them!), so you could also create inverse kinematics for tentacles, or multilegged robots, or anything that needs to reliably and realistically interact with the rest of a game world.

8.4 Masked Movement

Problem

You want to play an animation that applies only to certain body parts. For example, you might want a humanoid character to wave its hands around while running.

Solution

To demonstrate this, we'll build upon the character that can run around, and then we'll add another animation that affects only the arms:

1. Follow the steps in Recipe 8.2. We'll also modify one animation that comes with the Raw Mocap Data asset pack. In this example, we'll create an animation clip in which the character reaches out and grabs something in front of it with its right arm. To do this, we'll trim an existing clip to include only the motion we want.

2. Locate the IdleGrab_Neutral asset in the downloaded assets, and select it.

3. In the Inspector, go to the Animation tab.

4. Set the animation Start and End frames to 151 and 253, respectively (Figure 8-9). This is the range of the animation clip that contains the motion we want.

 You may see a notice about warnings found when importing the rig. These can be safely ignored in this case—they don't affect the work we're doing here.

5. Click the Apply button at the bottom of the Inspector.

6. Select the character, and go to the Animator tab by opening the Window menu and choosing Animation → Animator.

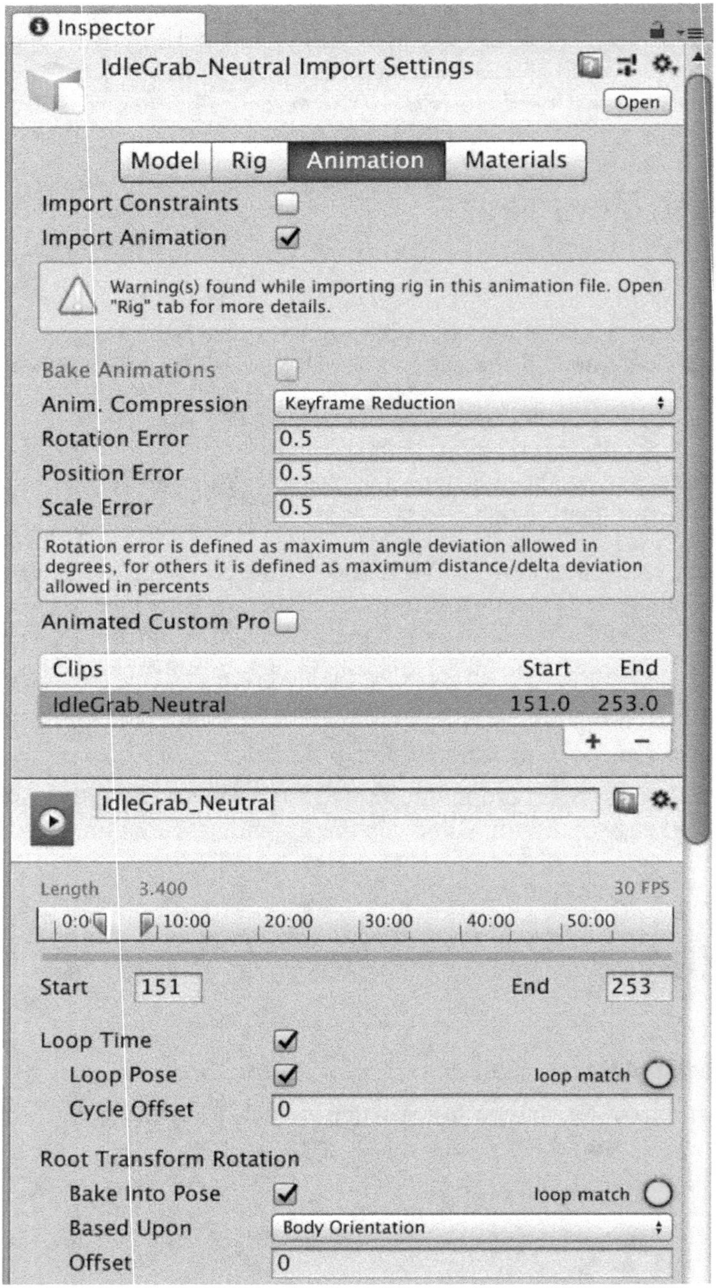

Figure 8-9. The import settings for the `IdleGrab_Neutral` *animation*

7. Create a new parameter by going to the Parameters tab and clicking the + button. Click Trigger in the menu that appears. Name the new trigger "Grab."

8. Create a new layer by going to the Layers tab and clicking the + button. Name the new layer "Arms." Click the Gear icon, and set the weight to 1.

9. Create a new state by right-clicking in the controller and choosing Create State → Empty. Name this new state "Passive."

10. Drag and drop the `IdleGrab_Neutral` animation into the `Animator`.

11. Right-click the `Passive` state, and choose Make Transition. Select the `Idle Grab_Neutral` animation, and a new transition will be made from `Passive` to `IdleGrab_Neutral`. Repeat the process in the other direction: make a transition from `IdleGrab_Neutral` to `Passive`.

12. Select the transition from `Passive` to `IdleGrab_Neutral`, and in the Inspector, turn off Has Exit Time. This will make the transition happen immediately.

13. While you're here, add a new condition to the transition by clicking the + button in the Conditions area and selecting the Grab parameter.

What we've done here is set up a layer that contains two animations: an empty animation named `Passive`, and an animation in which the character performs a grabbing motion. The grabbing motion is performed when the `Grab` trigger is used.

However, there's a problem: the `IdleGrab_Neutral` animation affects not just the arm, but the whole body. This means that we can't blend a grabbing animation with anything else, like walking. To make it so that the grabbing animation affects only the arm, we use an *avatar mask* to make the layer apply only to certain body parts:

1. Create a new avatar mask by opening the Assets menu and choosing Create → Avatar Mask.

2. Select the new mask, and click anywhere outside the figure of a person to deselect all body parts. Next, select the right arm. (This is on the left side of the image; pretend that the figure is facing you.) See Figure 8-10 for what the avatar settings should look like.

3. Go to the Arm layer in the `Animator`, and set the `Mask` property to the avatar mask you just created (Figure 8-11). This will make any animations playing on this layer affect only the specified body parts.

4. Test the animation by playing the game. As usual, you can move the character; when you select the `Grab` trigger parameter (by opening the `Animator`, selecting the Parameters pane, and clicking the `Grab` trigger), the character will extend its arm, and this will combine with other parts of the animation.

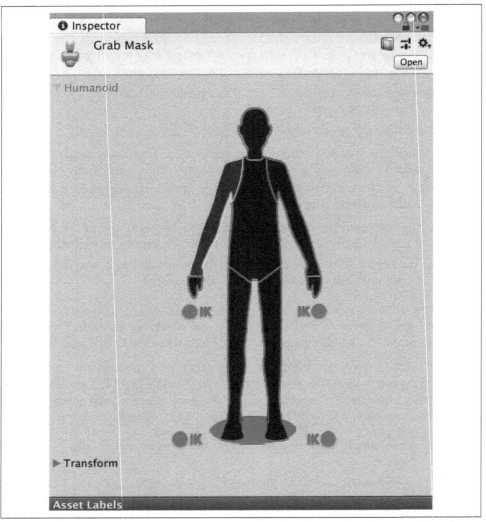

Figure 8-10. The avatar mask, with everything but the character's right arm selected

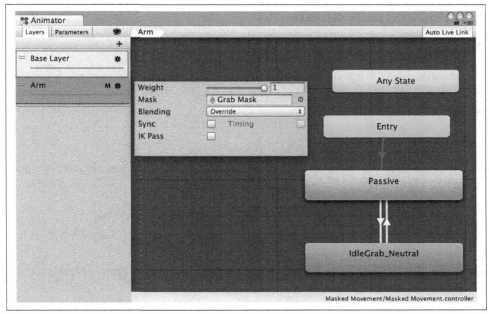

Figure 8-11. The Arm layer of the animator controller, configured to use the avatar mask

Discussion

Animation layers can be used to override or add to earlier layers. The different weights that can be set on each animation layer allow you to control how much influence that layer has over the final pose.

You can run multiple animations at the same time by creating multiple layers. Animation masks are used to control which parts of the rig are affected by which layers, and by adjusting the weight of different layers you can allow multiple animations to affect the *same* parts of the rig.

An avatar is a mapping of common components, such as arms or legs, to specific bones in the animation rig. This allows you to reuse animations across different meshes, even if the bones aren't quite the same.

8.5 Blended Movement

Problem

You want to blend between multiple animations. For example, you have a walking animation and a running animation, and you want to smoothly blend between the two as a character's speed increases.

Solution

Use a *blend tree*, which is an animation state that blends between two or more animation clips:

1. Add a floor to the scene, following the same steps as in Recipe 8.2.

2. Add the DefaultAvatar object to your scene. Rename it "Blended Movement Character."

3. Open the Assets menu, and choose Create → Animator Controller. Name the new asset "Blended Movement."

4. Select the Blended Movement character, and drag the Blended Movement controller that you just created into the `Animator` component's Controller slot.

5. With the Blended Movement character still selected, go to the Animator tab by opening the Window menu and choosing Animation → Animator.

6. Add a new `Float` parameter to the controller by going to the Parameters tab, clicking the +, and choosing Float. Name the new parameter "Speed."

7. Right-click in your animator controller, and choose Create State → From New Blend Tree.

8. Double-click the new state, and you'll be taken to the details of the blend tree.

9. Select the Blend Tree node, and set its parameter to "Speed." This is the parameter that the blend tree will use to decide which animation clips to use.

10. Drag the following animation clips into the blend tree's Inspector, and use the specified thresholds and speeds. When you're done, the Inspector should look like Figure 8-12, and the controller should look like Figure 8-13.

    • `WalkFWD`; threshold: −1.5, speed: −1

    • `Idle_Neutral_1`; threshold: 0, speed: 1

- WalkFWD; threshold: 1.5, speed: −1

- Run_Impulse; threshold: 5, speed: −1

11. Test the game by pressing the Play button. Hold down the up arrow to make the character walk forward. When the character's speed is 0, the character will stand at idle. As the speed increases, the character will transition through the walking animation to the running animation.

Adjust the Speed variable in the Character Movement script, and see how it affects the animation.

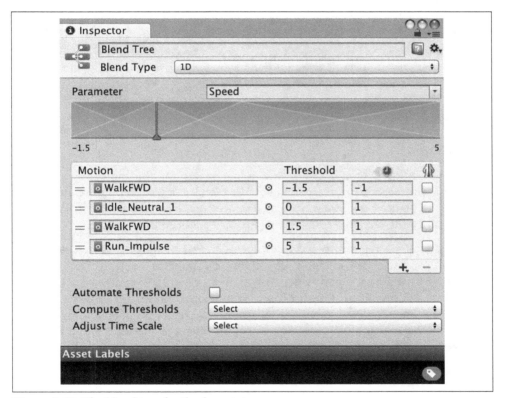

Figure 8-12. The blend tree for the four states

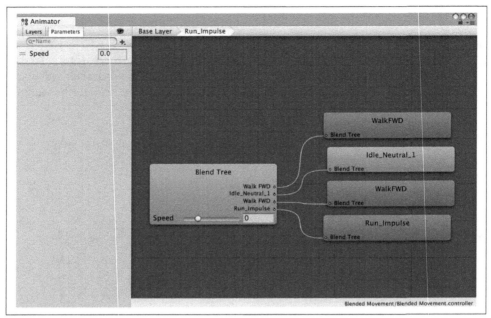

Figure 8-13. The controller for the blend tree

Discussion

Blend trees work in conjunction with a parameter on the animator controller. Depending on the value of the parameter, the blend tree will blend different animation clips. In Figure 8-12, you can see a blend tree that has four clips, which allow for walking backward, standing still, walking forward, and running forward.

There are multiple types of blend trees, including 2D blend trees. These are useful for when you have two kinds of directions you want to move in (for example, forward/backward and side-to-side). An example of a 2D blend tree can be seen in Figure 8-14; this blend tree uses two parameters, one for forward and reverse motion, and one for sideways motion. When the character is applying only forward motion, the regular running animation is played; when the character is applying only sideways motion, a turning animation is played; when both are applied at once, a running-while-turning animation is played.

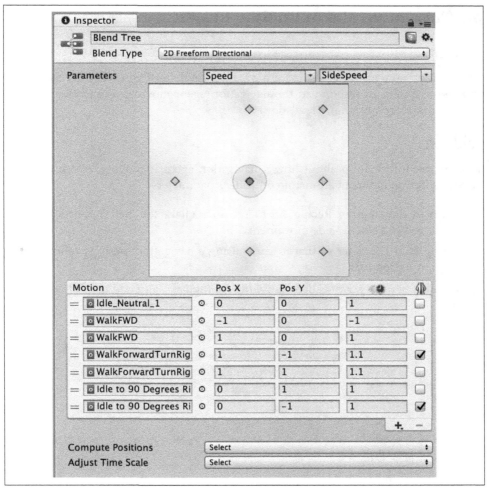

Figure 8-14. A 2D blend tree, with two independently controlled parameters

8.6 Navigation and Animating in Sync

Problem

You have a character set up to use a navigation mesh, and you want the character's animation system to respond to the navigation agent moving around the world so that the character looks more realistic.

Solution

You can get information about how a navigation agent is moving, and use that to provide information to an animator controller's parameters:

1. Perform the steps in Recipe 8.5 to set up a character that supports forward/backward and side-to-side movement.

2. Set up your character so that it works using a navigation mesh by following the steps in Recipe 10.3.

3. Create a new C# script called *NavigationAnimator.cs*, and add the following code to it:

```csharp
using UnityEngine.AI;

// Uses the NavMeshAgent to drive parameters on the Animator.
[RequireComponent(typeof(NavMeshAgent))]
[RequireComponent(typeof(Animator))]
public class NavigationAnimator : MonoBehaviour
{

    // Selects what the final position of the object is controlled by.
    enum Mode {
        // The agent directly controls the object's position. More
        // accurate, but causes foot sliding (because the animator isn't
        // moving at the exact speed of the agent).
        AgentControlsPosition,

        // The animator's root motion controls the object's position.
        // Looks better, but less accurate because the motion that
        // results won't precisely match what the agent wants to do.
        AnimatorControlsPosition
    }

    // The mode that this script is operating in.
    [SerializeField] Mode mode = Mode.AnimatorControlsPosition;

    // The names of the parameters that this script will control.
    [SerializeField] string isMovingParameterName = "Moving";
    [SerializeField] string sidewaysSpeedParameterName = "X Speed";
```

```
[SerializeField] string forwardSpeedParameterName = "Z Speed";

// Cached references to components we'll be accessing every frame.
Animator animator;
NavMeshAgent agent;

// Stores the movement we did last frame, so that we can smooth out
// our movement over time.
Vector2 smoothDeltaPosition = Vector2.zero;

void Start()
{
    // Cache references to the animator and the nav mesh agent.
    animator = GetComponent<Animator>();
    agent = GetComponent<NavMeshAgent>();

    // The animator will potentially be in charge of our position,
    // not the agent. Disable the agent's ability to directly set
    // this object's position. (The agent will retain the ability
    // to rotate the object.)

    agent.updatePosition = false;

}

void Update()
{
    // The agent stores where it wants to move next in
    // agent.nextPosition.

    // Calculate how far we currently are from where the agent
    // wants to be, in world space.
    Vector3 worldDeltaPosition =
        agent.nextPosition - transform.position;

    // Convert this to local space; we need to know how much of a
    // movement in the x and z planes this would be.
    float xMovement =
        Vector3.Dot(transform.right, worldDeltaPosition);
    float zMovement =
        Vector3.Dot(transform.forward, worldDeltaPosition);

    Vector2 localDeltaPosition = new Vector2(xMovement, zMovement);

    // Smooth out this movement by interpolating from the last
    // frame's movement to this one.
    float smooth = Mathf.Min(1.0f, Time.deltaTime / 0.15f);
    smoothDeltaPosition = Vector2.Lerp(smoothDeltaPosition,
                                       localDeltaPosition, smooth);
```

```
// Figure out our velocity.
var velocity = smoothDeltaPosition / Time.deltaTime;

// We need to tell the animator that we're moving when our
// velocity exceeds a threshold, and we're not too close
// to the destination.
bool shouldMove = velocity.magnitude > 0.5f &&
                  agent.remainingDistance > agent.radius;

// We now have all the information we need to tell the animator
// what to do. Update its parameters; the animator controller
// will play the right animation. This updates the animation's
// root position as well, which we can optionally use to control
// or influence the object's position.

// We're providing three parameters here.
// - 'Moving' is a bool that unambiguously indicates whether we
//    want to be idle or moving.
// - X and Z speed are intended to control a 2D blend tree.
// - Z speed is forward and backward, while X speed is left and
//    right.

// This can also work with a 1D blend tree, where Z speed is the
// only parameter, but if you do this, you should use this
// script in AgentControlsPosition mode.
//
// This is because if your animator controller doesn't have any
// animations that move the root position sideways, the animator
// will find it difficult to make the kinds of turns that the
// agent may try, and the result will be the visible object
// jumping around onscreen as a result of repeatedly moving too
// far from the agent. Play with your blend trees and
// animations to get good-feeling movement.

animator.SetBool(isMovingParameterName, shouldMove);
animator.SetFloat(sidewaysSpeedParameterName, velocity.x);
animator.SetFloat(forwardSpeedParameterName, velocity.y);

// Is the animator controlling our position, instead of
// the agent?
if (mode == Mode.AnimatorControlsPosition) {

    // If the animator is controlling our position, the agent
    // will start drifting away from the object. If this happens,
    // you'll start seeing visual glitches caused by the
    // navigation logic not matching the visible object onscreen.

    // To fix this, we'll detect if the object is significantly
    // far from the agent. "Significantly" means it's more
    // than one agent-radius away from the agent's position
```

```
                    // (that is, the object is outside the agent's cylinder).

                    // When this happens, we'll start bringing the object closer
                    // to the agent's position. This reduces animation realism
                    // slightly, because it's movement that's not reflected in
                    // the motion of the character, but it prevents larger
                    // errors from accumulating over time.

                    // Is the object's position far from where the agent wants
                    // to be?
                    if (worldDeltaPosition.magnitude > agent.radius)
                    {
                        // Bring us closer to where the agent wants to be
                        transform.position = Vector3.Lerp(transform.position,
                                                          agent.nextPosition,
                                                          Time.deltaTime / 0.15f);
                    }
                }
            }

            void OnAnimatorMove()
            {
                // Which mode is this script in?
                switch (mode)
                {
                    case Mode.AgentControlsPosition:
                        // Move the object directly where the agent wants
                        // to be.
                        transform.position = agent.nextPosition;
                        break;
                    case Mode.AnimatorControlsPosition:
                        // Update our position to where the animation system has
                        // placed us, following the animation's root movement.

                        // Override the movement in the y-axis to where the
                        // agent wants to be (otherwise, we'll just pass through
                        // hills, stairs, and other changes in ground height).

                        Vector3 position = animator.rootPosition;
                        position.y = agent.nextPosition.y;
                        transform.position = position;
                        break;
                }
            }
        }
```

4. Add a NavigationAnimator component to the object.

When the navigation agent starts moving to another location, it will update the parameters of the animator controller.

Discussion

Making the navigation agent animate as it moves involves a few things. The most important aspect is that, at each frame, a check is performed to see if the mode of the object is the agent controlling its position, or the animator controlling the position. The right animation system is then triggered, depending on the mode.

8.7 Cinematic Camera Tracking

Problem

You want to create a cinematic-style camera, and set it up so that it always keeps a certain object in view.

Solution

The best way to do this is to use the Cinemachine package. Cinemachine is a procedural camera system designed to provide a cinematic-style camera control system.

 If you read Unity's documentation, you might find references to Cinemachine being acquired from the Unity Asset Store. The latest version was moved from the Unity Asset Store to the Unity Package Manager some time ago, but some documentation about Cinemachine includes instructions to fetch it from the Asset Store; do not do this! The version in the Asset Store, while still available, is not the latest, will not be updated, and will not necessarily contain the features you expect or need. Make sure to always fetch a copy of Cinemachine from the Package Manager. For a refresher on the Package Manager, refer to Chapter 1.

First, install the Cinemachine package:

1. Open the Window menu, and choose Package Manager.
2. In the All tab, locate the Cinemachine package, and click Install.

Next, we'll set up a Cinemachine virtual camera:

1. Open the Cinemachine menu, and choose Create Virtual Camera (Figure 8-15). This will create and select a new virtual camera.
2. Position the virtual camera somewhere in your scene.
3. Drag the object that you want the camera to look at into the virtual camera's Look At slot (Figure 8-16).
4. Run the game. The camera will look at the target!

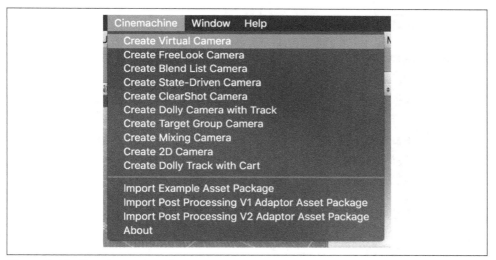

Figure 8-15. Creating a virtual camera

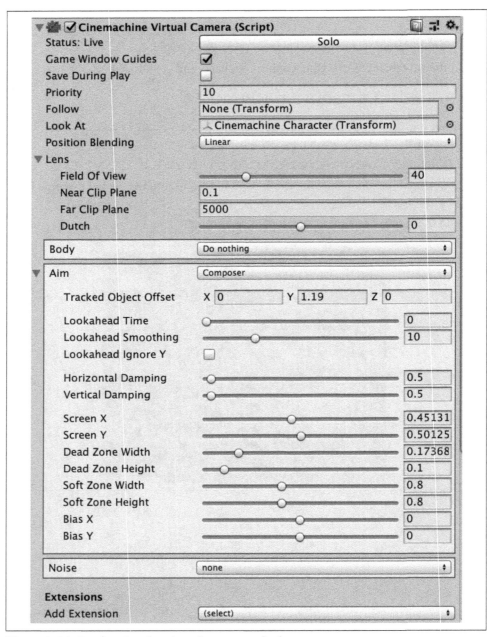

Figure 8-16. Configuring the virtual camera to look at a target

Discussion

Cinemachine works with virtual cameras, which are not really cameras: they behave more like a camera operator in the real world, and control the position, orientation, lens settings, and so on, of the real camera. The virtual cameras do no rendering on their own. Cinemachine virtual cameras are controlled by—the somewhat ominous-sounding—Cinemachine brains.

Cinemachine brains connect a real Unity camera with a virtual Cinemachine camera. Because there are likely to be multiple virtual cameras in most cinematic scenes, the brain monitors the situation, based on the priorities you assign it, and blends between cameras as necessary, applying the state of the virtual camera to the real camera, as shown in Figure 8-17.

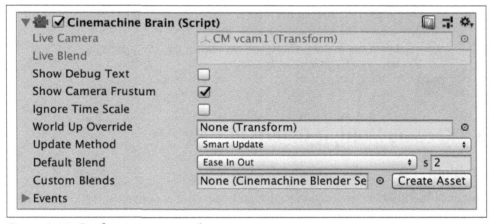

Figure 8-17. Configuring a camera brain

You can learn more about Cinemachine by reading the Cinemachine documentation (*https://oreil.ly/1JxsL*), and Unity's tutorial series for Cinemachine (*https://oreil.ly/zRohq*).

8.8 Automatically Switching Cameras

Problem

You have multiple cameras in the scene, and you want Cinemachine (see Recipe 8.7) to automatically switch between them so that a target object is always in view.

Solution

The solution here is to use a Cinemachine ClearShot camera:

1. Open the Cinemachine menu, and choose Create ClearShot Camera.

2. Select the ClearShot object, and drag the target you want to maintain a view of into the Look At field.

3. Add as many virtual cameras as you want as children of the ClearShot group.

Discussion

A ClearShot is an object that has one or more virtual cameras as its children, and is configured to look at a certain target. It will select from among its different children which camera has the best shot of the target.

 Learn more about ClearShot cameras in the Unity Scripting API reference (*https://oreil.ly/xAAmN*).

8.9 Keeping Multiple Objects in View

Problem

You have multiple objects in your scene, and you want a camera to try to keep them all in view at the same time.

Solution

To keep a lot of objects in view at the same time, you want to use a Cinemachine Look At Group. To create a Look At Group:

1. Create a new, empty game object, and name it "Look At Group."

2. Add a new `CinemachineTargetGroup` component to it.

3. In the list of targets, you can specify the list of Transforms that you want the Look At Group to refer to (Figure 8-18).

4. When you want a camera to look at the entire group, set the camera's Look At property to refer to the Look At Group, rather than the target itself.

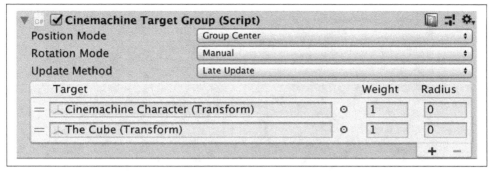

Figure 8-18. Creating a Look At Group

Discussion

This pretty much does what it says on the tin. You can learn a little more in the Unity Scripting API reference (*https://oreil.ly/MZSx5*).

8.10 Dollying a Camera

Problem

You want a camera to move around to keep an object in frame, but you want to ensure that the camera moves around only on a fixed track. This is called a dolly camera.

Solution

To create a dolly camera:

1. Open the Cinemachine menu, and choose Dolly Camera with Track.

   This will create two objects: a camera and a track for it to follow. The camera will always be positioned somewhere on the track, though it can rotate freely to look at its Look At target. It will reposition itself along the track to be close to its Follow target.

2. Configure the camera's Look At and Follow properties to refer to the object you want to track (Figure 8-19).

3. Select the Dolly Track, and configure the points that you want the track to go from and to. You can also create points between the start and finish to create a curving track (Figure 8-20).

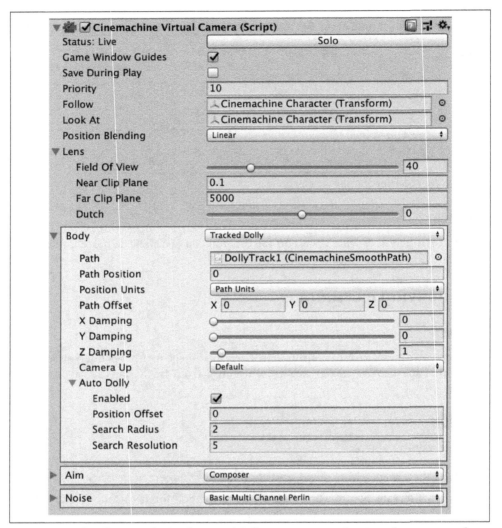

Figure 8-19. Configuring the Look At and Follow properties of a virtual camera config-ured to follow a dolly track

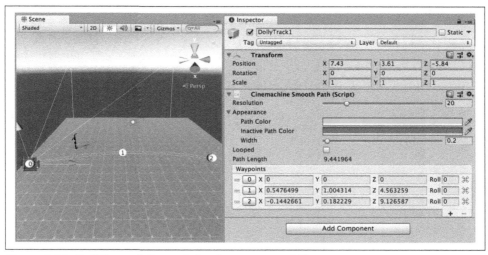

Figure 8-20. Building a dolly track for the camera to follow

Discussion

"Dolly camera" is terminology from filmmaking: a dolly is a cart with wheels that a real, physical camera is placed on to create smooth horizontal movement. A dolly camera is useful when you want to smoothly move past something or create more cinematic effects in your game.

 You can also use a dolly camera to create a *dolly zoom*, where the camera moves toward something while a zoom out is performed at the same time. This makes the object in focus appear to stay the same size, while everything else undergoes a perspective warp. We're fans of it since it's used to such great effect in the *Battlestar Galactica* TV series, when the ship jumps!

CHAPTER 9

Logic and Gameplay

Logic and gameplay take many different guises, and can mean many different things: from making something behave like a car, to letting the player select objects with the mouse, to camera behavior. In this chapter, we'll provide recipes and solutions to some of the in-project or in-game features that, as Unity developers, we find ourselves having to build over and over again. These are the basic building blocks of many Unity projects, but are not necessarily provided by Unity.

This chapter is far from containing all the gameplay solutions you'll need! Articles posted by game developers on Game Developer (*https://www.gamedeveloper.com*) are a great resource for more of this sort of thing. In your game development career, you'll find yourself implementing many of the recipes in this chapter time and time again, game after game.

9.1 Loading a New Scene File

Problem

You want to load a new scene file.

Loading a new scene file is a good way to load a different level of your game! But it's a generic technique that doesn't only apply to levels. Because scenes can be used for anything, including menus, scoreboards, and beyond, transitioning to a new scene doesn't always mean loading a new level.

Solution

To load a scene, you first need to tell Unity that you'd like to include that scene in your project. If you don't, the scene won't be included in any built versions, and you won't be able to load it.

To manage the list of scenes in your project, open the File menu and choose Build Settings. The Build Settings screen will appear (Figure 9-1). To mark a scene as loadable, drag and drop it from the *Assets* folder in the Project tab into the list at the top of the screen.

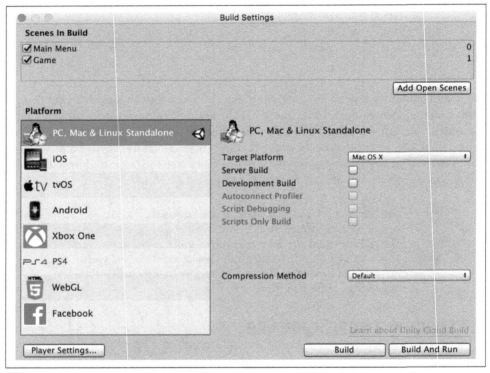

Figure 9-1. The scene list in the Build Settings screen, with two scenes added

You're now ready to write code that loads a scene. To use the `SceneManager` class, which handles scene loading for you, you'll need to include the following `using` directive at the top of your script:

```
using UnityEngine.SceneManagement;
```

Loading a new scene is as simple as calling `SceneManager.LoadScene` and providing the name of the scene. Unity will then load the new scene and unload the current one:

```
// Loads the scene named "Game," replacing the current scene; stops the
// game until loading is done (so don't load big scenes this way!)
SceneManager.LoadScene("Game");
```

It's important to remember that if you load a scene this way, your project will pause while the new scene is loaded. If loading takes a while, it can be an annoyance to the user, who might assume that the project has frozen or crashed.

To avoid this, you can load a scene in the background. Use the `SceneManager` class's `LoadSceneAsync` method, which starts loading a scene in the background and returns an object that you can use to measure how long it's going to take, and whether it's done loading:

```
public void LoadLevelAsync() {
    // Start loading the scene; we'll get back an object that represents
    // the scene loading operation

    var operation = SceneManager.LoadSceneAsync("Game");

    Debug.Log("begin load...");

    // Don't proceed to the scene once loading has finished
    operation.allowSceneActivation = false;

    // Start a coroutine that will run while the scene loads, and will run
    // some code after loading finishes
    StartCoroutine(WaitForLoading(operation));

}
IEnumerator WaitForLoading(AsyncOperation operation)
{

    // Wait for the scene load to reach at least 90%
    while (operation.progress < 0.9f)
    {
        yield return null;
    }

    // We're done!

    Debug.Log("Done load.");

    // Enabling scene activation will immediately start loading the scene
    operation.allowSceneActivation = true;
}
```

Your project can load multiple scenes at the same time. For example, you might have one scene that contains important objects like logic or gameplay managers, input systems, and the UI, and then have a separate scene for the levels in a game.

To load one scene on top of another, specify the `LoadSceneMode` as `Additive` when calling `LoadScene`. This will load the scene and add it on top of the currently loaded scenes. You can load as many scenes as will fit in memory:

```
public void LoadLevelAdditive() {
    // Load the scene in addition to the current one
    SceneManager.LoadScene("Game", LoadSceneMode.Additive);
}
```

You can also unload a level that was additively loaded, removing it and its contents from the project. Do this by calling `UnloadSceneAsync`:

```
public void UnloadLevel() {
    // Unloading a scene is an async operation, much like loading can be
    var unloadOperation = SceneManager.UnloadSceneAsync("Game");

    // If you want to run code after the unloading has completed, start a
    // coroutine (again, just like loading)
    StartCoroutine(WaitForUnloading(unloadOperation));
}

IEnumerator WaitForUnloading(AsyncOperation operation) {

    yield return new WaitUntil(() => operation.isDone);

    // Unloading has completed, and all objects that were in the scene
    // have been removed. However, Unity will not unload the assets that
    // those objects referred to, like the textures. These stay in memory
    // for later use by other objects; to free up the memory, do this:

    Resources.UnloadUnusedAssets();

}
```

Discussion

You can also load multiple scenes in the editor. To do this, right-click the scene you want to open and choose Open Scene Additive. The additional scene will appear in the Hierarchy (Figure 9-2). When two scenes are open, you can drag and drop objects between them.

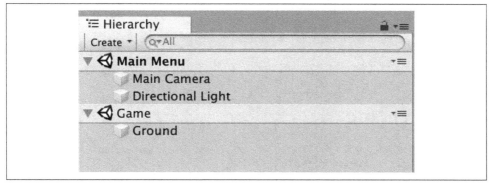

Figure 9-2. The Hierarchy tab, with two scenes loaded at the same time

9.2 Managing Hit Points

Problem

You want objects to take damage when another kind of object hits them. When they take enough damage, they're destroyed.

Solution

The first part of the solution is to create three scripts:

1. Create a new C# script called *DamageReceiver.cs* that can receive a signal that an object has taken damage, and has a number of *hit points* that can be diminished:

```csharp
public class DamageReceiver : MonoBehaviour {

    UnityEngine.Events.UnityEvent onDeath;

    [SerializeField] int hitPoints = 5;

    int currentHitPoints;

    private void Awake()
    {
        currentHitPoints = hitPoints;
    }
```

```
    public void TakeDamage(int damageAmount)
    {
        currentHitPoints -= damageAmount;

        if (currentHitPoints <= 0)
        {
            if (onDeath != null)
            {
                onDeath.Invoke();
            }

            Destroy(gameObject);
        }
    }
}
```

2. Next, create a new C# script called *DamageGiver.cs* that detects if one object has collided with another; if that other object has a `DamageReceiver` on it, it is told it has taken damage:

```
public class DamageGiver : MonoBehaviour {

    [SerializeField] int damageAmount = 1;

    // Called when the object collides with another
    private void OnCollisionEnter(Collision collision)
    {
        // Does the object we hit have a damage receiver?

        var otherDamageReceiver = collision
            .gameObject.GetComponent<DamageReceiver>();

        if (otherDamageReceiver != null) {
            // Tell it to take damage.
            otherDamageReceiver.TakeDamage(damageAmount);
        }

        // Destroy this projectile
        Destroy(gameObject);

    }
}
```

3. To test this, we'll create a script that creates and emits projectiles. Create a brand new C# script called *ProjectileShooter.cs*, and add the following code to it:

```
public class ProjectileShooter : MonoBehaviour {

    // The projectile to instantiate copies of
    [SerializeField] GameObject projectilePrefab = null;
```

```
// The amount of time to wait before creating another projectile
[SerializeField] float timeBetweenShots = 1;

// The speed that new projectiles should be moving at
[SerializeField] float projectileSpeed = 10;

// On start, begin shooting projectiles
void Start () {
    // Start creating projectiles
    StartCoroutine(ShootProjectiles());
}

// Loop forever, creating a projectile every 'timeBetweenShots'
// seconds
IEnumerator ShootProjectiles() {
    while (true) {
        ShootNewProjectile();

        yield return new WaitForSeconds(timeBetweenShots);
    }
}

// Creates a new projectile and starts it moving
void ShootNewProjectile() {

    // Spawn the new object with the emitter's position and rotation
    var projectile = Instantiate(
        projectilePrefab,
        transform.position,
        transform.rotation
    );

    // Get the rigidbody on the new projectile
    var rigidbody = projectile.GetComponent<Rigidbody>();

    if (rigidbody == null) {
        Debug.LogError("Projectile prefab has no rigidbody!");
        return;
    }

    // Make it move away from the emitter's forward direction at
    // 'projectileSpeed' units per second
    rigidbody.velocity = transform.forward * projectileSpeed;

    // Get both the projectile's collider and the emitter's
    // collider
    var collider = projectile.GetComponent<Collider>();
    var myCollider = this.GetComponent<Collider>();
```

```
// If both of them are valid, tell the physics system to ignore
// collisions between them (to prevent projectiles from
// colliding with their source)
if (collider != null && myCollider != null) {
    Physics.IgnoreCollision(collider, myCollider);
}

    }
}
```

Now, we'll set up some objects that demonstrate the system in action:

1. Create a cube, name it "Damage Receiver," and attach the *DamageReceiver.cs* script to it.

2. Create a sphere, and name it "Projectile."

3. Attach a `Rigidbody` component to the sphere. Disable gravity on the `Rigidbody`.

4. Attach a `DamageGiver` component to the sphere.

5. Drag the sphere from the Hierarchy into the Project tab. This will create a prefab.

6. Delete the original sphere from the scene.

7. Create a cylinder, and name it "Shooter."

8. Attach the *ProjectileShooter.cs* script to the cylinder.

9. Drag the Projectile prefab into the cylinder's Projectile Prefab field.

10. Position and orient the cylinder so that its forward direction—that is, its blue arrow—is aimed at the Damage Receiver.

11. Start the game. The shooter will fire spheres at the target. After enough of them hit it, the target will be removed from the scene.

Discussion

Our hit point system is only one possible way this behavior could be implemented. You could globally keep track of all objects with hit points in a grand central list of some kind and manage it there, for example.

 Repeatedly instantiating objects that you know will be destroyed later can be inefficient, because you're continuously allocating and freeing memory. We're doing it in this recipe for the sake of keeping the demo simple, but for a real game, consider using an object pool, which we discuss in Recipe 2.8.

9.3 Creating a Top-Down Camera

Problem

You want to create a camera system that looks down at the world. You want to be able to move the camera around, and limit the range that it can move around in.

Solution

Top-down cameras usually look best when they're looking down at an angle, not when they're aiming straight down the *y*-axis. However, we want the camera to move around only on the *x* and *z* directions, parallel to the ground:

1. Create an empty game object, and call it "Camera Rig."
2. Move the main Camera object into the Camera Rig.
3. Set the local position of the main Camera object to (0, 0, 0) so that it's at the same location as the Camera Rig.
4. Rotate the camera (not the Camera Rig!) around the *x*-axis so that it's looking down at the world.

Next, we'll add the code that moves the camera:

1. Create a new C# script called *TopDownCameraMovement.cs*, and add the following code to it:

```csharp
// Allows for limited top-down movement of a camera.
public class TopDownCameraMovement : MonoBehaviour {

    // The speed that the camera will move, in units per second
    [SerializeField] float movementSpeed = 20;

    // The lower-left position of the camera, on its current X-Z plane.
    [SerializeField] Vector2 minimumLimit = -Vector2.one;

    // The upper-right position of the camera, on its current X-Z plane.
    [SerializeField] Vector2 maximumLimit = Vector2.one;

    // Every frame, update the camera's position
    void Update()
    {
        // Get how much the user wants to move the camera
        var horizontal = Input.GetAxis("Horizontal");
        var vertical = Input.GetAxis("Vertical");

        // Compute how much movement to apply this frame, in world space
        var offset = new Vector3(horizontal, 0, vertical)
```

```
                * Time.deltaTime * movementSpeed;

            // Figure out what our new position would be.
            var newPosition = transform.position + offset;

            // Is this new position within our permitted bounds?
            if (bounds.Contains(newPosition)) {
                // Then move to it.
                transform.position = newPosition;
            } else {
                // Otherwise, figure out the closest point to the boundary,
                // and move there instead.
                transform.position = bounds.ClosestPoint(newPosition);
            }
        }

        // Computes the bounding box that the camera is allowed to be in.
        Bounds bounds {
            get {

                // We'll create a bounding box that's zero units high, and
                // positioned at the current height of the camera.
                var cameraHeight = transform.position.y;

                // Figure out the position of the corners of the boxes in
                // world space
                Vector3 minLimit = new Vector3(minimumLimit.x,
                    cameraHeight, minimumLimit.y);
                Vector3 maxLimit = new Vector3(maximumLimit.x,
                    cameraHeight, maximumLimit.y);
                // Create a new Bounds using these values and return it
                var newBounds = new Bounds();
                newBounds.min = minLimit;
                newBounds.max = maxLimit;
                return newBounds;
            }
        }

        // Draw the bounding box.
        private void OnDrawGizmos()
        {
            Gizmos.color = Color.red;
            Gizmos.DrawWireCube(bounds.center, bounds.size);
        }
    }
```

2. Attach a *TopDownCameraMovement.cs* script to the Camera Rig. A red rectangle
   will appear on the same level as the camera (see Figure 9-3).

---

3. Adjust the minimum and maximum points in the Inspector so that they cover the area that you want the camera to move around in.

4. Play the game. The camera will move when you press the arrow keys, and won't leave the red rectangle. If the camera is outside the rectangle before the game starts, it will move inside it.

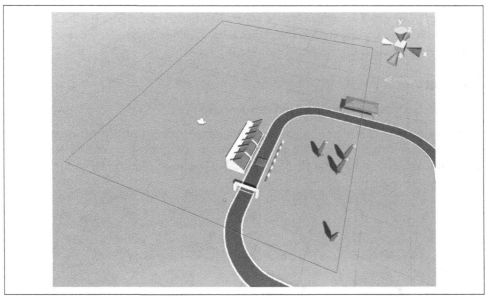

Figure 9-3. Positioning a top-down 2D camera above an example game level

Discussion

There's not much to say here. In each frame, we check how much the player wants to move the camera, figure out how much we need to move in a frame, calculate a new position within our allowed bounds, and move the camera there. Our top-down camera system, again, is only one possible way of implementing this sort of behavior! You could also use a more advanced system, such as Cinemachine.

> We use a *gizmo* (*https://oreil.ly/Q97F5*) as an aid in figuring out what's going on in the Scene view. Gizmos are elements in the Scene view that help you navigate it or understand what's going on.

9.4 Managing Quests

Problem

You want to manage a quest structure, where the player needs to complete certain objectives to finish a quest.

As part of your quest structure, you want some objectives to be optional, and some objectives to not be presented to the player until they're achieved. If an objective fails and it isn't optional, then the entire quest fails.

Solution

Before we can manage a quest structure, we need a quest.

First, let's define a simple quest: we'll position the camera in front of some colored blocks, and say that the player has to click them to complete the quest. However, one of the blocks is forbidden, and clicking it will fail the quest (Figure 9-4).

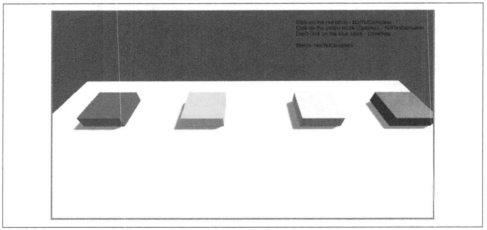

Figure 9-4. Clicking the forbidden block will fail the quest

We'll need to create the scene for our quest:

1. Create four cubes, and place them in front of the camera.

2. For each of the cubes, create a material and add it by dragging and dropping it onto the cube in the Scene view.

3. Change the color of the material for each cube. Make one red, one green, one yellow, and one blue. (If any of these colors are hard to tell apart, change the colors to whatever suits you best.)

Now the cube is set up (Figure 9-5).

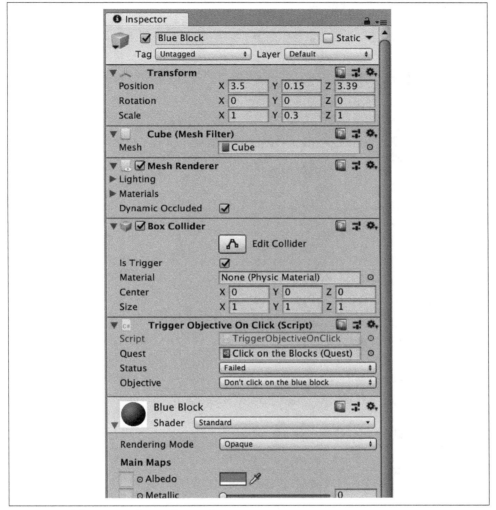

Figure 9-5. The setup of one of our cubes

Next, we'll handle displaying the status of the quest and its objectives:

1. Select the main Camera object, and add a Physics Raycaster to it.

2. Create a new canvas that displays the status of the quest and its objectives.

3. Add a game object with a Text component in it.

4. Resize this object so that it can comfortably contain a paragraph of text.

Now we'll set up the type of object that stores information about a quest. Create a new C# script called *Quest.cs*, and add the following code to it:

```
#if UNITY_EDITOR
using UnityEditor;
#endif

// A Quest stores information about a quest: its name and its
// objectives.

// CreateAssetMenu makes the Create Asset menu contain an entry that
// creates a new Quest asset.
[CreateAssetMenu(fileName = "New Quest", menuName = "Quest",
order = 100)]
public class Quest : ScriptableObject
{

    // Represents the status of objectives and quests
    public enum Status {
        NotYetComplete, // the objective or quest has not yet been
                        // completed
        Complete,       // the objective or quest has been successfully
                        // completed
        Failed          // the objective or quest has failed
    }

    // The name of the quest
    public string questName;

    // The list of objectives that form this quest
    public List<Objective> objectives;

    // Objectives are the specific tasks that make up a quest.
    [System.Serializable]
    public class Objective
    {
        // The visible name that's shown to the player
        public string name = "New Objective";

        // If true, this objective doesn't need to be complete for the
        // quest to be considered complete.
        public bool optional = false;

        // If false, the objective will not be shown to the user if
        // it's not yet complete. (It will be shown if it's Complete
        // or Failed.)
        public bool visible = true;

        // The status of the objective when the quest begins. Usually
        // this will be "not yet complete," but you might want an
        // objective that starts as Complete, and can be Failed.
        public Status initialStatus = Status.NotYetComplete;
```

```
        }

    }

#if UNITY_EDITOR
// Draw a custom editor that lets you build the list of objectives.
[CustomEditor(typeof(Quest))]
public class QuestEditor : Editor {

    // Called when Unity wants to draw the Inspector for a quest.
    public override void OnInspectorGUI()
    {

        // Ensure that the object we're displaying has had any pending
        // changes done.
        serializedObject.Update();

        // Draw the name of the quest.
        EditorGUILayout.PropertyField(
            serializedObject.FindProperty("questName"),
            new GUIContent("Name")
        );

        // Draw a header for the list of objectives
        EditorGUILayout.LabelField("Objectives");

        // Get the property that contains the list of objectives
        var objectiveList = serializedObject.FindProperty("objectives");

        // Indent the objectives
        EditorGUI.indentLevel += 1;

        // For each objective in the list, draw an entry
        for (int i = 0; i < objectiveList.arraySize; i++)
        {
            // Draw a single line of controls
            EditorGUILayout.BeginHorizontal();

            // Draw the objective itself (its name and its flags)
            EditorGUILayout.PropertyField(
                objectiveList.GetArrayElementAtIndex(i),
                includeChildren: true
            );

            // Draw a button that moves the item up in the list
            if (GUILayout.Button("Up", EditorStyles.miniButtonLeft,
                             GUILayout.Width(25)))
            {
                objectiveList.MoveArrayElement(i, i - 1);
            }

            // Draw a button that moves the item down in the list
```

```
                    if (GUILayout.Button("Down", EditorStyles.miniButtonMid,
                                    GUILayout.Width(40)))
                    {
                        objectiveList.MoveArrayElement(i, i + 1);
                    }

                    // Draw a button that removes the item from the list
                    if (GUILayout.Button("-", EditorStyles.miniButtonRight,
                                    GUILayout.Width(25)))
                    {
                        objectiveList.DeleteArrayElementAtIndex(i);
                    }

                    EditorGUILayout.EndHorizontal();

                }

                // Remove the indentation
                EditorGUI.indentLevel -= 1;

                // Draw a button that adds a new objective to the list
                if (GUILayout.Button("Add Objective"))
                {
                    objectiveList.arraySize += 1;
                }

                // Save any changes
                serializedObject.ApplyModifiedProperties();

        }
    }

#endif
```

 For more information on the ScriptableObject class, which we use to store information about quests as assets, see Recipe 2.9.

We can now create a quest asset:

1. Open the Assets menu, and choose Create → Quest. Name the new quest "Click on the Blocks."

2. Click Add Objective. Name the new objective "Click on the red block." Turn on the Visible checkbox.

3. Repeat this process two more times—once each for the green and yellow blocks. Make one of them optional, and one of them optional and not visible.

4. Add one more objective, for the blue block. For this one, set its name to "Don't click on the blue block." Set its Initial Status to "Complete."

When you're done, the Inspector should look something like Figure 9-6.

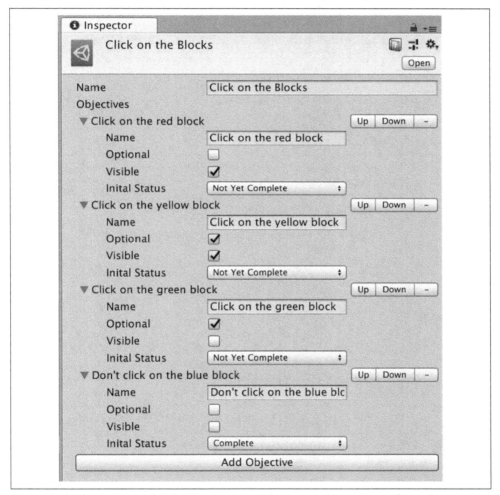

Figure 9-6. The Inspector for the quest asset, with several objectives configured

We'll now set up the code that manages the quest:

1. Create a new C# script called *QuestManager.cs*, and add the following code to it:

```csharp
// Represents the player's current progress through a quest.
public class QuestStatus {

    // The underlying data object that describes the quest.
    public Quest questData;

    // The map of objective identifiers.
    public Dictionary<int, Quest.Status> objectiveStatuses;

    // The constructor. Pass a Quest to this to set it up.
    public QuestStatus(Quest questData)
    {
        // Store the quest info
        this.questData = questData;

        // Create the map of objective numbers to their status
        objectiveStatuses = new Dictionary<int, Quest.Status>();

        for (int i = 0; i < questData.objectives.Count; i += 1)
        {
            var objectiveData = questData.objectives[i];

            objectiveStatuses[i] = objectiveData.initialStatus;
        }
    }

    // Returns the state of the entire quest.
    // If all nonoptional objectives are complete, the quest is complete.
    // If any nonoptional objective is failed, the quest is failed.
    // Otherwise, the quest is not yet complete.
    public Quest.Status questStatus {
        get {

            for (int i = 0; i < questData.objectives.Count; i += 1) {

                var objectiveData = questData.objectives[i];

                // Optional objectives do not matter to the overall
                // quest status
                if (objectiveData.optional)
                    continue;

                var objectiveStatus = objectiveStatuses[i];

                // This is a mandatory objective
                if (objectiveStatus == Quest.Status.Failed)
```

```
        {
            // If a mandatory objective is failed, the whole
            // quest is failed
            return Quest.Status.Failed;
        }
        else if (objectiveStatus != Quest.Status.Complete)
        {
            // If a mandatory objective is not yet complete,
            // the whole quest is not yet complete
            return Quest.Status.NotYetComplete;
        }
    }

    // All mandatory objectives are complete, so this quest is
    // complete
    return Quest.Status.Complete;

}
}

// Returns a string containing the list of objectives, their
// statuses, and the status of the quest.
public override string ToString()
{
    var stringBuilder = new System.Text.StringBuilder();

    for (int i = 0; i < questData.objectives.Count; i += 1)
    {
        // Get the objective and its status
        var objectiveData = questData.objectives[i];
        var objectiveStatus = objectiveStatuses[i];

        // Don't show hidden objectives that haven't been finished
        if (objectiveData.visible == false &&
            objectiveStatus == Quest.Status.NotYetComplete)
        {
            continue;
        }

        // If this objective is optional, display "(Optional)" after
        // its name
        if (objectiveData.optional)
        {
            stringBuilder.AppendFormat("{0} (Optional) - {1}\n",
                                objectiveData.name,
                                objectiveStatus.ToString());
        }
        else
        {
            stringBuilder.AppendFormat("{0} - {1}\n",
```

```
                                                  objectiveData.name,
                                                  objectiveStatus.ToString());
            }

        }

        // Add a blank line followed by the quest status
        stringBuilder.AppendLine();
        stringBuilder.AppendFormat(
            "Status: {0}", this.questStatus.ToString());

        return stringBuilder.ToString();
    }
}

// Manages a quest.
public class QuestManager : MonoBehaviour {

    // The quest that starts when the game starts.
    [SerializeField] Quest startingQuest = null;

    // A label to show the state of the quest.
    [SerializeField] UnityEngine.UI.Text objectiveSummary = null;

    // Tracks the state of the current quest.
    QuestStatus activeQuest;

    // Start a new quest when the game starts
    void Start () {

        if (startingQuest != null)
        {
            StartQuest(startingQuest);
        }
    }

    // Begins tracking a new quest
    public void StartQuest(Quest quest) {

        activeQuest = new QuestStatus(quest);

        UpdateObjectiveSummaryText();

        Debug.LogFormat("Started quest {0}", activeQuest.questData.name);
    }

    // Updates the label that displays the status of the quest and
    // its objectives
    void UpdateObjectiveSummaryText() {
```

```
        string label;

        if (activeQuest == null) {
            label = "No active quest.";
        } else {
            label = activeQuest.ToString();
        }

        objectiveSummary.text = label;
    }

    // Called by other objects to indicate that an objective has changed
    // status
    public void UpdateObjectiveStatus(
        Quest quest, int objectiveNumber, Quest.Status status) {

        if (activeQuest == null) {
            Debug.LogError(
                "Tried to set an objective status, but no quest" +
                "is active"
            );
            return;
        }

        if (activeQuest.questData != quest) {

            Debug.LogWarningFormat("Tried to set an objective status " +
                "for quest {0}, but this is not the active quest. " +
                "Ignoring.",
                quest.questName);

            return;
        }

        // Update the objective status
        activeQuest.objectiveStatuses[objectiveNumber] = status;

        // Update the display label
        UpdateObjectiveSummaryText();
    }

}
```

2. Create a new, empty game object, and add a `QuestManager` component to it.

3. Drag the quest asset you created into its Starting Quest field.

4. Drag the Text object that you set up earlier into its Objective Summary field.

5. Next, we'll set up a class that represents a change to an objective's status and can be applied when something happens. Create a new C# script called *Objective Trigger.cs*, and add the following code to it:

```csharp
#if UNITY_EDITOR
using UnityEditor;
using System.Linq;
#endif

// Combines a quest, an objective in that quest, and an objective
// status to use.
[System.Serializable]
public class ObjectiveTrigger
{

    // The quest that we're referring to
    public Quest quest;

    // The status we want to apply to the objective
    public Quest.Status statusToApply;

    // The location of this objective in the quest's objective list
    public int objectiveNumber;

    public void Invoke() {
        // Find the quest manager
        var manager = Object.FindObjectOfType<QuestManager>();

        // And tell it to update our objective
        manager.UpdateObjectiveStatus(quest,
                                      objectiveNumber,
                                      statusToApply);
    }
}

#if UNITY_EDITOR
// Custom property drawers override how a type of property appears in
// the Inspector.
[CustomPropertyDrawer(typeof(ObjectiveTrigger))]
public class ObjectiveTriggerDrawer : PropertyDrawer {

    // Called when Unity needs to draw an ObjectiveTrigger property
    // in the Inspector.
    public override void OnGUI(Rect position,
                               SerializedProperty property,
                               GUIContent label)
    {
        // Wrap this in Begin/EndProperty to ensure that undo works
        // on the entire ObjectiveTrigger property
        EditorGUI.BeginProperty(position, label, property);
```

```
// Get a reference to the three properties in the
// ObjectiveTrigger.
var questProperty =
    property.FindPropertyRelative("quest");
var statusProperty =
    property.FindPropertyRelative("statusToApply");
var objectiveNumberProperty =
    property.FindPropertyRelative("objectiveNumber");

// We want to display three controls:
// - An Object field for dropping a Quest object into
// - A pop-up field for selecting a Quest.Status from
// - A pop-up field for selecting the specific objective from;
//   it should show the name of the objective.
//
//   If no Quest has been specified, or if the Quest has no
//   objectives, the objective pop-up should be empty and
//   disabled.

// Calculate the rectangles in which we're displaying.
var lineSpacing = 2;

// Calculate the rectangle for the first line
var firstLinePosition = position;

firstLinePosition.height =
    base.GetPropertyHeight(questProperty, label);

// And for the second line (same as the first line, but shifted
// down one line)
var secondLinePosition = position;
secondLinePosition.y = firstLinePosition.y +
    firstLinePosition.height + lineSpacing;
secondLinePosition.height =
    base.GetPropertyHeight(statusProperty, label);

// Repeat for the third line (same as the second line, but
// shifted down)
var thirdLinePosition = position;
thirdLinePosition.y = secondLinePosition.y +
    secondLinePosition.height + lineSpacing;
thirdLinePosition.height =
    base.GetPropertyHeight(objectiveNumberProperty, label);

// Draw the quest and status properties, using the automatic
// property fields
EditorGUI.PropertyField(firstLinePosition, questProperty,
                    new GUIContent("Quest"));
EditorGUI.PropertyField(secondLinePosition, statusProperty,
```

```
                new GUIContent("Status"));

    // Now we draw our custom property for the object.
    // Draw a label on the lefthand side, and get a new rectangle
    // to draw the pop-up in
    thirdLinePosition = EditorGUI.PrefixLabel(thirdLinePosition,
                        new GUIContent("Objective"));

    // Draw the UI for choosing a property
    var quest = questProperty.objectReferenceValue as Quest;

    // Only draw this if we have a quest, and it has objectives
    if (quest != null && quest.objectives.Count > 0)
    {
        // Get the name of every objective, as an array
        var objectiveNames =
            quest.objectives.Select(o => o.name).ToArray();

        // Get the index of the currently selected objective
        var selectedObjective = objectiveNumberProperty.intValue;

        // If we somehow are referring to an object that's not
        // present in the list, reset it to the first objective
        if (selectedObjective >= quest.objectives.Count) {
            selectedObjective = 0;
        }

        // Draw the pop-up, and get back the new selection
        var newSelectedObjective = EditorGUI.Popup(thirdLinePosition,
                                        selectedObjective,
                                        objectiveNames);

        // If it was different, store it in the property
        if (newSelectedObjective != selectedObjective)
        {
            objectiveNumberProperty.intValue = newSelectedObjective;
        }

    } else {
        // Draw a disabled pop-up as a visual placeholder
        using (new EditorGUI.DisabledGroupScope(true)) {
            // Show a pop-up with a single entry: the string "-".
            // Ignore its return value, since it's not interactive
            // anyway.
            EditorGUI.Popup(thirdLinePosition, 0, new[] { "-" });
        }
    }

    EditorGUI.EndProperty();
}
```

```
// Called by Unity to figure out the height of this property.
public override float GetPropertyHeight(SerializedProperty property,
                                        GUIContent label)
{
    // The number of lines in this property
    var lineCount = 3;

    // The number of pixels between each line
    var lineSpacing = 2;

    // The height of each line
    var lineHeight = base.GetPropertyHeight(property, label);

    // The height of this property is the number of lines times the
    // height of each line, plus the spacing between each line
    return (lineHeight * lineCount) +
                        (lineSpacing * (lineCount - 1));
}
}
#endif
```

Finally, we'll set up the cubes so that they complete or fail objectives when they're clicked:

1. Create a new C# script called *TriggerObjectiveOnClick.cs*, and add the following code to it:

```
using UnityEngine.EventSystems;

// Triggers an objective when an object enters it.
public class TriggerObjectiveOnClick :
    MonoBehaviour, IPointerClickHandler {

    // The objective to trigger, and how to trigger it.
    [SerializeField] ObjectiveTrigger objective = new ObjectiveTrigger();

    // Called when the player clicks on this object
    void IPointerClickHandler.OnPointerClick(PointerEventData eventData)
    {
        // We just completed or failed this objective!
        objective.Invoke();

        // Disable this component so that it doesn't get run twice
        this.enabled = false;
    }
}
```

2. Add a `TriggerObjectiveOnClick` component to each cube. For each one, drag the quest asset into its Quest field, and select the appropriate status for the objective (that is, set the blue cube to Failed, and the rest to Complete).

Figure 9-7 shows an example of the red cube's `TriggerObjectiveOnClick` scripts after it's been configured.

 The canvas itself may block your raycasts unless you disable the text as a raycast target.

3. Play the game. The state of the quest is shown on the screen, and changes as you click different cubes.

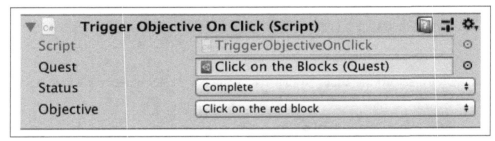

Figure 9-7. The Inspector for `TriggerObjectiveOnClick`

Discussion

So that was a long one! Don't worry, the discussion won't be as long as the solution.

 You can learn more about UIs in Chapter 12.

Creating a quest system here involves creating something to be a quest (the cubes), a UI to show the status of the quest, and then some actual quests. When you're building a system like this, it's important to think through the different combinations of states that the objects can be involved in. Think about what a mischievous, malicious, confused, or unlucky player might do: they might do things out of order, skip over content, or find ways to do what your code doesn't expect.

9.5 Dragging a Box to Select Objects

Problem

You want to click and drag the mouse to create a visible rectangle onscreen. When you release the mouse, you want to know which objects are inside that rectangle.

Solution

First, we'll create the canvas that draws the box, and the box object itself:

1. Open the GameObject menu, and choose UI → Canvas.
2. From the GameObject menu, choose UI → Image.
3. Name the new image "Selection Box."

Next, we'll create a script that outputs a message when it's selected:

1. Create a new C# script called *BoxSelectable.cs*, and add the following code to it:

    ```csharp
    // Handles the input and display of a selection box.
    public class BoxSelectable: MonoBehaviour {

        public void Selected() {

            Debug.LogFormat("{0} was selected!", gameObject.name);

        }

    }
    ```

2. Create some objects—it doesn't matter what they are; cubes will do—and place them so that the camera can see them.

3. Add the *BoxSelectable.cs* script to each object.

Now we'll create a script that updates the position and size of the selection box, and reports on which objects were selected:

1. Create a new C# script called *BoxSelection.cs*, and add the following code to it:

    ```csharp
    // Handles the input and display of a selection box.
    public class BoxSelection : MonoBehaviour
    {

        // Draggable inspector reference to the Image GameObject's
        // RectTransform.
        public RectTransform selectionBox;
    ```

```
// This variable will store the location of wherever we first click
// before dragging.
private Vector2 initialClickPosition = Vector2.zero;

// The rectangle that the box has dragged, in screen space.
public Rect SelectionRect { get; private set; }

// If true, the user is actively dragging a box
public bool IsSelecting { get; private set; }

// Configure the visible box
private void Start()
{
    // Setting the anchors to be positioned at zero-zero means that
    // the box's size won't change as its parent changes size
    selectionBox.anchorMin = Vector2.zero;
    selectionBox.anchorMax = Vector2.zero;

    // Setting the pivot point to zero means that the box will pivot
    // around its lower-left corner
    selectionBox.pivot = Vector2.zero;

    // Hide the box at the start
    selectionBox.gameObject.SetActive(false);
}

void Update()
{
    // When we start dragging, record the position of the mouse, and
    // start showing the box
    if (Input.GetMouseButtonDown(0))
    {
        // Get the initial click position of the mouse. No need to
        // convert to GUI space since we are using the lower left as
        // anchor and pivot.
        initialClickPosition =
            new Vector2(Input.mousePosition.x,
                        Input.mousePosition.y);

        // Show the box
        selectionBox.gameObject.SetActive(true);
    }

    // While we are dragging, update the position and size of the
    // box based on the mouse position.
    if (Input.GetMouseButton(0))
    {
        // Store the current mouse position in screen space.
        Vector2 currentMousePosition =
            new Vector2(Input.mousePosition.x,
```

```
                    Input.mousePosition.y);

        // Figure out the lower-left corner, and the upper-right
        // corner
        var xMin =
            Mathf.Min(currentMousePosition.x,
                        initialClickPosition.x);
        var xMax =
            Mathf.Max(currentMousePosition.x,
                        initialClickPosition.x);
        var yMin =
            Mathf.Min(currentMousePosition.y,
                        initialClickPosition.y);
        var yMax =
            Mathf.Max(currentMousePosition.y,
                        initialClickPosition.y);

        // Build a rectangle from these corners
        var screenSpaceRect = Rect.MinMaxRect(xMin, yMin,
                                                xMax, yMax);

        // The anchor of the box has been configured to be its
        // lower-left corner, so by setting its anchoredPosition, we
        // set its lower-left corner.
        selectionBox.anchoredPosition = screenSpaceRect.position;

        // The size delta is how far the box extends from its anchor.
        // Because the anchor's minimum and maximum are the same
        // point, changing its size delta directly changes its
        // final size.
        selectionBox.sizeDelta = screenSpaceRect.size;

        // Update our selection box
        SelectionRect = screenSpaceRect;
    }

    // When we release the mouse button, hide the box, and record
    // that we're no longer selecting
    if (Input.GetMouseButtonUp(0))
    {
        SelectionComplete();

        // Hide the box
        selectionBox.gameObject.SetActive(false);

        // We're no longer selecting
        IsSelecting = false;
    }
}
```

```
// Called when the user finishes dragging a selection box.
void SelectionComplete()
{
    // Get the component attached to this scene
    Camera mainCamera = GetComponent<Camera>();

    // Get the bottom-left and top-right corners of the screen-space
    // selection view, and convert them to viewport space
    var min = mainCamera.ScreenToViewportPoint(
        new Vector3(SelectionRect.xMin, SelectionRect.yMin));
    var max = mainCamera.ScreenToViewportPoint(
        new Vector3(SelectionRect.xMax, SelectionRect.yMax));

    // We want to create a bounding box in viewport space. We have
    // the x and y coordinates of the bottom-left and top-right
    // corners; now we'll include the z coordinates.
    min.z = mainCamera.nearClipPlane;
    max.z = mainCamera.farClipPlane;

    // Construct our bounding box
    var viewportBounds = new Bounds();
    viewportBounds.SetMinMax(min, max);

    // Check each object that has a Selectable component
    foreach (var selectable in FindObjectsOfType<BoxSelectable>()) {

        // Figure out where this object is in viewport space
        var selectedPosition = selectable.transform.position;

        var viewportPoint =
            mainCamera.WorldToViewportPoint(selectedPosition);

        // Is that point within our viewport bounding box? If it is,
        // they're selected.
        var selected = viewportBounds.Contains(viewportPoint);

        if (selected) {
            // Let them know.
            selectable.Selected();
        }
    }

    }
}
```

2. Attach a BoxSelection component to the main camera.

3. Drag the Selection Box image onto the Selection Box field.

---

4. Run the game. You can click and drag to create the box. When you release the mouse, all objects within the rectangle that have a `BoxSelectable` component will log that they were selected.

Discussion

The most interesting part of this solution is the use of viewport space, which is normalized and relative to the camera.

 If you use a sliced sprite, your selection box can have borders.

9.6 Creating a Menu Structure

Problem

You want to create a collection of menu pages in which only one menu is visible at a time.

Solution

To create a collection of menu pages:

1. Create a new script called *Menu.cs*:

```
// Contains UnityEvent, which this script uses
using UnityEngine.Events;

public class Menu : MonoBehaviour {

    // Invoked when a menu appears onscreen.
    public UnityEvent menuDidAppear = new UnityEvent();

    // Invoked when a menu is removed from the screen.
    public UnityEvent menuWillDisappear = new UnityEvent();

}
```

2. Create a new script called *MenuManager.cs*:

```
public class MenuManager : MonoBehaviour {

    [SerializeField] List<Menu> menus = new List<Menu>();

    private void Start()
```

```
{
    // Show the first menu on start
    ShowMenu(menus[0]);
}

public void ShowMenu(Menu menuToShow) {

    // Ensure that this menu is one that we're tracking.
    if (menus.Contains(menuToShow) == false) {

        Debug.LogErrorFormat(
            "{0} is not in the list of menus",
            menuToShow.name
        );
        return;
    }

    // Enable this menu, and disable the others
    foreach (var otherMenu in menus) {

        // Is this the menu we want to display?
        if (otherMenu == menuToShow) {

            // Mark it as active
            otherMenu.gameObject.SetActive(true);

            // Tell the Menu object to invoke its "did appear"
            // action
            otherMenu.menuDidAppear.Invoke();

        } else {

            // Is this menu currently active?
            if (otherMenu.gameObject.activeInHierarchy)
            {
                // If so, tell the Menu object to invoke its "will
                // disappear" action
                otherMenu.menuWillDisappear.Invoke();
            }

            // And mark it as inactive
            otherMenu.gameObject.SetActive(false);
        }
    }
}

}
```

Now we'll create a sample menu. It'll have two screens—a main menu and an options menu:

1. Create a new game object, and call it "Menu Manager."
2. Add the *MenuManager.cs* script to this object.
3. Create a canvas.
4. Create a new child game object called "Main Menu." This will act as a container for the menu's controls.
5. Add the *Menu.cs* script to this object.
6. Add a button game object to the Main Menu object. Name this button "Show Options Menu Button."
7. Set its text to "Options Menu."
8. Duplicate the Main Menu object, and rename it to "Options Menu."
9. Rename its "Show Options Menu Button" text to "Show Main Menu Button."
10. Change its text to "Back."
11. Select the Menu Manager object.
12. Drag the Main Menu object onto the Menus slot.
13. Drag the Options Menu object onto the Menus slot.

Next, we'll make the buttons show the appropriate menus:

1. Select the "Show Options Menu Button" inside the Main Menu object.
2. Add a new entry in the button's On Click event.
3. Drag the Menu Manager into the object field.
4. In the Function drop-down menu, choose MenuManager → ShowMenu.
5. Drag the Options Menu object into the parameter field.
6. When you're done, the On Click event should look like Figure 9-8.
7. Select the "Show Main Menu Button" inside the Options Menu object.
8. Add a new entry in the button's On Click event.
9. Drag the Menu Manager into the object field.
10. In the Function drop-down menu, choose MenuManager → ShowMenu.
11. Drag the Main Menu object into the parameter field.
12. When you're done, the On Click event should look like Figure 9-9.

13. Run the game. The main menu will appear. Clicking the Options button will hide it and show the options menu, and clicking the Back button will return you to the main menu.

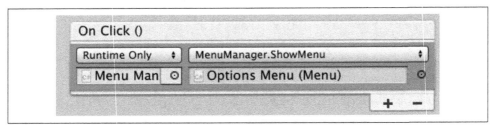

Figure 9-8. Configuring the On Click event for the Show Options Menu button

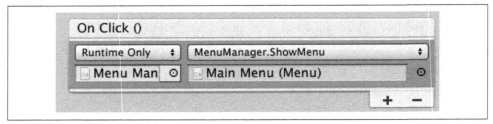

Figure 9-9. Configuring the On Click event for the Show Main Menu button

Discussion

You can also add other function calls to each menu; see Figure 9-10.

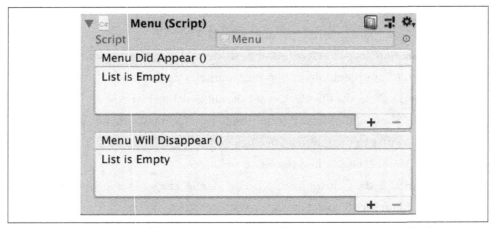

Figure 9-10. The Menu Did Appear and Menu Will Disappear events, to which you can add function calls

9.7 Creating a Wheeled Vehicle

Problem

You want to implement a vehicle with wheels, like a car.

Solution

To create a wheeled vehicle:

1. Create an empty object called "Vehicle."

2. Add a rigidbody to it.

3. Set its mass to 750, and its drag to 0.1.

4. If you have a car mesh to use, add it as a child of the Vehicle object. If you don't have a mesh, add a cube as a child and scale it so that it's the right shape and size for a car. If you do this, make sure you remove the box collider that comes with the cube. In either case, make sure that your visible object's position is (0, 0, 0), so that it's in the right place.

5. Create an empty game object as a child, and call it "Colliders."

6. Add an empty game object to "Colliders," and name it "Body."

7. Add a box collider to the Body object.

8. Click Edit Collider, and click and drag the box so that it fits closely around the visible car object.

9. Create a new, empty child object of Colliders, and name it "Wheel Front Left."

10. Add a wheel collider to this new object.

11. Position this near where you want the front-left tire to be. If you're using a car mesh, place it in the middle of the visible tire.

12. Adjust the radius of the wheel to the size you want. (It's OK if the wheel collider goes inside the body collider.)

13. Duplicate the wheel three times—one for each of the other three tires. Move each to one of the other tires, and rename them appropriately. When you're done, the colliders should look something like Figure 9-11.

Figure 9-11. Placing the vehicle's wheels

14. Create a new script, and call it *Vehicle.cs*. Add the following code to it:

```
// Configures a single wheel's control parameters.
[System.Serializable]
public class Wheel {
    // The collider this wheel uses
    public WheelCollider collider;

    // Whether this wheel should be powered by the engine
    public bool powered;

    // Whether this wheel is steerable
    public bool steerable;

    // Whether this wheel can apply brakes
    public bool hasBrakes;
}

// Controls the power, braking, and steering applied to wheels.
public class Vehicle : MonoBehaviour {

    // The list of wheels on this vehicle
    [SerializeField] Wheel[] wheels = {};

    // The settings used for controlling the wheels:
```

```csharp
// Maximum motor torque
[SerializeField] float motorTorque = 1000;

// Maximum brake torque
[SerializeField] float brakeTorque = 2000;

// Maximum steering angle
[SerializeField] float steeringAngle = 45;

private void Update() {

    // If the vertical axis is positive, apply motor torque and no
    // brake torque. If it's negative, apply brake torque and no
    // motor torque.
    var vertical = Input.GetAxis("Vertical");

    float motorTorqueToApply;
    float brakeTorqueToApply;

    if (vertical >= 0) {
        motorTorqueToApply = vertical * motorTorque;
        brakeTorqueToApply = 0;
    } else {
        // If the vertical axis is negative, cut the engine and step
        // on the brakes.

        // We use Mathf.Abs here to ensure that we use the positive
        // value of "vertical" (because applying negative braking
        // torque would lead to weirdness).
        motorTorqueToApply = 0;
        brakeTorqueToApply = Mathf.Abs(vertical) * brakeTorque;
    }

    // Scale the maximum steering angle by the horizontal axis.
    var currentSteeringAngle =
        Input.GetAxis("Horizontal") * steeringAngle;

    // Update all wheels

    // Using a for loop, rather than a foreach loop, because foreach
    // loops allocate temporary memory, which is turned into garbage
    // at the end of the frame. We want to minimize garbage, because
    // the more garbage that gets generated, the more often the
    // garbage collector has to run, which causes performance
    // problems.
    for (int wheelNum = 0; wheelNum < wheels.Length; wheelNum++) {

        var wheel = wheels[wheelNum];
```

```
// If a wheel is powered, it updates its motor torque
if (wheel.powered) {
    wheel.collider.motorTorque = motorTorqueToApply;
}

// If a wheel is steerable, it updates its steer angle
if (wheel.steerable) {
    wheel.collider.steerAngle = currentSteeringAngle;
}

// If a wheel has brakes, it updates its brake torque
if (wheel.hasBrakes) {
    wheel.collider.brakeTorque = brakeTorqueToApply;
}
            }
        }
    }
```

15. Add the *Vehicle.cs* script to the Vehicle object.

16. Select the Vehicle object, and add four entries to the Wheels list.

17. For each of the entries:

    a. Add one of the wheel colliders.

    b. If it's a rear wheel, turn on Powered.

    c. If it's a front wheel, turn on Steerable.

    d. Turn on Has Brakes.

18. Play the game. You should be able to drive the car around.

Discussion

You could also consider adding an orbiting camera to follow the vehicle as it moves, as per Recipe 9.10.

When building a vehicle, consider what happens when all of the wheels are steerable, or all of them are powered.

 Try modifying the mass of the vehicle or the torque values. See what happens!

In Unity, wheel colliders define their own suspension parameters. Play with them for interesting effects.

9.8 Keeping a Car from Tipping Over

Problem

You want your car to not flip over when taking sharp turns.

Solution

Your car tips over because it's rotating around its center of mass, which is too high. When the center of mass is lower, any rotation around it will force the wheels into the ground harder, instead of flipping the entire car over.

To keep a car from tipping over:

1. Create a new C# script called *AdjustCenterOfMass.cs*, with the following code:

```
[RequireComponent(typeof(Rigidbody))]
public class AdjustCenterOfMass : MonoBehaviour {

    // How far the center of mass should be moved from its default
    // position
    [SerializeField] Vector3 centerOfMass = Vector3.zero;

    private void Start()
    {
        // Override the center of mass, to enhance stability
        GetComponent<Rigidbody>().centerOfMass += centerOfMass;
    }

    // Called by the editor to show "gizmos" in the Scene view. Used to
    // help visualize the overridden center of mass.
    private void OnDrawGizmosSelected()
    {
        // Draw a green sphere where the updated center of mass will be.
        Gizmos.color = Color.green;

        var currentCenterOfMass =
            this.GetComponent<Rigidbody>().worldCenterOfMass;

        Gizmos.DrawSphere(currentCenterOfMass + centerOfMass, 0.125f);
    }
}
```

2. Add this component to the game object containing your vehicle's rigidbody.

3. Move the center of mass's y coordinate down a bit, so that it's just at the floor of the vehicle. The lower the center of mass, the more stable the vehicle will be.

Discussion

In Unity, rigidbodies usually compute their center of mass from their colliders, but you can override it.

In real life, a car's center of mass is low because of heavy objects like the transmission and engine being under the floor. The way we've implemented it here (and how it's typically implemented in games) is less realistic but makes for better gameplay.

9.9 Creating Speed Boosts

Problem

You want to create objects on your race track that give a temporary speed boost to vehicles that drive over them.

Solution

First, create the visible component of the speed boost. In this example, we'll go for a simple, cartoonish look:

1. Create a new material, and call it "Speed Boost."

2. Set its albedo color to red.

3. Open the GameObject menu, and choose 3D Object → Plane.

4. Position and scale the object appropriately on your track.

5. Name the object "Speed Boost."

6. Drag the Speed Boost material onto it.

7. Remove the mesh collider from the object.

8. Add a box collider.

9. Turn on Is Trigger.

10. Adjust the size and position to create a volume big enough for a car (for example, see Figure 9-12).

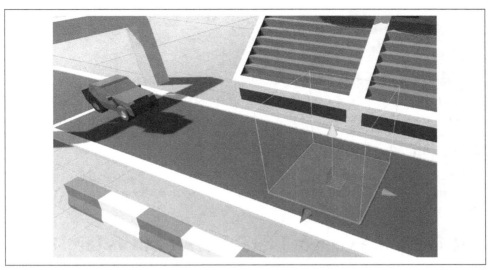

Figure 9-12. The Speed Boost object, with a box collider big enough for a car to fit into

11. Create a new C# script called *SpeedBoost.cs*, and add the following code to it:

```
public class SpeedBoost : MonoBehaviour {

    // The amount of time the boost should apply
    [SerializeField] float boostDuration = 1;

    // The amount of force to apply in the forward direction
    [SerializeField] float boostForce = 50;

    // Called when a rigidbody enters the trigger
    private void OnTriggerEnter(Collider other)
    {
        // Ensure this collider has a rigidbody, either on itself
        // or on a parent object
        var body = other.GetComponentInParent<Rigidbody>();

        if (body == null) {
            return;
        }

        // Attach a ConstantForce component to it
        var boost = body.gameObject.AddComponent<ConstantForce>();

        // Make the ConstantForce boost the object forward by the
        // specified amount
        boost.relativeForce = Vector3.forward * boostForce;
```

```
        // Remove this ConstantForce after boostDuration seconds
        Destroy(boost, boostDuration);
    }
}
```

12. Attach a `SpeedBoost` component to the Speed Boost object.

13. Test the game. When a vehicle enters the boost area, it will be boosted forward for a short duration.

Discussion

Our speed boost is nothing complex: just an object with a collider and a trigger, and a call to the physics system to apply some force to the object that needs to get the speed increase. A boost!

9.10 Creating a Camera That Orbits Around Its Target

Problem

You want to create a camera that rotates around a target's position at a fixed distance.

Solution

To create an orbiting camera:

1. Add a camera to the scene.

2. Create a new C# script called *OrbitingCamera.cs*, and replace its code with the following:

```
public class OrbitingCamera : MonoBehaviour
{

    // The object we're orbiting around
    [SerializeField] Transform target;

    // The speed at which we change our rotation and elevation
    [SerializeField] float rotationSpeed = 120.0f;
    [SerializeField] float elevationSpeed = 120.0f;

    // The minimum and maximum angle of elevation
    [SerializeField] float elevationMinLimit = -20f;
    [SerializeField] float elevationMaxLimit = 80f;

    // The distance we're at from the target
    [SerializeField] float distance = 5.0f;
    [SerializeField] float distanceMin = .5f;
    [SerializeField] float distanceMax = 15f;
```

```csharp
// The angle at which we're rotated around the target
float rotationAroundTarget = 0.0f;

// The angle at which we're looking down or up at the target
float elevationToTarget = 0.0f;

// Use this for initialization
void Start()
{
    Vector3 angles = transform.eulerAngles;
    rotationAroundTarget = angles.y;
    elevationToTarget = angles.x;

    if (target) {
        // Take the current distance from the camera to the target
        float currentDistance =
            (transform.position - target.position).magnitude;

        // Clamp it to our required minimum/maximum
        distance = Mathf.Clamp(
            currentDistance, distanceMin, distanceMax);
    }
}

// Every frame, after all Update functions are called, update the
// camera position and rotation
//
// We do this in LateUpdate so that if the object we're tracking has
// its position changed in the Update method, the camera will be
// correctly positioned, because LateUpdate is always run afterward.
void LateUpdate()
{
    if (target)
    {
        // Update our rotation and elevation based on mouse movement
        rotationAroundTarget +=
            Input.GetAxis("Mouse X")
                * rotationSpeed * distance * 0.02f;

        elevationToTarget -=
            Input.GetAxis("Mouse Y") * elevationSpeed * 0.02f;

        // Limit the elevation to between the minimum and
        // the maximum
        elevationToTarget = ClampAngle(
            elevationToTarget,
            elevationMinLimit,
            elevationMaxLimit
        );
```

```
// Compute the rotation based on these two angles
Quaternion rotation = Quaternion.Euler(
    elevationToTarget,
    rotationAroundTarget,
    0
);

// Update the distance based on mouse movement
distance = distance - Input.GetAxis("Mouse ScrollWheel") * 5;

// And limit it to the minimum and maximum
distance = Mathf.Clamp(distance, distanceMin, distanceMax);

// Figure out a position that's "distance" units away
// from the target in the reverse direction to where
// we're looking
Vector3 negDistance = new Vector3(0.0f, 0.0f, -distance);
Vector3 position = rotation * negDistance + target.position;

// Update the position
transform.position = position;

// Update the rotation so we're looking at the target
transform.rotation = rotation;
        }
    }

    // Clamps an angle between "min" and "max," wrapping it if it's less
    // than 360 degrees or higher than 360 degrees.
    public static float ClampAngle(float angle, float min, float max)
    {

        // Wrap the angle at -360 and 360
        if (angle < -360F)
            angle += 360F;
        if (angle > 360F)
            angle -= 360F;

        // Clamp this wrapped angle
        return Mathf.Clamp(angle, min, max);
    }
}
```

3. Add a cube to the scene.

4. Select the camera, and drag the cube's entry in the Hierarchy into the Target field.

5. Run the game. As you move the mouse, the camera will rotate around the target.

Discussion

This kind of camera is sometimes referred to as a "chase camera." We do most of the work in the LateUpdate function here, because we want to make sure that the camera is in the correct position if the object it's tracking has its position change in the Update function. LateUpdate (*https://oreil.ly/119Fb*) is always run after Update.

You can learn about the execution order of events in the Unity manual (*https://oreil.ly/_qAMr*).

9.11 Creating an Orbiting Camera That Won't Clip Through Walls

Problem

You want to detect when there's an object between the camera and the target, and move the camera closer.

This recipe builds upon Recipe 9.10.

Solution

To create a camera that won't clip through walls:

1. Add the following variable to the OrbitingCamera class:

```
// When true, the camera will adjust its distance when there's a
// collider between it and the target
[SerializeField] bool clipCamera;
```

2. Add the following code to the class's LateUpdate method:

```
if (clipCamera) {

    // We'll cast out a ray from the target to the position we just
    // computed. If the ray hits something, we'll update our
    // position to where the ray hit.

    // Store info about any hit in here.
    RaycastHit hitInfo;
```

```
// Generate a ray from the target to the camera
var ray =
    new Ray(target.position, position - target.position);

// Perform the ray cast; if it hit anything, it returns true,
// and updates the hitInfo variable
var hit = Physics.Raycast(ray, out hitInfo, distance);

if (hit) {
    // We hit something. Update the camera position to where the
    // ray hit an object.
    position = hitInfo.point;
}
}
```

3. Turn on Clip Camera on your orbiting camera, and play the game.

The camera will now move closer to the target if there's a collider between the camera and the target.

Discussion

Raycasts will only hit colliders. If there's an object that blocks the camera but doesn't have a collider attached, the script won't know to move closer.

9.12 Detecting When the Player Has Completed a Lap

Problem

You want to detect when the player has completed a lap around a race circuit. You also want to detect if the player is going the wrong way, or cheating by taking too much of a shortcut.

Solution

You can solve this by creating a set of checkpoints that the player must pass, in order. If the player is passing checkpoints in the wrong order, they're going the wrong way:

1. Start by laying out your track, so that both you and the player will know the path to take. See Figure 9-13.

The assets we're using for the racing recipes in this chapter are from Kenney's racing kit (*https://oreil.ly/J3GMy*), which is free and under a permissive Creative Commons Zero license.

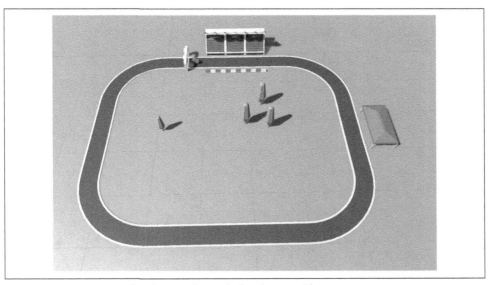

Figure 9-13. An example of a simple track that laps itself

2. Add a vehicle to the scene, and ensure that you're able to drive around (just to make sure that the driving component works).

3. Create a new C# script called *Checkpoint.cs*, and add the following code to it. Note that it contains two classes; one of them is special, editor-only code that adds buttons to the Inspector to help build the track:

```csharp
#if UNITY_EDITOR
// Include the UnityEditor namespace when this class is being used
// in the Editor.
using UnityEditor;
#endif

public class Checkpoint : MonoBehaviour
{

    // If true, this is the start of the circuit
    [SerializeField] public bool isLapStart;

    // The next checkpoint in the circuit. If we're visiting these in
    // reverse, or skipping too many, then we're going the wrong way.
```

```csharp
    [SerializeField] public Checkpoint next;

    // The index number, used by LapTracker to figure out if we're going
    // the wrong way.
    internal int index = 0;

    // Checkpoints are invisible, so we draw a marker in the Scene view
    // to make it easier to visualize.
    private void OnDrawGizmos()
    {
        // Draw the markers as a blue sphere, except for the lap start,
        // which is yellow.
        if (isLapStart)
        {
            Gizmos.color = Color.yellow;
        }
        else
        {
            Gizmos.color = Color.blue;
        }

        Gizmos.DrawSphere(transform.position, 0.5f);

        // If we have a next node set up, draw a blue line to it.
        if (next != null)
        {
            Gizmos.color = Color.blue;
            Gizmos.DrawLine(transform.position, next.transform.position);
        }
    }
}

#if UNITY_EDITOR
// Code that adds further controls for building a track to the
// Checkpoint Inspector.
[CustomEditor(typeof(Checkpoint))]
public class CheckpointEditor : Editor {

    // Called when Unity needs to display the Inspector for this
    // Checkpoint component.
    public override void OnInspectorGUI()
    {
        // First, draw the Inspector contents that we'd normally get.
        DrawDefaultInspector();

        // Get a reference to the Checkpoint component we're editing, by
        // casting 'target' (which is just an Object) to Checkpoint.
        var checkpoint = this.target as Checkpoint;

        // Display a button that inserts a new checkpoint between us and
```

```
// the next one. GUILayout.Button both displays the button and
// returns true if it was clicked.
if (GUILayout.Button("Insert Checkpoint")) {

    // Make a new object, and add a Checkpoint component to it
    var newCheckpoint = new GameObject("Checkpoint")
        .AddComponent<Checkpoint>();

    // Make it point to our next one, and make us point to
    // it (in other words, insert it between us and our next
    // checkpoint)
    newCheckpoint.next = checkpoint.next;
    checkpoint.next = newCheckpoint;

    // Make it one of our siblings
    newCheckpoint.transform
        .SetParent(checkpoint.transform.parent, true);

    // Position it as our next sibling in the Hierarchy.
    // Not technically needed, and doesn't affect the game at
    // all, but it looks nicer.
    var nextSiblingIndex =
        checkpoint.transform.GetSiblingIndex() + 1;

    newCheckpoint.transform.SetSiblingIndex(nextSiblingIndex);

    // Move it slightly so that it's visibly not the same one
    newCheckpoint.transform.position =
        checkpoint.transform.position + new Vector3(1, 0, 0);

    // Select it, so that we can immediately start moving it
    Selection.activeGameObject = newCheckpoint.gameObject;
}

// Disable this button if we don't have a next checkpoint, or if
// the next checkpoint is the lap start

var disableRemoveButton = checkpoint.next == null ||
                                    checkpoint.next.isLapStart;

using (new EditorGUI.DisabledGroupScope(disableRemoveButton)) {
    // Display a button that removes the next checkpoint
    if (GUILayout.Button("Remove Next Checkpoint"))
    {
        // Get the node that this next checkpoint was linking to
        var next = checkpoint.next.next;

        // Remove the next one
        DestroyImmediate(checkpoint.next.gameObject);
```

```
                    // Aim ourselves at what it was pointing at
                    checkpoint.next = next;
                }
            }
        }
    }
#endif
```

4. Create a new, empty game object called "Checkpoints."

5. Add a new, empty game object as a child of Checkpoints. Name it "Checkpoint," and add a `Checkpoint` component to it.

6. Position this checkpoint at the start of the racetrack.

7. Turn on Is Lap Start.

8. Click Insert Checkpoint in the Inspector. A new checkpoint will be added and selected. Position it further along the track.

9. Continue inserting new checkpoints. You can also select an earlier checkpoint and click Insert Checkpoint to insert a new checkpoint between two existing points, or delete a checkpoint by selecting the previous checkpoint and clicking Delete Next Checkpoint.

10. When you've completed the circuit, select the last checkpoint and drag the Lap Start checkpoint (the one with a yellow marker) into its Next field.

 If the connections between checkpoints get messed up, you can fix them by changing the Next field on the checkpoints.

When you're done, the circuit should look something like Figure 9-14.

11. Position the final checkpoint so that the finish line of the circuit is right in the middle of the first and last checkpoints, which should be quite close together. See Figure 9-15.

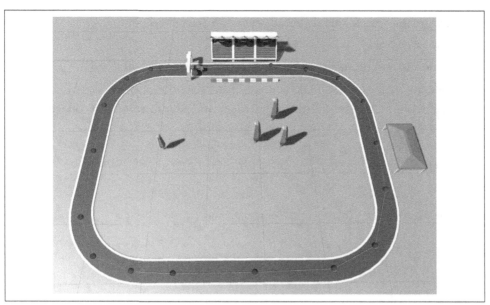

Figure 9-14. The checkpoints placed around the track

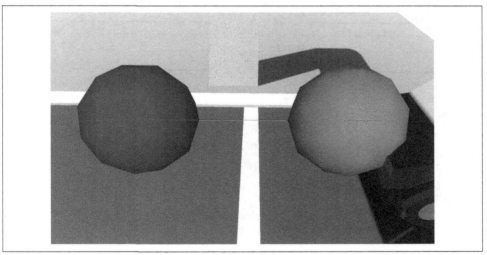

Figure 9-15. The final checkpoint, placed so that the finish line is between the first and last checkpoint

12. Position the vehicle slightly ahead of the Lap Start checkpoint.

13. Create a canvas.

14. Create and add two game objects with a Text component attached.

15. Make one display the text "Wrong Way!" and the other display "Lap 1."

16. Create a new C# script called *LapTracker.cs*, and add the following code to it:

```csharp
// We use LINQ to help figure out the start of the circuit with fewer
// lines of code. Using LINQ allocates memory, which is something we
// try to avoid, but because we only do it once (at scene start), it's
// not as bad.
using System.Linq;

public class LapTracker : MonoBehaviour {

    // The object that we're tracking as it makes laps around the
    // circuit.
    [SerializeField] Transform target = null;

    // The number of nodes in the list we're permitted to skip. This
    // prevents the player from just driving a tiny circle from the
    // start of the track to the end ("I crossed the finish line
    // three times! That means I win!"). Increase this number to permit
    // longer shortcuts. Set this to 0 to forbid any shortcuts.
    [SerializeField] int longestPermittedShortcut = 2;

    // The UI element that appears to let the player know they're
    // going the wrong way.
    [SerializeField] GameObject wrongWayIndicator;

    // A text field that displays the number of laps the player has
    // completed.
    [SerializeField] UnityEngine.UI.Text lapCounter;

    // The number of laps the player has completed.
    int lapsComplete = 0;

    // The checkpoint that the player was near most recently.
    Checkpoint lastSeenCheckpoint;

    // The list of all checkpoints on the circuit. We keep a copy of it
    // here, because we need to use this list every frame, and because
    // using FindObjectsOfType to regenerate the list every frame
    // would be slow.
    Checkpoint[] allCheckpoints;

    // The start checkpoint is the first (and hopefully only) checkpoint
    // that has isLapStart turned on.
```

```
Checkpoint StartCheckpoint {
    get {
        // Get the checkpoint marked as the start of the lap
        return FindObjectsOfType<Checkpoint>()
            .Where(c => c.isLapStart)
            .FirstOrDefault();
    }
}

void Start () {

    // Ensure that the counter says "lap 1"
    UpdateLapCounter();

    // The player isn't going the wrong way at the start
    wrongWayIndicator.SetActive(false);

    // Create the list of all checkpoints which Update will make
    // use of
    allCheckpoints = FindObjectsOfType<Checkpoint>();

    // Create the circuit of connected checkpoints
    CreateCircuit();

    // Begin the race at the start of the circuit
    lastSeenCheckpoint = StartCheckpoint;
}

private void Update()
{
    // What's the nearest checkpoint?
    var nearestCheckpoint = NearestCheckpoint();

    if (nearestCheckpoint == null) {
        // No checkpoints! Bail out.
        return;
    }

    if (nearestCheckpoint.index == lastSeenCheckpoint.index) {
        // Nothing to do; the nearest checkpoint has not changed.
    } else if (nearestCheckpoint.index > lastSeenCheckpoint.index) {

        var distance =
            nearestCheckpoint.index - lastSeenCheckpoint.index;

        if (distance > longestPermittedShortcut + 1) {
            // The player has skipped too many checkpoints.
            // Treat this as going the wrong way.
            wrongWayIndicator.SetActive(true);
        } else {
```

```
                    // We are near the next checkpoint; the player is going
                    // the right way.
                    lastSeenCheckpoint = nearestCheckpoint;

                    wrongWayIndicator.SetActive(false);
                }

            } else if (nearestCheckpoint.isLapStart &&
                    lastSeenCheckpoint.next.isLapStart) {
                // If the last checkpoint we saw is the last in the circuit,
                // and our nearest is now the start of the circuit, we just
                // completed a lap!

                lastSeenCheckpoint = nearestCheckpoint;

                lapsComplete += 1;
                UpdateLapCounter();

            } else {
                // This checkpoint is lower than the last one we saw. The
                // player is going the wrong way.
                wrongWayIndicator.SetActive(true);
            }
        }

        // Calculates the nearest checkpoint to the player.
        Checkpoint NearestCheckpoint() {

            // If we don't have a list of checkpoints to use, exit
            // immediately
            if (allCheckpoints == null) {
                return null;
            }

            // Loop through the list of all checkpoints, and find the
            // nearest one to the player's position.
            Checkpoint nearestSoFar = null;
            float nearestDistanceSoFar = float.PositiveInfinity;

            for (int c = 0; c < allCheckpoints.Length; c++) {
                var checkpoint = allCheckpoints[c];
                var distance =
                    (target.position - checkpoint.transform.position)
                    .sqrMagnitude;

                if (distance < nearestDistanceSoFar) {
                    nearestSoFar = checkpoint;
                    nearestDistanceSoFar = distance;
                }
            }
```

```
        return nearestSoFar;
}

// Walks the list of checkpoints, and makes sure that they all have
// an index that's one higher than the previous one (except for
// the start checkpoint)
void CreateCircuit() {

    var index = 0;

    // Start at the start of the checkpoint
    var currentCheckpoint = StartCheckpoint;

    do
    {
        // Update the index for this checkpoint
        currentCheckpoint.index = index;
        index += 1;

        // Move to the checkpoint it's pointing to
        currentCheckpoint = currentCheckpoint.next;

        // We should not reach the end of the list; that means that
        // the circuit does not form a loop
        if (currentCheckpoint == null)
        {
            Debug.LogError("The circuit is not closed!");
            return;
        }

        // loop until we reach the start again
    } while (currentCheckpoint.isLapStart == false);

}

// Update the text that's shown to the user
void UpdateLapCounter()
{
    lapCounter.text = string.Format("Lap {0}", lapsComplete + 1);
}

// Draw a line indicating the nearest checkpoint to the player in
// the Scene view. (Useful for debugging.)
private void OnDrawGizmos()
{
    var nearest = NearestCheckpoint();

    if (target != null && nearest != null) {
```

```
                Gizmos.color = Color.red;
                Gizmos.DrawLine(target.position, nearest.transform.position);

            }
        }
    }
```

17. Create a new, empty game object, and add the `LapTracker` component to it.

18. Set the Target field to the vehicle.

19. Set the Wrong Way Indicator field to the label that says "Wrong Way!"

20. Set the Lap Counter field to the label that says "Lap 1."

21. Play the game.

Discussion

When you drive the circuit in the right direction, the lap counter will go up when you cross the finish line. If you drive in the wrong direction or take too much of a shortcut, the "Wrong Way!" indicator will appear.

All we're doing is checking if we're visiting the checkpoints in reverse or skipping too many! Magic.

 This won't magically know if there's a flaw in the game that allows a player to cheat in all situations. It's just tracking that the player is going in the right direction, not holistically exploring the game state to prevent cheating. You'll still need to manually test your game!

CHAPTER 10

Behavior, Simulation, and AI

The appearance of intelligent, decision-based behavior is a core facet of building an engaging world or game. Video game artificial intelligence isn't like the rest of the AI field. It's mostly fakery, tricks, and illusions of complexity. You don't need to be an AI or machine learning wizard to build complex, engaging behaviors into video games. In this chapter, we'll explore solutions to some of the most common problems game developers encounter when giving entities behavior and AI.

We'll use two different techniques: behavior programming and machine learning.

You can use Unity to work with genuine AI and machine learning! The last few recipes in this chapter explore using Unity ML-Agents, but it's a big topic. To learn more, check out our book *Practical Simulations for Machine Learning* (O'Reilly).

10.1 Enemies Detecting When They Can See the Player

Problem

You want an object to be able to detect when it can "see" its target; that is, the target is both close enough to the object and in front of the object. You want to be able to visualize and configure the area in which targets can be seen.

Obviously, the most common use for this technique is making sure enemies can find the player they need to attack!

Solution

This solution starts with a script:

1. Create a new script called *EnemyVisibility.cs*, and add the following code to it:

```
#if UNITY_EDITOR
using UnityEditor;
#endif

// Detects when a given target is visible to this object. A target is
// visible when it's both in range and in front of the target. Both the
// range and the angle of visibility are configurable.
public class EnemyVisibility : MonoBehaviour
{

    // The object we're looking for.
    public Transform target = null;

    // If the object is more than this distance away, we can't see it.
    public float maxDistance = 10f;

    // The angle of our arc of visibility.
    [Range(0f, 360f)]
    public float angle = 45f;

    // If true, visualize changes in visibility by changing
    // material color
    [SerializeField] bool visualize = true;

    // A property that other classes can access to determine if we can
    // currently see our target.
    public bool targetIsVisible { get; private set; }

    // Check to see if we can see the target every frame.
    void Update()
    {
        targetIsVisible = CheckVisibility();

        if (visualize) {
            // Update our color: yellow if we can see the target,
            // white if we can't
            var color = targetIsVisible ? Color.yellow : Color.white;

            GetComponent<Renderer>().material.color = color;
        }

    }
```

```csharp
// Returns true if this object can see the specified position.
public bool CheckVisibilityToPoint(Vector3 worldPoint) {

    // Calculate the direction from our location to the point
    var directionToTarget = worldPoint - transform.position;

    // Calculate the number of degrees from the forward direction.
    var degreesToTarget =
        Vector3.Angle(transform.forward, directionToTarget);

    // The target is within the arc if it's within half of the
    // specified angle. If it's not within the arc, it's not visible.
    var withinArc = degreesToTarget < (angle / 2);

    if (withinArc == false)
    {
        return false;
    }

    // Figure out the distance to the target
    var distanceToTarget = directionToTarget.magnitude;

    // Take into account our maximum distance
    var rayDistance = Mathf.Min(maxDistance, distanceToTarget);

    // Create a new ray that goes from our current location, in the
    // specified direction
    var ray = new Ray(transform.position, directionToTarget);

    // Stores information about anything we hit
    RaycastHit hit;

    // Perform the raycast. Did it hit anything?
    if (Physics.Raycast(ray, out hit, rayDistance)) {
        // We hit something.
        if (hit.collider.transform == target) {
            // It was the target itself. We can see the target point.
            return true;
        }
        // It's something between us and the target. We cannot see
        // the target point.
        return false;
    } else {
        // There's an unobstructed line of sight between us and the
        // target point, so we can see it.
        return true;
    }
}
```

```csharp
// Returns true if a straight line can be drawn between this object
// and the target. The target must be within range, and within the
// visible arc.
public bool CheckVisibility()
{
    // Compute the direction to the target
    var directionToTarget = target.position - transform.position;

    // Calculate the number of degrees from the forward direction.
    var degreesToTarget =
        Vector3.Angle(transform.forward, directionToTarget);

    // The target is within the arc if it's within half of the
    // specified angle. If it's not within the arc, it's not visible.
    var withinArc = degreesToTarget < (angle / 2);

    if (withinArc == false) {
        return false;
    }

    // Compute the distance to the point
    var distanceToTarget = directionToTarget.magnitude;

    // Our ray should go as far as the target is or the maximum
    // distance, whichever is shorter
    var rayDistance = Mathf.Min(maxDistance, distanceToTarget);

    // Create a ray that fires out from our position to the target
    var ray = new Ray(transform.position, directionToTarget);

    // Store information about what was hit in this variable
    RaycastHit hit;

    // Records info about whether the target is in range and not
    // occluded
    var canSee = false;

    // Fire the raycast. Did it hit anything?
    if (Physics.Raycast(ray, out hit, rayDistance))
    {
        // Did the ray hit our target?
        if (hit.collider.transform == target)
        {
            // Then we can see it (that is, the ray didn't hit an
            // obstacle between us and the target)
            canSee = true;
        }

        // Visualize the ray.
        Debug.DrawLine(transform.position, hit.point);
```

```
        }
        else
        {
            // The ray didn't hit anything. This means that it reached
            // the maximum distance and stopped, which means we didn't
            // hit our target. It must be out of range.

            // Visualize the ray.
            Debug.DrawRay(transform.position,
                        directionToTarget.normalized * rayDistance);
        }

        // Is it visible?
        return canSee;

    }
}

#if UNITY_EDITOR
// A custom editor for the EnemyVisibility class. Visualizes and allows
// for editing the visible range.
[CustomEditor(typeof(EnemyVisibility))]
public class EnemyVisibilityEditor : Editor {

    // Called when Unity needs to draw the Scene view.
    private void OnSceneGUI()
    {
        // Get a reference to the EnemyVisibility script we're
        // looking at
        var visibility = target as EnemyVisibility;

        // Start drawing at 10% opacity
        Handles.color = new Color(1, 1, 1, 0.1f);

        // Drawing an arc sweeps from the point you give it. We want to
        // draw the arc such that the middle of the arc is in front of
        // the object, so we'll take the forward direction and rotate
        // it by half the angle.

        var forwardPointMinusHalfAngle =
            // rotate around the y-axis by half the angle
            Quaternion.Euler(0, -visibility.angle / 2, 0)
                    // rotate the forward direction by this
                    * visibility.transform.forward;

        // Draw the arc to visualize the visibility arc
        Vector3 arcStart =
            forwardPointMinusHalfAngle * visibility.maxDistance;
```

```
Handles.DrawSolidArc(
    visibility.transform.position,  // Center of the arc
    Vector3.up,                     // Up direction of the arc
    arcStart,                       // Point where it begins
    visibility.angle,               // Angle of the arc
    visibility.maxDistance          // Radius of the arc
);

// Draw a scale handle at the edge of the arc; if the user drags
// it, update the arc size.

// Reset the handle color to full opacity
Handles.color = Color.white;

// Compute the position of the handle, based on the object's
// position, the direction it's facing, and the distance
Vector3 handlePosition =
    visibility.transform.position +
        visibility.transform.forward * visibility.maxDistance;

// Draw the handle, and store its result.
visibility.maxDistance = Handles.ScaleValueHandle(
    visibility.maxDistance,          // current value
    handlePosition,                  // handle position
    visibility.transform.rotation,   // orientation
    1,                               // size
    Handles.ConeHandleCap,           // cap to draw
    0.25f);                          // snap to multiples of this
                                     // if the snapping key is
                                     // held down
        }
    }
    #endif
```

2. Create two capsules in the scene by opening the GameObject menu and choosing 3D Object → Capsule.

3. Add an `EnemyVisibility` component to one capsule. Make its Target field refer to the other capsule. Note that you can see the visibility arc (Figure 10-1).

4. Play the game. The capsule with the `EnemyVisibility` component will turn bright yellow when it can see its target.

Figure 10-1. Displaying the visibility arc

Discussion

The *EnemyVisibility.cs* script that we created sets things up so that a given target is visible when it's both within a certain range of the object and in front of the object. At every frame, there's a check to see if the target is visible.

We also created a custom editor for the class we've made, which both visualizes the visibility range in the editor and allows us to edit it without having to go into scripting!

 You can learn more about customizing the editor to make your life easier in Chapter 12.

10.2 Defining a Path That AI Entities and the Player Can Follow

Problem

You want to allow entities in your game to find paths around a scene.

Solution

Navigation meshes are easiest to set up when your level is made of objects that you don't expect to move during gameplay, such as the ground, walls, and other obstacles. To define a path:

1. Select the objects that you don't expect to move.
2. At the top right of the Inspector, click the drop-down arrow and choose Navigation Static (Figure 10-2).

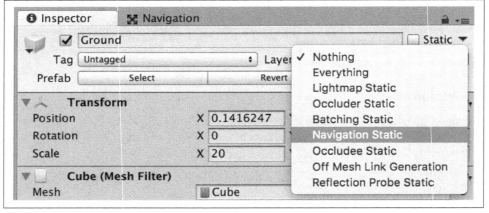

Figure 10-2. Setting a game object to be Navigation Static from the Static menu

With at least one object marked as Navigation Static, you can bake a navigation mesh:

1. Open the Window menu, and choose Navigation.
2. Go to the Bake tab, and click Bake. A navigation mesh will be generated (Figure 10-3). Note how the mesh stops at the edges of the ground and around the perimeter of the obstacles (which are marked as Navigation Static).

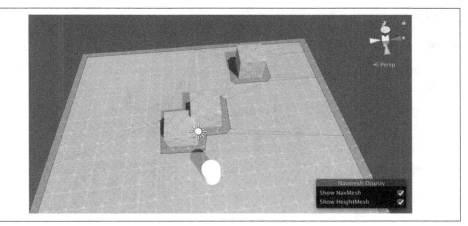

Figure 10-3. A navigation mesh

 You can also select the Static checkbox, which will mark the selected objects static for all other purposes as well.

Discussion

A navigation mesh essentially defines an area of a game environment that can be traversed by entities that have to move around the area. Typically your game world's navigation mesh will define the parts of a scene that aren't obstructed. For example, in a forest scene, dense parts of the forest would not be included in your navigation mesh.

You can learn how to use the navigation mesh you've created in Recipe 10.3.

10.3 Letting Entities in Your Game Follow a Path

Problem

You want to create an object that can find a path from its current location to a given destination, avoiding walls and other obstacles. You want to test this feature by clicking different places in the world and making the object try to move to where you clicked.

Solution

To have an object follow a path:

1. First, ensure that your scene has a navigation mesh by following the steps in Recipe 10.2.
2. Create a new cylinder by opening the GameObject menu and choosing 3D Object → Cylinder.
3. Add a NavMeshAgent component to the cylinder.
4. Create a new C# script called *MoveToPoint.cs*, and add the following code to it:

```csharp
using UnityEngine.AI;
// When the player clicks on a part of the world, the NavMeshAgent moves
// to that position.
[RequireComponent(typeof(NavMeshAgent))]
public class MoveToPoint : MonoBehaviour
{

    // The agent we'll be moving around.
    NavMeshAgent agent;

    void Start()
    {
        // Cache a reference to the NavMeshAgent on game start
        agent = GetComponent<NavMeshAgent>();
    }

    // When the user clicks, move the agent.
    void Update()
    {

        // Did the user just click the left mouse button?
        if (Input.GetMouseButtonDown(0))
        {

            // Get the position onscreen, in screen coordinates (i.e.,
            // pixels).
            var mousePosition = Input.mousePosition;

            // Convert this position into a ray that starts at the
            // camera and moves toward where the mouse cursor is.
            var ray = Camera.main.ScreenPointToRay(mousePosition);

            // Store information about any raycast hit in this variable.
            RaycastHit hit;

            // Did the ray hit something?
            if (Physics.Raycast(ray, out hit))
```

```
                        {
                            // Figure out where the ray hit an object.
                            var selectedPoint = hit.point;

                            // Tell the agent to start moving to that point.
                            agent.destination = selectedPoint;

                        }
                    }
                }
            }
```

5. Add a `MoveToPoint` component to the cylinder.

6. Play the game. Click somewhere in the world, and the cylinder will start moving to the point you clicked.

Discussion

A `NavMeshAgent` will do its best to find and follow a useful path to get to where it needs to go, but it might not always succeed. It's a best-effort situation, rather than a guarantee that it'll find a path to the end point.

The inner workings of the navigation system are not actually too complicated once you unpack them. If you're interested in learning more about how it works in Unity, check out the Unity manual (*https://oreil.ly/32v1g*).

10.4 Finding a Good Distribution of Random Points (Poisson Disc)

Problem

You want to efficiently find a random collection of points in a given area.

Solution

Use a Poisson disc distribution:

1. Create a new C# script called *PoissonDiscSampler.cs*, and add the following code to it:

```
// With thanks to Gregory Schlomoff, who wrote this implementation and
// released it into the public domain, and to Robert Bridson of the
// University of British Columbia, for developing the efficient
// algorithm that this code implements.

// http://gregschlom.com/devlog/2014/06/29/
```

```
//          Poisson-disc-sampling-Unity.html
// http://www.cs.ubc.ca/~rbridson/docs/
//          bridson-siggraph07-poissondisk.pdf

// Generates a distribution of 2D points that aren't too close to each
// other. Operates in O(N) time.
public class PoissonDiscSampler
{
    // Maximum number of attempts before marking a sample as inactive.
    private const int k = 30;

    // The rectangle in which points will be placed
    private readonly Rect rect;

    // radius squared
    private readonly float radius2;

    // The cell size of the grid of points
    private readonly float cellSize;

    // The grid of points
    private Vector2[,] grid;

    // The list of locations near which we're trying to add new
    // points.
    private  List<Vector2> activeSamples = new List<Vector2>();

    // Create a sampler with the following parameters:
    //
    // - width:  each sample's x coordinate will be between [0, width]
    // - height: each sample's y coordinate will be between [0, height]
    // - radius: each sample will be at least `radius` units away from
    //    any other sample, and at most 2 * `radius`.
    public PoissonDiscSampler(float width, float height, float radius)
    {
        rect = new Rect(0, 0, width, height);
        radius2 = radius * radius;
        cellSize = radius / Mathf.Sqrt(2);
        grid = new Vector2[Mathf.CeilToInt(width / cellSize),
                        Mathf.CeilToInt(height / cellSize)];
    }

    // Return a lazy sequence of samples. You typically want to call
    // this in a foreach loop, like so:
    //    foreach (Vector2 sample in sampler.Samples()) { ... }
    public IEnumerable<Vector2> Samples()
    {
        // First sample is chosen randomly
        Vector2 firstSample = new Vector2(Random.value * rect.width,
                                        Random.value * rect.height);
```

```
yield return AddSample(firstSample);

while (activeSamples.Count > 0) {

    // Pick a random active sample
    int i = (int) Random.value * activeSamples.Count;
    Vector2 sample = activeSamples[i];

    // Try `k` random candidates between [radius, 2 * radius]
    // from that sample.
    bool found = false;
    for (int j = 0; j < k; ++j) {

        float angle = 2 * Mathf.PI * Random.value;

        float r = Mathf.Sqrt(Random.value * 3 * (2 * radius2));

        Vector2 candidate = sample + r * new Vector2(
            Mathf.Cos(angle), Mathf.Sin(angle));

        // Accept candidates if it's inside the rect and farther
        // than 2 * radius to any existing sample.
        if (rect.Contains(candidate) &&
                        IsFarEnough(candidate)) {
            found = true;
            yield return AddSample(candidate);
            break;
        }
    }

    // If we couldn't find a valid candidate after k attempts,
    // remove this sample from the active samples queue
    if (!found) {
        activeSamples[i] =
                activeSamples[activeSamples.Count - 1];
        activeSamples.RemoveAt(activeSamples.Count - 1);
    }
}
}

private bool IsFarEnough(Vector2 sample)
{
    GridPos pos = new GridPos(sample, cellSize);

    int xmin = Mathf.Max(pos.x - 2, 0);
    int ymin = Mathf.Max(pos.y - 2, 0);
    int xmax = Mathf.Min(pos.x + 2, grid.GetLength(0) - 1);
    int ymax = Mathf.Min(pos.y + 2, grid.GetLength(1) - 1);
```

```
        for (int y = ymin; y <= ymax; y++) {
            for (int x = xmin; x <= xmax; x++) {
                Vector2 s = grid[x, y];
                if (s != Vector2.zero) {
                    Vector2 d = s - sample;
                    if (d.x * d.x + d.y * d.y < radius2) return false;
                }
            }
        }

        return true;

        // Note: we use the zero vector to denote an unfilled cell in
        // the grid. This means that if we were to randomly pick (0, 0)
        // as a sample, it would be ignored for the purposes of
        // proximity testing and we might end up with another sample
        // too close from (0, 0). This is a very minor issue.
    }

    // Adds the sample to the active samples queue and the grid before
    // returning it
    private Vector2 AddSample(Vector2 sample)
    {
        activeSamples.Add(sample);
        GridPos pos = new GridPos(sample, cellSize);
        grid[pos.x, pos.y] = sample;
        return sample;
    }

    // Helper struct to calculate the x and y indices of a sample in the
    // grid
    private struct GridPos
    {
        public int x;
        public int y;

        public GridPos(Vector2 sample, float cellSize)
        {
            x = (int)(sample.x / cellSize);
            y = (int)(sample.y / cellSize);
        }
    }
}
```

This script doesn't define a new component. Instead, it defines a class that other scripts will be able to use. You won't see `PoissonDiscSampler` appear in the Add Component menu, because it's not a subclass of `MonoBehaviour`.

2. To test this, create a new C# script called *PoissonDiscDemo.cs*, and add the following code to it:

```csharp
public class PoissonDiscDemo : MonoBehaviour {

    // The area in which we'll place our points
    [SerializeField] Vector2 size = new Vector2(10,10);

    // The points won't be any closer than this to each other
    [SerializeField] float cellSize = 0.5f;

    // The list of points we'll show
    List<Vector3> points;

    // Calculate the points to show when the game starts
    private void Awake()
    {
        // Create a list of points from the sampler
        points = new List<Vector3>();

        var sampler = new PoissonDiscSampler(size.x, size.y, cellSize);

        foreach (var point in sampler.Samples()) {
            points.Add(
                new Vector3(point.x, transform.position.y, point.y)
            );
        }
    }

    // Visualize the points we've calculated
    private void OnDrawGizmos()
    {
        // Early out if we have no list to use
        if (points == null) {
            return;
        }

        Gizmos.color = Color.white;
```

```
        // Draw each point in the scene
        foreach (var point in points) {
            Gizmos.DrawSphere(transform.position + point, 0.1f);
        }
    }

}
```

3. Create an empty game object and add a `PoissonDiscDemo` component to it. Play the game, and notice how it creates a randomly positioned field of dots. Note also that the dots are fairly evenly distributed—they don't bunch up together, and there are no sparse areas (see Figure 10-4).

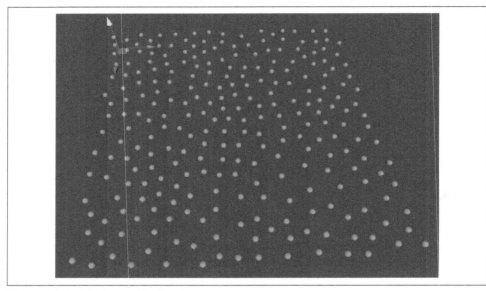

Figure 10-4. A Poisson distribution

Discussion

Random noise is an incredibly useful tool for game development. Random noise makes things look far less artificial than they otherwise would, and can serve as the basis for making decisions about things like pathfinding.

This recipe uses random noise in a relatively abstract way, but hopefully you see how it can be useful for game development and design. We'll explore other uses of random noise in one or two other recipes in this book.

10.5 Enemies Detecting Where They Can Take Cover

Problem

You want to create an object that hides from another object, taking into account that object's ability to see things and the surrounding environment.

Solution

To create an object that hides from another object:

1. Create a new C# script called *EnemyAvoider.cs*, and add the following code to it:

```csharp
using UnityEngine.AI;

// Detects if the target can see us, and if it can, navigates to
// somewhere it can't.
[RequireComponent(typeof(NavMeshAgent))]
public class EnemyAvoider : MonoBehaviour {

    // The object that's looking for us. We'll use it to determine if it
    // can see us, and if it can see the places we're considering hiding.
    [SerializeField] EnemyVisibility visibility = null;

    // The size of the area where we're considering hiding.
    [SerializeField] float searchAreaSize = 10f;

    // The density of the search field. Larger numbers means fewer
    // hiding places are considered, but it's more efficient.
    [SerializeField] float searchCellSize = 1f;

    // If true, lines will be drawn indicating where we're considering
    // hiding.
    [SerializeField] bool visualize = true;

    // The navigation agent, which will navigate to the best
    // hiding place.
    NavMeshAgent agent;

    // The Start method is a coroutine; when the game starts, it will
    // start a continuous cycle of avoiding the target.
    IEnumerator Start()
    {
        // Cache a reference to our navigation agent
        agent = GetComponent<NavMeshAgent>();

        // Do this forever:
        while (true) {
```

```
// Can the target see us?
if (visibility.targetIsVisible) {

    // Find a place to run to where it can't see us anymore.
    Vector3 hidingSpot;

    if (FindHidingSpot(out hidingSpot) == false) {

        // We didn't find anywhere to hide! wait a second
        // and try again.
        yield return new WaitForSeconds(1.0f);
        continue;
    }

    // Tell the agent to start moving to this location
    agent.destination = hidingSpot;
}

// Wait a bit, and then check to see if the target can still
// see us.
yield return new WaitForSeconds(0.1f);
    }
}

// Attempts to find a nearby place where the target can't see us.
// Returns true if one was found; if it was, put the position in the
// hidingSpot variable.
bool FindHidingSpot(out Vector3 hidingSpot) {

    var distribution = new PoissonDiscSampler(
        searchAreaSize, searchAreaSize, searchCellSize);

    var candidateHidingSpots = new List<Vector3>();

    foreach (var point in distribution.Samples()) {

        var searchPoint = point;

        // Reposition the point so that the middle of the search
        // area is at (0, 0)
        searchPoint.x -= searchAreaSize / 2f;
        searchPoint.y -= searchAreaSize / 2f;

        var searchPointLocalSpace = new Vector3(
            searchPoint.x,
            transform.localPosition.y,
            searchPoint.y
        );

        // Can it see us from here?
```

```
var searchPointWorldSpace =
    transform.TransformPoint(searchPointLocalSpace);

// Find the nearest point on the navmesh
NavMeshHit hit;

bool foundPoint;

foundPoint = NavMesh.SamplePosition(
    searchPointWorldSpace,
    out hit,
    5,
    NavMesh.AllAreas
);

if (foundPoint == false) {
    // We can't get here. Disregard as a place to hide.
    continue;
}

searchPointWorldSpace = hit.position;

var canSee =
    visibility.CheckVisibilityToPoint(searchPointWorldSpace);

if (canSee == false) {
    // We can't see the target from this position.
    // Return it!
    candidateHidingSpots.Add(searchPointWorldSpace);

}

if (visualize) {
    Color debugColor = canSee ? Color.red : Color.green;

    Debug.DrawLine(
        transform.position, searchPointWorldSpace,
        debugColor, 0.1f);
}

}

if (candidateHidingSpots.Count == 0) {
    // We didn't find a hiding spot.

    // Provide a dummy value
    hidingSpot = Vector3.zero;

    // Indicate our failure
    return false;
```

```
}

// For each of our candidate points, calculate the length of the
// path needed to reach it.

// Build a list of candidate points, matched with the length of
// the path needed to reach it.
List<KeyValuePair<Vector3, float>> paths;

// For each point, calculate the length
paths = candidateHidingSpots.ConvertAll(
    (Vector3 point) => {

    // Create a new path that reaches this point
    var path = new NavMeshPath();
    agent.CalculatePath(point, path);

    // Store the distance needed for this path
    float distance;

    if (path.status != NavMeshPathStatus.PathComplete)
    {
        // If this path doesn't reach the target, consider it
        // infinitely far away
        distance = Mathf.Infinity;
    }
    else
    {

        // Get up to 32 of the points on this path
        var corners = new Vector3[32];
        var cornerCount = path.GetCornersNonAlloc(corners);

        // Start with the first point
        Vector3 current = corners[0];

        distance = 0;
```

```
            // Figure out the cumulative distance for each point
            for (int c = 1; c < cornerCount; c++)
            {
                var next = corners[c];
                distance += Vector3.Distance(current, next);
                current = next;
            }
        }

        // Build the pair of point and distance
        return new KeyValuePair<Vector3, float>(point, distance);
    });

    // Sort this list based on distance, so that the shortest path
    // is at the front of the list
    paths.Sort((a, b) =>
    {
        return a.Value.CompareTo(b.Value);
    });

    // Return the point that's the shortest to reach
    hidingSpot = paths[0].Key;
    return true;

    }

}
```

2. Add the *EnemyAvoider.cs* script to the object that should be hiding from the target.

3. Ensure that the target has an `EnemyVisibility` component (from Recipe 10.1).

4. Set the Visibility field to the target.

5. Play the game. When the avoider can be seen by the target, it looks for a place where it can't be seen and moves there. In Figure 10-5, red lines point to places where it can be seen, while green lines point to places where it can't be seen.

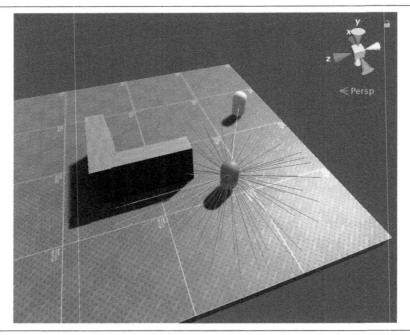

Figure 10-5. The avoider in the process of looking for a place to hide

Discussion

Every so often, this algorithm checks to see if the target can see us. If the target can see us, the algorithm generates a collection of random points nearby and, for each point, figures out if the target can see that point. Any point that can be seen is then discarded, all remaining points are tested, and again any point that can be seen is discarded. Finally, each remaining point is tested to find the length of the path to reach it, and the shortest is selected.

 For better performance, you can increase the Search Cell Size to reduce the number of possible hiding spots that are tested. If you've still got too many points, you can also reduce the Search Area Size to reduce the range of overall possible hiding spots.

10.6 Building and Using a State Machine

Problem

You want to use a state machine, which is a programming pattern that lets you manage the various possible object states.

Solution

Create a new C# script called *StateMachine.cs*, and add the following code to it:

```csharp
// Manages a collection of states, which can be transitioned from and to.
public class StateMachine {

    // A single state.
    public class State
    {
        // The state's visible name. Also used to identify the state to
        // the state machine.
        public string name;

        // Called every frame while the state is active.
        public System.Action onFrame;

        // Called when the state is transitioned to from another state.
        public System.Action onEnter;

        // Called when the state is transitioning to another state.
        public System.Action onExit;

        public override string ToString()
        {
            return name;
        }
    }

    // The collection of named states.
    Dictionary<string, State> states = new Dictionary<string, State>();

    // The state that we're currently in.
    public State currentState { get; private set; }

    // The state that we'll start in.
    public State initialState;

    // Creates, registers, and returns a new named state.
    public State CreateState(string name) {

        // Create the state
        var newState = new State();

        // Give it a name
        newState.name = name;

        // If this is the first state, it will be our initial state
        if (states.Count == 0)
        {
            initialState = newState;
        }
```

```
        // Add it to the dictionary
        states[name] = newState;

        // And return it, so that it can be further configured
        return newState;
    }

    // Updates the current state.
    public void Update() {

        // If we don't have any states to use, log the error.
        if (states.Count == 0 || initialState == null) {
            Debug.LogErrorFormat("State machine has no states!");
            return;
        }

        // If we don't currently have a state, transition to
        // the initial state.
        if (currentState == null) {
            TransitionTo(initialState);
        }

        // If the current state has an onFrame method, call it.
        if (currentState.onFrame != null) {
            currentState.onFrame();
        }
    }

    // Transitions to the specified state.
    public void TransitionTo(State newState) {

        // Ensure we weren't passed null
        if (newState == null)
        {
            Debug.LogErrorFormat("Cannot transition to a null state!");
            return;
        }

        // If we have a current state and that state has an onExit
        // method, call it
        if (currentState != null && currentState.onExit != null)
        {
            currentState.onExit();
        }

        Debug.LogFormat(
            "Transitioning from '{0}' to '{1}'", currentState, newState);

        // This is now our current state
        currentState = newState;
```

```
        // If the new state has an on enter method, call it
        if (newState.onEnter != null)
        {
            newState.onEnter();
        }
    }

    // Transitions to a named state.
    public void TransitionTo(string name) {

        if (states.ContainsKey(name) == false) {
            Debug.LogErrorFormat("State machine doesn't contain a state"
                                + "named {0}!", name);
            return;
        }

        // Find the state in the dictionary
        var newState = states[name];

        // Transition to it
        TransitionTo(newState);

    }

}
```

This **StateMachine** class can be used like this:

```
// Demonstrates a state machine. This object has two states: 'searching'
// and 'aiming'. When the target is in range, it transitions from
// 'searching' to 'aiming'; when the target leaves range, it
// transitions back.
public class Turret : MonoBehaviour {

    // The object we'll rotate to aim
    [SerializeField] Transform weapon;

    // The object we're trying to aim at
    [SerializeField] Transform target;

    // Aim at the target when it's within this range
    [SerializeField] float range = 5f;

    // The arc that we'll turn in while the target is out of range
    [SerializeField] float arc = 45;

    // The state machine that manages this object
    StateMachine stateMachine;

    // Use this for initialization
    void Start () {

        // Create the state machine
```

```csharp
stateMachine = new StateMachine();

// The first state we register will be the initial state
var searching = stateMachine.CreateState("searching");

// Log when we enter the state
searching.onEnter = delegate {
    Debug.Log("Now searching for the target...");
};

// Each frame, animate the turret and also check to see if the
// target is in range
searching.onFrame = delegate {

    // Sweep from side to side
    var angle = Mathf.Sin(Time.time) * arc / 2f;
    weapon.eulerAngles = Vector3.up * angle;

    // Find the distance to our target
    float distanceToTarget =
        Vector3.Distance(transform.position, target.position);

    // Are they in range?
    if (distanceToTarget <= range) {
        // Then transition to the aiming state
        stateMachine.TransitionTo("aiming");
    }
};

// The aiming state runs when the target is in range.
var aiming = stateMachine.CreateState("aiming");

// Every frame, keep the turret aimed at the target. Detect
// when the target leaves range.
aiming.onFrame = delegate {

    // Aim the weapon at the target
    weapon.LookAt(target.position);

    // Transition back to 'searching' when it's out of range
    float distanceToTarget =
        Vector3.Distance(transform.position, target.position);

    if (distanceToTarget > range)
    {
        stateMachine.TransitionTo("searching");
    }
};

//
aiming.onEnter = delegate {
    Debug.Log("Target is in range!");
```

```
        };

        aiming.onExit = delegate {
            Debug.Log("Target went out of range!");
        };
    }

    void Update () {
        // Update the state machine's current state
        stateMachine.Update();
    }
}
```

Discussion

State machines are great when you have a system where you need an absolute guarantee that there can be only one state at a time. When you have a fixed set of states—for example, a character that can move, jump, or crawl—you never want the character to be simultaneously jumping and crawling.

10.7 Building a Simulation Environment for Machine Learning

Problem

You want to create a simulation environment that contains a ball that, using reinforcement machine learning, learns to roll itself toward a specific target on a platform.

Solution

Unity provides a package called ML-Agents Toolkit, which gives you everything you need to create and train simulations using real machine learning inside Unity. The basic steps to solve this problem are:

1. Design and build an environment in Unity for the agents to work inside. This is just a Unity scene!

2. Create an Agent, which requires you to subclass Agent (supplied by Unity ML-Agents), and script it to observe its environment, perform the actions it needs to do, and be rewarded accordingly.

3. Attach the Agent scripts to the simulation environment.

To build the environment:

1. Create a new 3D project, and name it "BallAgent."

2. Add the ML-Agents package to the project by using the Unity Package Manager.

3. Create a floor for your ball agent by adding a Plane to the scene. Name it "Floor," and set its Position and Rotation to (0, 0, 0), and its Scale to (1, 1, 1).

4. Create a target by adding a Cube to the scene. Name it "Target," and set its Position to (3, 0.5, 3), Rotation to (0, 0, 0), and Scale to (1, 1, 1).

5. Create the agent, which will roll to the target, by adding a Sphere to the scene. Name it "BallAgent," and set its Position to (0, 0.5, 0), Rotation to (0, 0, 0), and Scale to (1, 1, 1).

6. Use the Inspector to add a `Rigidbody` component to the sphere.

7. Group the floor, target, and agent under a new GameObject in the Hierarchy, and name it "Training Area," or similar.

Next, create the agent script:

1. Select the BallAgent, and choose the Add Component button in the Inspector. Choose New Script, and name the new script "BallAgent," then click Create and Add.

2. Open the new script, and replace the code with the following:

```
using Unity.MLAgents;
using Unity.MLAgents.Sensors;
using Unity.MLAgents.Actuators;

public class BallAgent: Agent
{
    Rigidbody rBody;
    void Start () {
        rBody = GetComponent<Rigidbody>();
    }

    public Transform Target;

    public override void OnEpisodeBegin()
    {
        // If the Agent fell, zero its momentum
        if (this.transform.localPosition.y < 0)
        {
            this.rBody.angularVelocity = Vector3.zero;
            this.rBody.velocity = Vector3.zero;
            this.transform.localPosition = new Vector3( 0, 0.5f, 0);
        }
```

```csharp
        // Move the target to a new spot
        Target.localPosition = new Vector3(Random.value * 8 - 4,
                                           0.5f,
                                           Random.value * 8 - 4);
    }

    public override void CollectObservations(VectorSensor sensor)
    {
        // Target and Agent positions
        sensor.AddObservation(Target.localPosition);
        sensor.AddObservation(this.transform.localPosition);

        // Agent velocity
        sensor.AddObservation(rBody.velocity.x);
        sensor.AddObservation(rBody.velocity.z);
    }

    public float forceMultiplier = 10;
    public override void OnActionReceived(ActionBuffers actionBuffers)
    {
        // Actions, size = 2
        Vector3 controlSignal = Vector3.zero;
        controlSignal.x = actionBuffers.ContinuousActions[0];
        controlSignal.z = actionBuffers.ContinuousActions[1];
        rBody.AddForce(controlSignal * forceMultiplier);

        // Rewards
        float distanceToTarget = Vector3.Distance(
            this.transform.localPosition, Target.localPosition);

        // Reached target
        if (distanceToTarget < 1.42f)
        {
            SetReward(1.0f);
            EndEpisode();
        }

        // Fell off platform
        else if (this.transform.localPosition.y < 0)
        {
            EndEpisode();
        }
    }

    public override void Heuristic(in ActionBuffers actionsOut)
    {
        var continuousActionsOut = actionsOut.ContinuousActions;
        continuousActionsOut[0] = Input.GetAxis("Horizontal");
```

```
                continuousActionsOut[1] = Input.GetAxis("Vertical");
        }

    }
```

This class does a few interesting things:

- It descends from `Agent`, which comes from the ML-Agents package, instead of `MonoBehaviour`.

- It extends four methods from the `Agent` class in order to know what to do when an episode starts (`OnEpisodeBegin`), how to collect observations to learn about the simulation (`CollectObservations`), how to take actions (`OnAction Received`), and to allow a user to drive the agent (`Heuristic`).

- In `OnEpisodeBegin`, we set up the simulation environment for a new episode. An episode is a period during which the agent attempts to solve the case, and lasts until it does, fails, or runs out of time. `OnEpisodeBegin` initializes the scene by placing the target in a random position, and resetting the agent to being back on the platform if it fell off in a previous episode.

- `CollectObservations` sends the agent information about its environment. In this case, we send the position of the target, the position of the agent, and the velocity of the agent. This helps it get to the target, and helps it learn to manipulate its speed so that it does not roll off the platform.

- `OnActionReceived` receives actions, and assigns a reward for the action. This agent has two actions: the force applied on the x-axis and the force applied on the z-axis. We also assign it a reward: if it reaches the target, it gets a reward of `1.0`, and we end the episode; if it falls off the platform, it ends the episode with no reward.

- Finally, `Heuristic` allows using keyboard controls to move the agent around to test the simulation.

Next, we need to set up the agent inside the Unity editor:

1. Select the agent, and drag the Target from the Hierarchy into the Target field in the Inspector (which comes from the script we just made).

2. Use the Add Component button to add a Decision Requester component, and set its Decision Period to 10.

3. Use the Add Component button to add a Behavior Parameters component. Name it "BallAgent," and set its Vector Observation Space Size to 8, and its Continuous Actions to 2.

We can test the agent by choosing Heuristic Only under Behavior Type in the Behavior Parameters component of the BallAgent. With this done, press Play and use the arrow keys to drive the ball agent around the scene. If you hit the target, the scene (and episode) should reset with the target in a new location.

Finally, we'll train the agent:

1. Using your favorite text editor, create a new file called *BallAgentConfig.yaml*, and add the following:

```
behaviors:
  RollerBall:
    trainer_type: ppo
    hyperparameters:
      batch_size: 10
      buffer_size: 100
      learning_rate: 3.0e-4
      beta: 5.0e-4
      epsilon: 0.2
      lambd: 0.99
      num_epoch: 3
      learning_rate_schedule: linear
      beta_schedule: constant
      epsilon_schedule: linear
    network_settings:
      normalize: false
      hidden_units: 128
      num_layers: 2
    reward_signals:
      extrinsic:
        gamma: 0.99
        strength: 1.0
    max_steps: 500000
    time_horizon: 64
    summary_freq: 10000
```

2. Train the agent by running `mlagents-learn path/tp//BallAgentConfig.yaml --run-id=BallAgent1`.

> You can use Tensorboard to monitor the training by running `tensorboard --logdir results --port 6006`.

Once the agent has completed training (this might take some time, depending on the power of your machine), you can drag the resulting *.nnx* model into the appropriate slot of the agent's Inspector, and run it again using the trained model.

CHAPTER 11

Sound and Music

Audio can be one of the most important parts of an interactive experience, especially when you're building a game. Unity has a wide range of tools for both simple and complex audio setups. In this chapter, we'll discuss both the basics of how to get audio working in your scenes and more advanced ways to control how your project sounds.

 Sound and music are far, far more important than you might suspect. If you're building a game, don't leave out sound, music, and audio.

As with other chapters, this chapter is far from an exhaustive collection of recipes covering everything you might ever need to do with audio in Unity. Instead, we try to cover the things that, as Unity developers, we find ourselves implementing over and over again, game after game, project after project.

11.1 Playing Sounds

Problem

You want to play sound and music in your project.

Solution

To play an audio clip, you first need an audio file to play. If you already have one in mind, drag and drop it into your project.

If you need sound effects for your game, there are places where you can find some for free. Kenney (*https://kenney.nl*) has a decent collection of public-domain sound effects; community sites like Freesound (*https://freesound.org*) have a wider range of both material and quality. You can also create your own. Bfxr (*https://www.bfxr.net*) is a free app for Windows and Mac that generates retro-style sound effects. Humble Bundle (*https://oreil.ly/grINu*) also often runs great deals for large collections of game resources.

Once you've added the audio asset to your project, configure how Unity imports it by selecting it and looking at the Inspector (Figure 11-1). Unity supports *.aif*, *.wav*, *.mp3*, and *.ogg* audio. It also supports the tracker formats *.xm*, *.mod*, *.it*, and *.s3m*. Unity will convert audio into the format that you specify.

Figure 11-1. The import settings for an AudioClip asset

Once you've imported your audio clip, it's ready to be played. In Unity, audio is played from `AudioSource` components attached to game objects. To create an `AudioSource` component:

1. Open the GameObject menu, and choose Audio → Audio Source. A new game object will be created, with an `AudioSource` component attached.

You can also add an `AudioSource` component to an existing object by selecting the game object, clicking the Add Component button at the bottom of the Inspector, and choosing Audio → Audio Source.

2. Once you have an audio source, attach the audio clip that you want to play by dragging the asset from the Project tab into the AudioClip slot (Figure 11-2).

3. Play the project in Unity. The audio will begin playing.

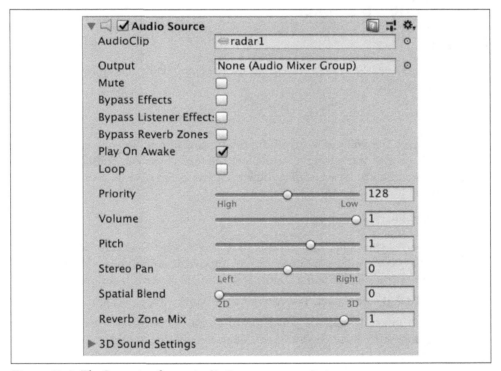

Figure 11-2. The Inspector for an `AudioSource` *component*

You can configure whether an audio source begins playing when the object first becomes active by enabling the Play On Awake option.

Discussion

The player's speakers or headphones play audio when an `AudioSource` component that's currently playing audio is in range of an `AudioListener` component. When you create a new scene, the main Camera object that's included in all objects comes with an `AudioListener` component attached.

 You should only have one `AudioListener` in the scene at a time. If you have more than one, Unity will warn you, and only one of them will work.

11.2 Setting Up a Mixer

Problem

You want to manage the levels and settings for the audio being played by your project in a central location.

Solution

You can manage the volume levels of different groups of audio sources by creating an audio mixer asset and setting up groups in the mixer. You can configure an audio source to route its audio to a specific group; each group can have its own volume level and effects.

To create an audio mixer:

1. Open the Assets menu, and choose Assets → Create → Audio Mixer. A new audio mixer asset will be created; rename it to whatever you like. ("Audio Mixer" is common; you might not need more than a single mixer in your project.)

2. Double-click the new asset. The Audio Mixer panel will open (Figure 11-3).

3. The audio mixer manages a collection of *groups*. Groups have a volume slider and can have effects attached to them. They can also have children, which means that changing the volume of the parent affects the volume of its children. There's always one group, called Master; all other groups are children of Master.

4. Create a new group by clicking the + button at the right of groups. (For example, you can create a group called "Music," and another called "Sound Effects.")

5. To make use of the groups you've created, you can route an audio source to a group. Select the audio source, and drag and drop the mixer group from the Group list in the Audio Mixer panel onto the audio source's Output slot. Any audio played by the audio source will be sent to the mixer group.

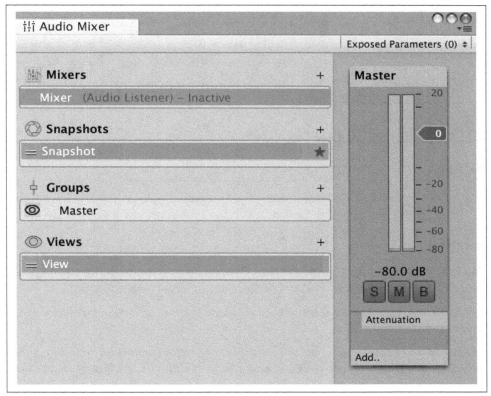

Figure 11-3. The Audio Mixer panel

 The audio subsystem of most game engines, Unity included, still, unfortunately, uses the Master terminology, as it borrows from the long-standing use of this term in the audio space. This isn't a good thing, and we hope the industry will update the term as soon as possible.

Discussion

In addition to the volume level for each group, you can also selectively control which groups are active:

M (mute) button
    Mutes the group

S (solo) button
    Mutes all *other* groups

B (bypass) button
    Disables audio effects (discussed in Recipe 11.3)

11.3 Using Audio Effects

Problem

You want to apply effects that change the way audio sounds in your scene. For example, you want to apply an echoing effect.

Solution

You can modify how audio is processed by the audio system by adding audio effects, which can filter the frequency ranges of the sound, apply reverb, and more.

You can set up effects in three different places: an audio mixer group, an audio source, or an audio listener.

Effects on an audio source or an audio listener are components, just like other nonaudio components, such as renderers or physics colliders. To add an effect on an audio source:

1. Select the game object that contains the audio source you want to modify, and click the Add Component button.

2. Click Audio, and select an effect you want to add. The component will be added, and any audio played by the audio source will be modified by the filter (Figure 11-4).

To add an effect on an audio listener, the process is identical, except that the effect will modify any audio *received* by the listener (see Figure 11-5).

Figure 11-4. An audio effect component, attached to a game object with an audio source

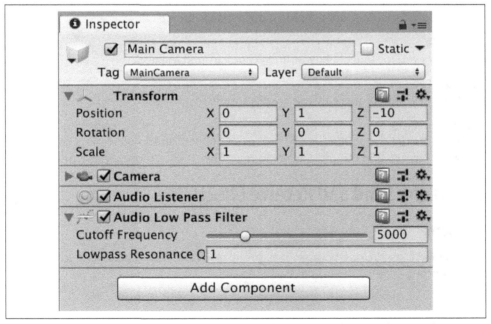

Figure 11-5. An audio effect component, attached to a game object with an audio listener

The ordering of the components is important, because it controls the order in which the effects are applied to the audio.

In addition to adding effects to audio sources and listeners, you can also add effects on groups in the mixer:

1. If you don't already have one, create a mixer group by following the steps in Recipe 11.2.
2. Under the mixer for your group, click Add and select an effect.
3. Select the effect under the group.

The B button in a mixer group bypasses effects, temporarily disabling them.

Discussion

There's a huge variety of audio effects available, and each one can be configured to support the effect you're after. Some of the most useful include:

Reverb effect
Allows you to simulate how sound echoes around a space

Low-Pass Filter effect
Cuts out high frequencies and creates a muffled sound

Compressor filter
Reduces the dynamic range between the quietest and loudest parts of a sound, which means that the audio tends to sound like it's at a more consistent level

11.4 Using Send and Receive Effects

Problem

You want effects on one audio mixer group to work with signals that come from another group.

Solution

Use Send and Receive effects on your audio groups:

1. Set up at least two mixer groups on an audio mixer by following the steps in Recipe 11.2.

2. Add a Receive effect on the mixer group that should receive the audio by clicking the Add button at the bottom of the group.

3. Add a Send effect on the mixer group that should send audio. Your groups should now look something like Figure 11-6. Once you've added a Send effect, you need to set up where it sends its audio.

4. Select the Send effect, and in its Inspector, set the Receiver to the Receive effect you added (Figure 11-7).

5. Play the game, and play some audio through the group that has the Send effect. The audio will also play through the group that has the Receive effect, and will be modified by any effects on the receiving group.

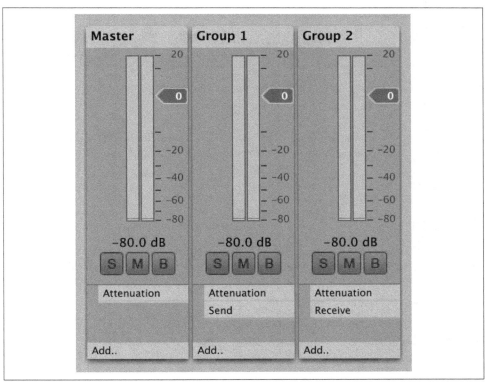

Figure 11-6. An audio mixer, with a Send effect on one group and a Receive effect on another

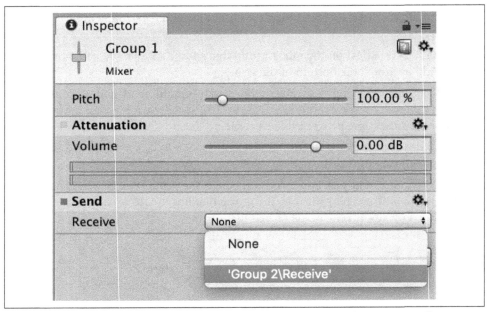

Figure 11-7. Configuring a Send effect to send audio to the specified Receive effect on another group

By default, the Send effect is set to the lowest level. You'll need to increase the send level for any audio to be sent to the receiver.

Discussion

Send and Receive effects aren't hugely useful on their own, since all they do is duplicate an audio signal. They become useful when you want to have finer control over how audio is routed, and when you want to apply audio effects that make use of multiple audio signals at the same time.

Some effects act as their own receivers—you don't need to add a Receive effect on them as well. For example, the Duck Volume effect (discussed in Recipe 11.5) can act as a receiver.

11.5 Ducking

Problem

You want to make one group of sounds grow quiet when another group is active. For example, you want to reduce the volume of sound effects when speech is playing, to make it clearer.

Solution

In a *ducking* effect, the level of one signal causes the level of another signal to lower. To implement this, you add a Duck Volume effect to the group that should lower its volume, and add Send effects to the groups that should trigger the volume lowering.

For example, imagine that you've got a mixer group that plays music and another that plays speech, and you want to automatically lower the music volume when speech is playing:

1. Set up at least two mixer groups on an audio mixer by following the steps in Recipe 11.2. Name one mixer "Voice," and the other mixer "Music."

2. Set up two audio sources: make one send to the Voice group, and the other send to the Music group. Attach whatever audio clip you like to each source, and make the source that's sending to Music loop.

3. Select the Music group, which should lower its volume when Voice is playing, and add a new Duck Volume effect.

4. Select the Voice group, which should cause the Music group to lower its volume, and add a Send effect.

5. Select the Send effect, and set its Receiver to the Duck Volume effect.

6. Increase the send level to its maximum (0 dB).

You're now ready to test:

1. Play the game. You won't hear much of an effect yet; you'll need to tune the setting to figure out what values to set.

2. Make the Voice source play its sound; for example, you can use a script to control the audio source (see Recipe 11.7).

3. Select the Duck Volume effect, and click the Edit in Playmode button at the top of the Inspector.

4. As it's playing, adjust the Threshold slider to control at what point the ducking takes effect.

Discussion

You can also configure the Ratio and Knee parameters to adjust how the Duck Volume effect modifies its volume. Additionally, the Attack Time and Release Time settings give you control over how quickly the effect is applied, and how long it takes for it to go away.

11.6 Using Multiple Audio Zones

Problem

You want to create areas in which audio sounds different. For example, you want the game to have a deep echo when the player walks into a cave.

Solution

Use a *reverb zone* to create areas of a scene that apply different reverb settings to your audio listener. Reverb zones distort the sound heard by a listener, depending on where the listener is within the zone, and are used when you want to gradually apply an ambient effect to a place as the player enters it.

To create a reverb zone:

1. Open the GameObject menu, and choose Audio → Audio Reverb Zone.

2. Position the new zone in the area where you want the reverb to apply.

3. Click and drag the points on the two spheres to set the minimum and maximum radius of the effect (Figure 11-8).

4. In the Inspector (Figure 11-9), select what kind of effect you want to apply. There's a wide range of presets, including concert halls, caves, padded rooms, and everything in between.

5. Play the project, and move the camera into the reverb zone. As you enter the zone, the effect will begin to apply to any audio being received by the audio listener.

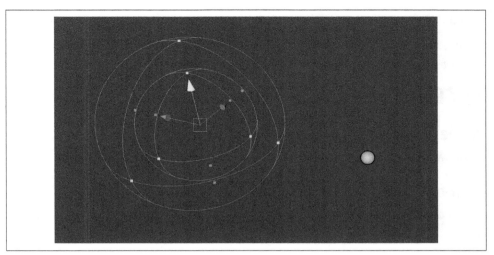

Figure 11-8. The Audio Reverb Zone in the scene

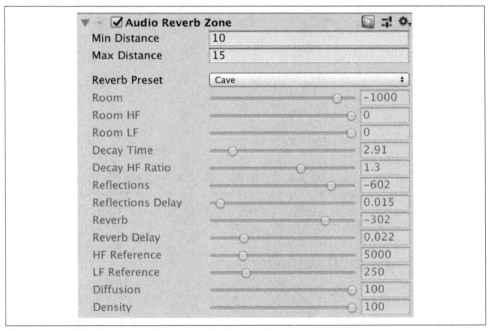

Figure 11-9. The Inspector for an Audio Reverb Zone

Discussion

If you set the Reverb Preset to Custom, you can modify the individual reverb settings and create a reverb effect that more precisely suits your needs.

11.7 Playing Audio with Scripts

Problem

You want to trigger audio playback from a script.

Solution

Use the `Play`, `PlayDelayed`, `PlayOneShot`, and `Stop` methods on an `AudioSource` component to control an audio source:

```
// Play the AudioClip that's currently set
source.Play();

// Play the AudioClip with a delay, measured in seconds
source.PlayDelayed(0.5f);

// Play a specified AudioClip; the volume scale is optional
source.PlayOneShot(clip, 0.5f); // play at half volume
source.PlayOneShot(clip, 1f); // play at full volume

// Stop playing the current clip
source.Stop();
```

Discussion

It's often useful to be able to play an audio clip that you only know the identity of during gameplay, because it means that you can set up an audio source with the appropriate volume level and audio mixer group at design time, and then have control over the sound itself during gameplay.

11.8 Using a Sound Manager

Problem

You want to build a system that allows sound effects to be triggered from arbitrary points in your code.

Solution

Create a system that allows other parts of your code to request that a sound effect be played. The code given in this class is a simple example, but it's designed to be a base from which you can add the specific features you need for your project.

This system works by defining an asset of the SoundEffect as a ScriptableObject class that contains references to audio clips (for more information on Scriptable Object, see Recipe 2.9). The AudioManager, which is a singleton, has a list of these SoundEffect assets, and can be asked to play one of them by passing the name of the effect. A random clip that's attached to the SoundEffect asset will be selected, allowing for some nice variation. The effect can be played either at the same position as the listener, or a position in the world can be passed as a parameter, and the selected audio clip will be played there.

 This script makes use of a singleton class, which we discuss in Recipe 2.6. Follow the steps in that recipe before you continue with this one.

To begin building this, we'll start by defining the SoundEffect asset:

1. Create a new C# script called *SoundEffect.cs*, and put the following code in it:

```
// An asset that contains a collection of audio clips.
[CreateAssetMenu]
public class SoundEffect : ScriptableObject {

    // The list of AudioClips that might be played when
    // this sound effect is played.
    public AudioClip[] clips;

    // Randomly selects an AudioClip from the 'clips' array,
    // if one is available.
    public AudioClip GetRandomClip() {
        if (clips.Length == 0) {
            return null;
        }
        return clips[Random.Range(0, clips.Length)];
    }
}
```

In a real game, you might want to exclude the most recently playing random sound from the next result, just to make the game feel like it's more interesting than it actually is!

2. Create `SoundEffect` assets by opening the Assets menu and choosing Create → Sound Effect. Name the new asset whatever you like.

3. Select the new asset, and in the Inspector, drag and drop the audio assets you'd like to use for this sound effect (see Figure 11-10).

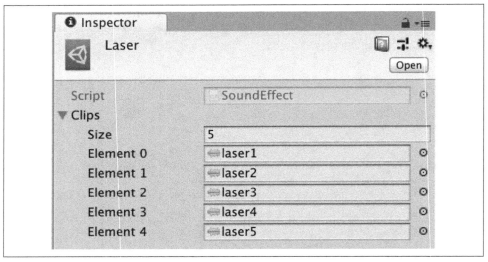

Figure 11-10. The Inspector for a SoundEffect *asset, with a collection of audio clips added to its list*

Next, we'll create the `AudioManager` class itself. Create a new C# script called *Audio Manager.cs*, and add the following code to it:

```csharp
public class AudioManager : Singleton<AudioManager> {

    // The list of references to SoundEffect assets.
    public SoundEffect[] effects;

    // A dictionary that maps the names of SoundEffects to the objects
    // themselves, to make it faster to look them up.
    private Dictionary<string, SoundEffect> _effectDictionary;

    // A reference to the current audio listener, which we use to place
    // audio clips.
    private AudioListener _listener;
```

```csharp
    private void Awake() {
        // When the manager wakes up, build a dictionary of named sounds, so
        // that we can quickly access them when needed
        _effectDictionary = new Dictionary<string, SoundEffect>();
        foreach (var effect in effects) {
            Debug.LogFormat("registered effect {0}", effect.name);
            _effectDictionary[effect.name] = effect;
        }

    }

    // Plays a sound effect by name, at the same position as the audio
    // listener.
    public void PlayEffect(string effectName) {
        // If we don't currently have a listener (or the reference we had
        // was destroyed), find one to use
        if (_listener == null) {
            _listener = FindObjectOfType<AudioListener>();
        }

        // Play the effect at the listener's position
        PlayEffect(effectName, _listener.transform.position);

    }

    // Plays a sound effect by name, at a specified position in the world
    public void PlayEffect(string effectName, Vector3 worldPosition) {

        // Does the sound effect exist?
        if (_effectDictionary.ContainsKey(effectName) == false) {
            Debug.LogWarningFormat(
                "Effect {0} is not registered.", effectName);
            return;
        }

        // Get a clip from the effect
        var clip = _effectDictionary[effectName].GetRandomClip();

        // Make sure it wasn't null
        if (clip == null) {
            Debug.LogWarningFormat(
                "Effect {0} has no clips to play.", effectName);
            return;
        }

        // Play the selected clip at the specified point
        AudioSource.PlayClipAtPoint(clip, worldPosition);

    }

}
```

Finally, we'll create the singleton instance, and add the audio clips we want to be available:

1. Create a new game object by opening the GameObject menu and choosing Create Empty. Name the new object "Audio Manager."

2. Select the new object.

3. Drag and drop the *AudioManager.cs* script onto the Inspector.

4. Add the SoundEffect asset that you created to the Effects list (Figure 11-11).

Figure 11-11. The Inspector for an Audio Manager, with a SoundEffect asset added to its list

You're now ready to trigger sound effects from your code. For example, if you created a SoundEffect named "Laser," you'd trigger it like so:

```
// Play a sound called "laser" at the same place as the listener
AudioManager.instance.PlayEffect("laser");

// Play the same sound at the origin
AudioManager.instance.PlayEffect("laser", Vector3.zero);
```

Discussion

As with any singleton, you're making a trade-off between ease of initial development and increased software complexity. See the Discussion of Recipe 2.6 for more details.

CHAPTER 12

User Interface

The UI system included with Unity is a powerful, flexible way to build your game's UI. It's useful for building everything from explicitly menu-based and interface-based pieces of your game, such as actual menus and configuration screens, to in-game UI, and for extending the Unity editor environment with helpful additional UI pieces to streamline your game development process.

If you've used Unity in the past, you'll be pleased to learn that the UI system has been totally replaced in recent years! Everything covered here involves the current UI system, which might sometimes be called the "new UI system" in Unity documentation.

The old Unity UI system focused on a programmer-based workflow, rather than the visual UI elements involved. It was designed the way a programmer might think, instead of how a UI needs to behave: visually! The new system fixes this, and we're all better off for it.

You don't need to add anything to your overarching project to begin using the Unity UI system. Everything is done through game objects belonging to the UI system.

The Unity UI system lets you create UIs for the player to interact with to start the game, modify settings, and so on (e.g., a main menu), as well as in-game UIs, such as those you might find on computer screens in a virtual world (e.g., computer consoles in a first-person-style game). You can learn about all the components of the Unity UI system in the Unity manual (*https://oreil.ly/m3-vy*).

12.1 Working with UI Controls

Problem

You want to build a user interface in Unity.

Solution

Building a UI in Unity is much like building anything in Unity: it's something that you construct out of game objects. Unity provides a range of UI elements as game objects, as shown in Figure 12-1.

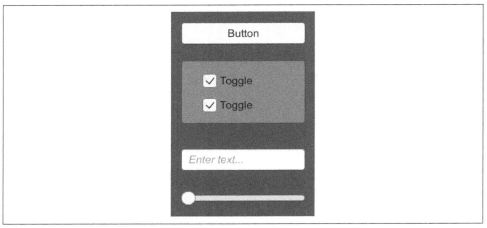

Figure 12-1. Game objects showing a range of UI elements

To draw a UI in Unity, you need a `Canvas` component. You can add a `Canvas` to a game object, but you can also add one directly to your scene to create a place to put your UI:

1. Open the GameObject menu, and choose UI → Canvas.

   All UI elements are added as children of a `Canvas`. We're going to add some text to our UI.

2. Select the newly added canvas, then open the GameObject menu again and choose UI → Text. A Text object will be added to the canvas.

3. Select the Rectangle tool, and drag the Text object to resize and reposition it.

4. Select the Text object, and modify its properties to change its text.

A UI that just shows some text isn't very helpful, so now we're going to write a script to log some text to the console, and then attach the script to a button:

1. Create a new C# script called *ButtonClicked.cs*, remove the two methods created by default, and add the following code to the class:

```
public void ButtonWasClicked() {
    Debug.Log("The button was clicked!");
}
```

This public method, `ButtonWasClicked`, will be connected to a button we'll add to our UI. It sends a message saying that the button was clicked to the debug log.

2. We can also add a public method that takes a parameter, allowing us to add a message to the logged output. Add the following method to the class:

```
public void ButtonWasClickedWithParameter(string parameter) {
    string message =
        string.Format("The button was clicked: {0}", parameter);

    Debug.Log(message);
}
```

We've defined two public methods: `ButtonWasClickedWithParameter`, which simply logs that the button was clicked, and `Format`, which does the same thing but includes a string parameter that we can use.

3. As an aside, we can also add private methods that won't be available to connect to UI elements. Add the following method to the class:

```
void PrivateButtonWasClicked() {
    Debug.Log(
        "This won't run as the direct result of a button click!"
    );
}
```

 All class methods are private by default in C#, so if you want to create a private method, you don't need to specify a protection level. Nothing is stopping you from including the `private` keyword if you want to, though.

Now we need to actually attach our new script to the UI we've been building:

1. Attach a `ButtonClicked` component (our new script) to the Canvas object, or to any other game object—for the purposes of this example, it doesn't matter which.

2. Open the GameObject menu one more time, and choose UI → Button.

3. Select the button you added, and click the + button under its On Click component.

4. Drag the object you attached the ButtonClicked component to in step 1 into the new object field that appears.

5. In the function drop-down that now appears, choose ButtonClicked → Button-WasClicked.

6. Your UI should look similar to Figure 12-2. Run the game. When you click the button, text will appear in the console.

7. Stop the game, and click the + button again. Drag the same object in, and choose ButtonClicked → ButtonWasClickedWithParameter. Note how this method lets you specify a string to send when the button is clicked.

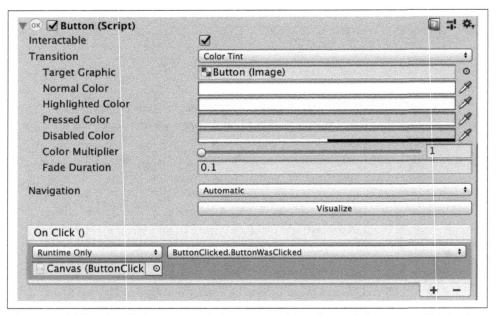

Figure 12-2. The On Click event for the button, configured to call the ButtonClicked *component's* ButtonWasClicked *method*

Because it's not public, the PrivateButtonWasClicked method will never appear in the list of methods you can choose.

Discussion

Beyond the obvious output—we added a button that makes something happen—there are a few moving pieces in play here that are useful to be aware of.

 Each canvas has a Canvas Scaler component attached, which allows you to control the scale and pixel density of the UI elements inside the canvas it's attached to. This is useful for making sure your UI behaves as expected when you're building a game that could run on multiple screen resolutions. Learn more about this component in Unity's documentation (*https://oreil.ly/I4ZfB*).

Every UI element exists on a canvas, and every UI element has a `RectTransform` component attached. If you're familiar with the `Transform` component (see Chapter 1 if you need a refresher), then it's simple to explain the `RectTransform`: it's the equivalent of `Transform` for a UI element, and it provides a position, rotation, and scale for UI elements inside their canvas.

Each `RectTransform` also has four small triangular handles, called *anchors*. These anchors define how the component is anchored to its parent. You can move the anchors around (or manipulate them in the Inspector) to, for example, allow a button to change its width in relation to its parent container, while ensuring that its height always stays the same and that it stays the same distance from the bottom of the container.

There's a button that resembles a target, shown in the upper lefthand corner of Figure 12-3, that allows you to pick from a preset anchor configuration.

▼ ⬡ **Rect Transform**			🖻 🖣 ⚙,
center	Pos X	Pos Y	Pos Z
	-130.5	-189.5	0
middle	Width	Height	
	160	30	⬚ R
▼ Anchors			
Min	X 0.5	Y 0.5	
Max	X 0.5	Y 0.5	
Pivot	X 0.5	Y 0.5	
Rotation	X 0	Y 0	Z 0
Scale	X 1	Y 1	Z 1

Figure 12-3. The button that looks like a target allows you to choose from a preset anchor configuration

12.2 Theming Controls

Problem

You're using your own artwork for your controls, rather than the built-in Unity artwork. You want this art to be able to scale as the controls change its size, without stretching.

Solution

When you're building game art, especially for a UI, you want to be sure your interface elements look their best at whatever resolution the game ends up running in. To do this for UI elements, you need to set the sprites you use to draw your UI in a certain way, and tell the Unity engine which bits can be scaled without looking bad:

1. Start by importing the textures you want to use.

 When working with UIs, you must ensure that the textures are configured to be imported as "Sprite / UI." For a reminder on how to set up asset import, see Chapter 1.

For this example, we'll customize a panel using art from the open source UI asset kit by Kenney (*https://oreil.ly/ft0xR*). We'll be using the *PNG* folder, and setting the textures as sprites in the importer.

There's a lot of free game art on the internet. Kenney makes some of our favorite material, and we refer to it frequently in this book! Check out all its packs (*http://kenney.nl*).

2. Open the GameObject menu, and choose UI → Panel to add a panel to your scene.

3. Select the Panel game object, and change its Source Image to the `blue_panel` image from the Kenney UI pack.

4. Resize the panel, and you'll see that the image stretches (Figure 12-4) and doesn't look very good. We can fix that!

Figure 12-4. A stretching panel with distorted corners

To fix it, we need to set up the panel's sprite so that only certain regions get stretched. In this texture, everything except the corners can be scaled without looking bad, so we'll set it up accordingly:

1. Select the `blue_panel` texture.

2. Click the Sprite Editor button.

3. In the Sprite Editor, drag the green dot that appears at the top of the screen down, until the green line is underneath the rounded corners of the image. You can also manually type in the change by setting the border's T value to 5.

4. Repeat this process for the other three edges. When you're done, the Sprite Editor window should look like Figure 12-5.

5. Click Apply, and close the Sprite Editor.

6. Select the Panel object.

7. Change the `Image` component's Image Type from Simple to Sliced.

8. The stretched appearance will go away because only the middle areas of the sprite are allowed to stretch, and the shape of the corners will be preserved (Figure 12-6).

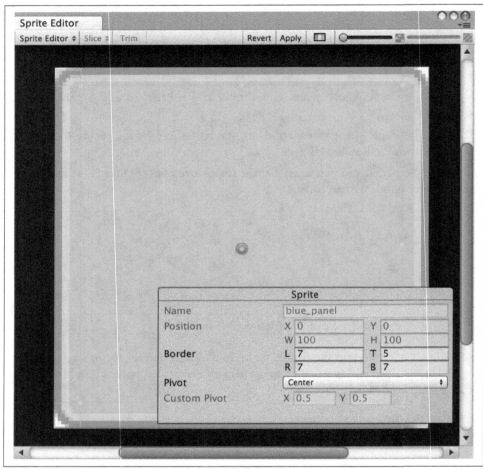

Figure 12-5. The Sprite Editor window, with the borders configured for the sprite

Figure 12-6. The same stretching panel from Figure 12-4, but with the sprite configured to only stretch in the middle

Discussion

The technique we're using here is sometimes called *9-slicing*, because of the nine areas of the image that are defined by the slicing process. It's nothing more complicated than using one single image asset with nine subsections, each with a different behavior: the corners aren't scaled, and the rest of the image is stretched as necessary.

You may notice that there are other options for the `Image` component's Image Type: Simple, Tiled, and Filled.

Simple scales the whole sprite equally. Tiled behaves similarly to the Sliced setting we're using here, but repeats the center part rather than stretching it. Filled behaves the same as Simple, but fills the sprite from a defined origin in a defined direction, method, and amount.

You can learn more about using images to style UI components in the Unity manual (*https://oreil.ly/Cf3VW*).

12.3 Animating the UI

Problem

You want to animate parts of the user interface.

Solution

UI animation is common in video games. Interfaces often need to draw attention to themselves, or are used to help the player feel like they've accomplished something special, or understand the impact of something they've done in the game. Unity makes animating elements of the UI as easy as animating anything else built inside Unity: pretty simple!

This is a different approach to animation than we took in Chapter 8. You could hook the system we used there up to a UI as well, if you wanted. But we're trying to show you a diversity of approaches to problem solving.

To demonstrate, we'll make a button spin when it's clicked. First, we'll need to create a new button:

1. Open the GameObject menu, and choose UI → Button to add a button to your scene.

You might notice that creating a button also creates a canvas as a parent to the button. Since all UI elements are required to be children of a canvas, one will be created for you if there isn't one in the scene when you add a new UI element. If there's already a canvas in the scene, new UI components will be added as children of it. For more on canvases, see Recipe 12.1 and the Unity manual (*https://oreil.ly/mAvF9*).

2. Next, we'll need to create a script that actually performs the animation for us. Create a new C# script called *SpinButton.cs*, remove the contents of the class, and add the following code inside it:

```
private IEnumerator StartSpinning()
{
    // Don't do any spinning if spin time is zero or less (
    if (spinTime <= 0) {
        yield break;
    }

    // Keep track of how long we've been spinning.
    float elapsed = 0f;

    while (elapsed < spinTime) {
        elapsed += Time.deltaTime;

        // Calculate how far along the animation we are, measured
        // between 0 and 1.
        var t = elapsed / spinTime;

        // Use this value to figure out how many degrees we should be
        // rotated at on this frame.
        var angle = curve.Evaluate(t) * 360f;

        // Calculate the rotation by rotating this many angles around
        // the x-axis.
        transform.localRotation =
            Quaternion.AngleAxis(angle, Vector3.right);

        // Wait a new frame.
        yield return null;
    }

    // The animation is now complete. Reset the rotation to normal.
```

```
        transform.localRotation = Quaternion.identity;
}
```

This code defines a method, `StartSpinning`, that we'll be calling as a coroutine, and which updates the rotation of the object it's attached to.

3. We'll also need to define some variables for the parameters of the rotation. Add the following to the method we just created:

```
// The amount of time needed to perform a full spin
[SerializeField] float spinTime = 0.5f;

// Controls the pacing of the animation.
[SerializeField] AnimationCurve curve =
    AnimationCurve.EaseInOut(0, 0, 1, 1);
```

 When you use the `SerializeField` attribute, you're letting Unity know that the contents of those variables should be saved to disk and displayed as an editable value in the Inspector.

4. We'll need to add a public method to start a coroutine, calling the `StartSpinning` method that we just created:

```
public void Spin() {

    // Start a spin.
    StartCoroutine(StartSpinning());

}
```

 When a coroutine is started, it pauses execution and returns control to Unity every time the `yield return` statement is encountered. If you need a refresher on coroutines, check out Chapter 2.

5. Attach a `SpinButton` component to the button we created earlier.
6. Click the + button in the On Click field.
7. Drag the button itself into the field.
8. In the pop-up menu, choose SpinButton → Spin.
9. Run the game. When you click the button, it will spin around! A masterpiece.

You can also adjust the curve to control the pacing of the animation, as well as its duration, using the variables we exposed to the editor, as shown in Figure 12-7.

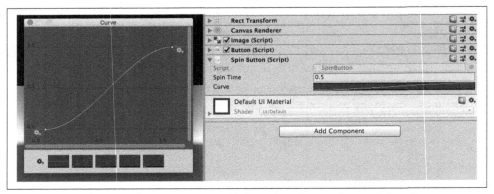

Figure 12-7. Adjusting the curve to control the animation pacing and duration

Discussion

An animation curve, used here, stores a collection of keyframes that can be evaluated over time.

 "Evaluating" in this context means sampling from the curve at a requested time in the curve: we're asking the curve to tell us what's going on at the specific time for which we're evaluating.

Using an animation curve for this instead of, say, incrementing the rotation every frame is a much more powerful and flexible way to animate. It removes much of the manual work, and allows us to focus on the desired movement of the UI, rather than coding complex animations.

As we've mentioned throughout this cookbook, pretty much any object, including objects on the canvas, can be animated (positioned, rotated, and so on) like everything else in Unity. You can also animate the properties of these objects! (Again, just like everything else in Unity.)

12.4 Creating a List of Items

Problem

You want to create a scrolling list of UI items.

Solution

Lists are a common UI element. You can use them for everything from menus to groups of items in an inventory.

First, we'll create the container for the list. The container for the list will be one of Unity's UI components: a scroll view. We're going to create a simple scrolling list like the one shown in Figure 12-8.

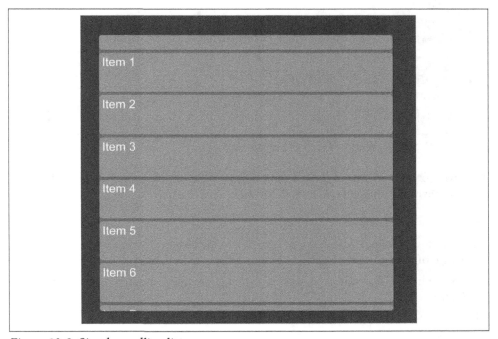

Figure 12-8. Simple scrolling list

Next, we'll need to do some setup:

1. Create a scroll view by opening the GameObject menu and choosing UI → Scroll View.
2. Select the Content object in the scroll view.
3. Add a Vertical Layout Group to the Content object.
4. Turn on the Width checkbox in Child Controls Size. This will make the objects inside the Content object expand their width to fill their parent, while still having control over their own height.
5. Add a Content Size Fitter component to the Content object.
6. Set the Vertical Fit setting to Preferred Size. This will make the Content object adjust its height to be the total height of its children. It should look like Figure 12-9.

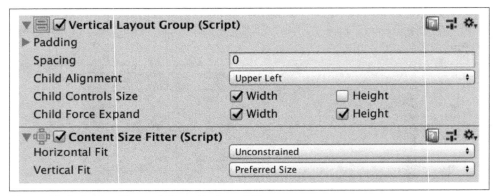

Figure 12-9. Setting Vertical Fit to Preferred Size

Now we'll create our prototype list item object. We'll be using the prototype list item as the basic object that gets re-created for each item in our list:

1. Create a panel. Name it "List Item."

2. Drag the List Item onto the Content object in the scroll view. It will resize to the width of the Content object.

3. Create a new Text object by opening the GameObject menu and choosing UI → Text.

4. Make the Text object a child of the List Item.

5. Set the Text object's minimum anchor to (0, 0) and its maximum anchor to (1, 1). This will make it define its size relative to the width and height of its parent.

6. Set the Text object's Left, Top, Bottom, and Right margins to 5. This will inset the Text object by 5 pixels on all edges.

Next, we'll add some code that lets each list item manage its content:

1. Create a new C# script called *ListItem.cs*. Remove the contents of the class, and add the following code to it:

```
[SerializeField] UnityEngine.UI.Text labelText;
```

This creates a label to store the text that will be used for a list item entry, and exposes it to the Unity Inspector.

2. Add the following property:

```
public string Label
{
    get
    {
        return labelText.text;
    }
    set
    {
        labelText.text = value;
    }
}
```

This exposes a string, allowing you to get or set the contents of the label.

For more information on the syntax for creating getters and setters, check out Chapter 2.

Now we need to add the script we've just created to the prototype object:

1. Add a ListItem script to the List Item.
2. Drag the Text object into the Label Text field.
3. Drag the List Item object from the Hierarchy into the Project tab. This will create a prefab.
4. Delete the List Item from the scene. You no longer need it, as you have the prefab!

For a refresher on prefabs and how they work within Unity, see Chapter 1.

Finally, we'll add code that populates the list with instances of the List Item:

1. Create a new C# script called *List.cs*. Add the following code to it:

```csharp
public class List : MonoBehaviour {

    // The number of items to create
    [SerializeField] int itemCount = 5;

    // Each list item will be of this type
    [SerializeField] ListItem itemPrefab;

    // The object that new items should be inserted into
    [SerializeField] RectTransform itemContainer;

    void Start () {

        // Create as many items as we need to
        for (int i = 0; i < itemCount; i++)
        {
            var label = string.Format("Item {0}", i);

            // Create a new item
            CreateNewListItem(label);

        }

    }

    public void CreateNewListItem(string label)
    {
        var newItem = Instantiate(itemPrefab);

        // Place it in the container; tell it to not keep its current
        // position or scale, so it will be laid out correctly by the
        // UI system
        newItem.transform.SetParent(
            itemContainer,
            worldPositionStays: false
        );

        // Give it a label
        newItem.Label = label;
    }

}
```

2. Add a `List` component to the scroll view.
3. Drag the List Item prefab into its List Item Prefab slot.

4. Drag the Content object into its List Container slot.

5. Run the game. The list will now contain a scrollable collection of items! It should look something like Figure 12-10.

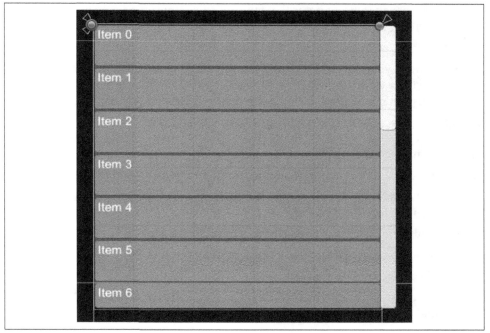

Figure 12-10. Running the game will show a list of scrollable items

Discussion

Scroll views are, obviously, really useful when you have content that doesn't quite fit on the screen. A scroll view is composed of a few pieces—most importantly, a clip area that controls how much is shown of another important piece, a content area.

12.5 Fading Out List Items

Problem

You want to manage a list of items that fade out some time after being removed.

Solution

So you've built your lovely list, based on the previous recipe, and now you want to make items vanish from it in a pleasing manner, as they're no longer needed. Attractive lists that look great as things are removed are very popular in video games.

To make your list cleanly fade items out as they get removed:

1. Start with the list example from Recipe 12.4.
2. Duplicate the List Item prefab, and name the new prefab "Fading List Item."
3. Select the Fading List Item prefab, and add a Canvas Group component. This will allow you to fade the entire object.
4. Configure the List object to use the new Fading List Item.
5. Add a new button to the scene, and set its text to read "Add Item."
6. Add a new entry in its On Click list.
7. Drag the List object into its object field, and select the List → CreateNewListItem method.
8. Type **New List Item** into the text field.
9. Create a new C# script called *FadeAfterDelay.cs*, remove the body of the class, and then add the following code:

```
// The number of seconds before a fade starts
[SerializeField] float delayBeforeFading = 2f;

// The amount of time to take while fading out
[SerializeField] float fadeTime = 0.25f;
```

10. After the necessary properties are added, add the following method:

```
// Notice the return type—this Start method is a coroutine!
IEnumerator Start () {

    // Wait the required amount of time
    yield return new WaitForSeconds(delayBeforeFading);

    // We need a canvas group in order to fade
    CanvasGroup canvasGroup = GetComponent<CanvasGroup>();

    if (canvasGroup == null) {
```

```
            Debug.LogWarning("Cannot fade - no canvas group attached!");
            yield break;
        }

        // Fade time must be more than 0 in order for a fade to be
        // animated
        if (fadeTime <= 0) {
            yield break;
        }

        // Keep track of how much time we've spent fading
        var fadeTimeElapsed = 0f;

        // Perform the fade every frame
        while (fadeTimeElapsed < fadeTime) {

            fadeTimeElapsed += Time.deltaTime;

            // Calculate the fraction of the fade time (between 0 and 1)
            var t = fadeTimeElapsed / fadeTime;

            // Calculate our alpha; it starts at 1, and goes to 0
            var alpha = 1f - t;

            // Apply the fade
            canvasGroup.alpha = alpha;

            // Wait for the next frame
            yield return null;
        }

        // Remove this game object from the scene
        Destroy(gameObject);
    }
```

11. Attach a `FadeAfterDelay` component to the Fading List Item.

12. Run the program. When you click the button, a new list item will appear; after a moment, it will fade out. We'd take a screenshot and show you, but it already faded away....

Discussion

You'll notice that the `Start` method is a coroutine, so other things can still happen while it runs and takes care of fading and deleting the object from memory.

12.6 Creating Onscreen Position Indicators

Problem

You want to display icons that highlight the position of objects onscreen, providing the player with a general direction for objects that they might not be able to see at the time.

Solution

To display the indicators, we'll use Unity's GUI system. This means that we'll set up a canvas and a prototype indicator to use as a prefab.

You'll need a sprite to use for your indicators. If you don't have one, Kenney's game icons pack (*https://oreil.ly/xjHu1*) has a good one. To create onscreen position indicators:

1. Create a new canvas by opening the GameObject menu and choosing UI → Canvas.
2. Create a new image by opening the GameObject menu and choosing UI → Image.
3. Set the sprite of the image to the sprite you want to use for your indicators.
4. Rename the image "Indicator."
5. Drag the Indicator image into the Project tab. This will create a prefab.
6. Delete the Indicator image from the scene.

Next, we'll create the code that creates, positions, and removes indicators as they're needed:

1. Create a new C# script called *IndicatorManager.cs*, and add the following code to it:

```
public class IndicatorManager : MonoBehaviour {

    // The indicator that appears over each tracked object.
    [SerializeField] RectTransform indicatorPrefab = null;

    // The object that all indicators will go into.
    [SerializeField] RectTransform indicatorContainer = null;

    // The single instance of the indicator manager.
    public static IndicatorManager manager;

    // Maps objects in the world to indicators onscreen.
    Dictionary<TrackedObject, RectTransform> indicators =
```

```
        new Dictionary<TrackedObject, RectTransform>();

private void Awake()
{
    // Set up the singleton variable to refer to this instance.
    manager = this;
}

private void LateUpdate()
{
    // We do this in LateUpdate so that the calculation of the
    // positions can happen after the objects have moved, which
    // prevents jitter.

    // Every frame, for each object that we're tracking, update the
    // position of its indicator.
    foreach (var pair in indicators) {
        TrackedObject target = pair.Key;
        RectTransform indicator = pair.Value;

        // Has the target been removed from the scene?
        if (target == null) {
            // Skip this indicator
            continue;
        }

        // Update the indicator's position in the canvas.
        indicator.anchoredPosition =
            GetCanvasPositionForTarget(target);
    }
}

// Returns the location in canvas space that an indicator should be
// for a given object
private Vector2 GetCanvasPositionForTarget(TrackedObject target)
{
    // Convert the position of the object from world space to
    // viewport space
    var indicatorPoint =
        Camera.main.WorldToViewportPoint(target.transform.position);

    // Viewport coordinates are (0, 0) to (1, 1); (0, 0) is the
    // bottom-left corner of the screen.

    // If a point is outside the screen, we clamp it to the edges.
    indicatorPoint.x = Mathf.Clamp01(indicatorPoint.x);
    indicatorPoint.y = Mathf.Clamp01(indicatorPoint.y);

    // If a point is behind the camera, we force it to the bottom of
    // the screen.
```

```
if (indicatorPoint.z < 0) {
    indicatorPoint.y = 0;

    // We also have to flip it on the x-axis for it to appear
    // correctly.
    indicatorPoint.x = 1f - indicatorPoint.x;
}

// Canvas coordinates are (0, 0) -> (width, height); (0, 0) is
// the bottom-left corner of the canvas.

// This means that we can scale by the canvas size to get the
// position in canvas space.

// Get the canvas
var canvas = indicatorContainer.GetComponentInParent<Canvas>();

// Get its size
Vector2 canvasSize =
    canvas.GetComponent<RectTransform>().sizeDelta;

// Scale it
indicatorPoint.Scale(canvasSize);

// We've now calculated where it belongs in the canvas!
return indicatorPoint;
}

public void AddTrackingIndicator(TrackedObject transform) {

    // Do we already have an indicator for this object?
    if (indicators.ContainsKey(transform)) {
        // Nothing to do; we already have an indicator for this
        // transform
        return;
    }

    // Create our indicator from the prefab
    var indicator = Instantiate(indicatorPrefab);

    // Give it a useful name
    indicator.name = string.Format("Indicator for {0}",
                                    transform.gameObject.name);

    // Move the indicator into the container
    indicator.SetParent(indicatorContainer, false);
```

```
        // Ensure the pivot point is in the center of the object, so
        // that the center of the image is right over the object's
        // position
        indicator.pivot = new Vector2(0.5f, 0.5f);

        // Ensure the object doesn't adjust its size and position based
        // on the size of its parent
        indicator.anchorMin = Vector2.zero;
        indicator.anchorMax = Vector2.zero;

        // Keep track of the relationship between the target and its
        // indicator
        indicators[transform] = indicator;

        // Place the indicator in the right location
        indicator.anchoredPosition =
                        GetCanvasPositionForTarget(transform);

    }

    // Stops tracking a target.
    public void RemoveTrackingIndicator(TrackedObject transform) {

        // If we have an indicator for this target object, remove it
        // from the scene
        if (indicators.ContainsKey(transform)) {
            // Destroy the indicator, if it isn't already gone from the
            // scene.
            if (indicators[transform] != null) {
                Destroy(indicators[transform].gameObject);
            }
        }

        // And remove it from the list, if it's present. (The Remove
        // method won't throw an exception if "transform" isn't in the
        // dictionary.)
        indicators.Remove(transform);
    }
}
```

2. Create an empty game object. Name it "Indicator Manager."

3. Add an `IndicatorManager` component to the Indicator Manager.

4. Drag the canvas into the Indicator Container field.

5. Drag the Indicator prefab into the Indicator Prefab field.

Next, we'll create a script that requests an indicator when it first appears, and removes it when it's removed from the scene. Create a new C# script called *TrackedObject.cs*, and add the following code to it:

```
public class TrackedObject : MonoBehaviour {

    void Start () {
        // When the object first appears, request an indicator.
        IndicatorManager.manager.AddTrackingIndicator(this);
    }

    // Tell the indicator manager to remove our tracking indicator.
    // OnDestroy is called when either the object is removed from the scene,
    // or the scene is being unloaded (including when we exit Play mode).
    private void OnDestroy()
    {
        IndicatorManager.manager.RemoveTrackingIndicator(this);

    }

}
```

Finally, we'll create an object that will have an indicator drawn over it:

1. Create a new sphere by opening the GameObject menu and choosing 3D Object → Sphere.
2. Move the sphere where the camera can see it.
3. Add a TrackedObject component to it.
4. Run the game. An indicator will be drawn over it; when you move the sphere around, the indicator will follow it. If you move the sphere behind the camera, its indicator will move to the bottom of the screen; when you delete the sphere, the indicator will be removed as well. You can also add as many TrackedObject components to the scene as you'd like.

Discussion

Don't forget that objects are destroyed when the Unity editor leaves Play mode!

12.7 Custom Editors

Problem

You want to customize the Inspector for a component.

Solution

Unity's editor is one of its best features. First appearances can be deceiving, and while the Unity editor looks like many other professional software packages, it's actually a flexible, friendly place to get your work done.

One of the most useful things you can do within the Unity editor is to create Inspectors for different components in your game. You've already seen how we can expose property variables to the Inspector; this technique takes it one step further.

We'll create a script that, when paired with a custom editor, allows you to quickly build a brick wall. When you add a `Wall` component, you'll specify the width and height of the wall, as well as a prefab to use for the brick texture. A button will appear in the Inspector; when you click it, it will create bricks as child objects.

First, we'll create the brick prefab:

1. Create a new cube, and name it "Brick."
2. Set its scale to (2, 1, 1).
3. Drag it from the Hierarchy tab into the Project tab. This will create a new prefab.
4. Delete the original Brick prefab from the scene.

Next, we'll write the code for the wall. This file will contain two classes—one for the `Wall` component, and one for the custom editor:

1. Create a new C# script called *Wall.cs*. Remove the contents of the class it created, and add the following code to it:

    ```
    [SerializeField] public int rows = 5;
    [SerializeField] public int columns = 5;

    [SerializeField] public Renderer brickPrefab;
    ```

    These variables are the properties a wall will need: a number of rows, a number of columns, and a place to store the prefab we'll be using for each brick in our brick wall.

2. Add another class below it, in the same script file. Open your class, named `WallEditor`, as follows:

    ```
    #if UNITY_EDITOR
    // The Editor object that will manage the Inspector for Wall components.
    [CustomEditor(typeof(Wall))]
    public class WallEditor : Editor {
    ```

This makes sure it descends from the Editor, rather than MonoBehaviour. This gives us access to editor features. You close it as follows:

```
}
#endif
```

3. Update the includes at the top of the file with the following, below the existing includes:

```
#if UNITY_EDITOR
using UnityEditor;
#endif
```

This makes sure we can use the UnityEditor namespace, and the if statement ensures it's included only when this script is being run within the editor environment. For more about this syntax, see Chapter 2.

4. Within the new WallEditor class, add the following method:

```
public override void OnInspectorGUI()
{
    // Make sure that we have the latest data
    serializedObject.Update();

    EditorGUILayout.PropertyField(
        serializedObject.FindProperty("rows"));

    EditorGUILayout.PropertyField(
        serializedObject.FindProperty("columns"));

    EditorGUILayout.PropertyField(
        serializedObject.FindProperty("brickPrefab"));

    serializedObject.ApplyModifiedProperties();

    if (GUILayout.Button("Create Wall")) {
        CreateWall();
    }
}
```

This method is called by the Unity editor when the contents of the Inspector for the object the script is attached to need to be drawn. The code here updates the copy of the object, adds UI elements to the Inspector panel for each of the properties, and creates a button labeled Create Wall, which will call another method, CreateWall, when it's clicked.

5. Create a new method called CreateWall, returning void. Inside it, add:

```
Undo.RegisterFullObjectHierarchyUndo(target, "Create Wall");
```

This registers the state of the object before we start making changes to it, so that users can undo what the script does. This is generally polite behavior for an editor enhancement.

6. Add some code to get a reference to the wall we want to work with:

```
var wall = target as Wall;

if (wall == null) {
    return;
}
```

`target` is a property of the superclass, the editor, and gives us a reference to the object currently represented in the Inspector.

 We can't call `DestroyImmediate` on objects in a list that we're iterating over, because the size of the list would change as we're iterating over it. Instead, we copy references to them into an array of fixed size, so we can destroy that.

7. Create a place to temporarily store all the current children so we can work with them:

```
GameObject[] allChildren =
    new GameObject[wall.transform.childCount];

int i = 0;
```

8. Now we can step through all the children and add them to our temporary storage:

```
foreach (Transform child in wall.transform)
{
    allChildren[i] = child.gameObject;
    i += 1;
}
```

9. We can now iterate through the array we've just made, and destroy each object:

```
foreach (GameObject child in allChildren)
{
    // Destroy the object, and also record it as an undoable
    // action
    DestroyImmediate(child.gameObject);
}
```

10. To replace them with new objects, bricks, we'll need a reference to the size of a brick, which we'll get from our prefab:

```
var brickSize =
    wall.brickPrefab.GetComponent<Renderer>().bounds.size;
```

11. Then we can go through each row, and through each column using a nested loop, and instantiate a copy of our brick prefab there:

```
for (int row = 0; row < wall.rows; row++) {

    // Figure out where the row should be
    var rowPosition = Vector3.zero;
    rowPosition.y += brickSize.y * row;

    for (int column = 0; column < wall.columns; column++)
    {
        // Figure out where the brick should be
        var columnPosition = rowPosition;
        columnPosition.x += brickSize.x * column;

        // Every second row is offset a bit
        if (row % 2 == 0) {
            columnPosition.x += brickSize.x / 2f;
        }

        // PrefabUtility.InstantiatePrefab is like Instantiate, but
        // it remembers that it was a prefab and maintains the
        // connection. (We have to cast it to GameObject because
        // there's no generic version of InstantiatePrefab—the
        // compiler won't figure out the type automatically based
        // on the type that was passed in.)

        var brick = PrefabUtility
            .InstantiatePrefab(wall.brickPrefab.gameObject)
            as GameObject;

        // Give it a name appropriate to its position
        brick.name = string.Format("{0} ({1},{2})",
                                    wall.brickPrefab.name,
                                    column,
                                    row);

        // Place it in the scene
        brick.transform.SetParent(wall.transform, false);

        // Update its position, relative to its parent
        brick.transform.localPosition = columnPosition;

        // Don't rotate it, relative to its parent
        brick.transform.localRotation = Quaternion.identity;

    }
}
```

Phew. That's a long piece of code. Now we can use it:

1. Create a new, empty game object, and name it "Wall." Add a Wall component to it.

2. Drag the Brick prefab into the Brick Prefab slot.

3. Click the Create Wall button. A wall of bricks will appear! You can see an example of the input in the custom Inspector, and the output, in Figure 12-11.

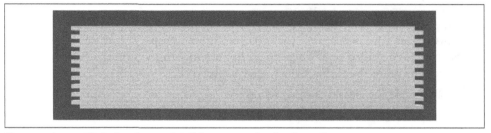

Figure 12-11. Click the Create Wall button and a brick wall appears

Discussion

EditorGUILayout and GUILayout both provide similar versions of common editor UI elements. It's important that, when designing Unity editors, you consider which set of controls you want to use.

 When you customize a Unity Inspector component, you replace the default layout with the script you create.

12.8 Property Drawers

Problem

You want to customize how the Inspector draws variables of a certain type. For example, you've got a custom class, and you want to customize how it appears.

Solution

We'll demonstrate how to do this by defining a new type, called `MultiValue`. This will contain a list of strings, one of which can be chosen in the Inspector:

1. Create a new C# script called *MultiValue.cs*. Remove the contents of the class, and then add the following code to the top, below the standard includes:

    ```
    #if UNITY_EDITOR
    using UnityEditor;
    #endif
    ```

    This makes sure we can use the `UnityEditor` namespace, and the `if` statement ensures it's included only when this script is being run within the editor environment. For more about this syntax, see Chapter 2.

2. Next, update the class to look as follows:

    ```
    [System.Serializable]
    public class MultiValue {

        // The index of the currently selected value.
        [SerializeField] int _selectedIndex = 0;

        // The list of available options
        [SerializeField] string[] options;

        // Manages the selected index, and keeps it from going out of bounds.
        public int SelectedIndex {
            get {
                return _selectedIndex;
            }
            set {
                value = Mathf.Clamp(value, 0, options.Length);
            }
        }

        // Creates a new chooser, using the specified values.
        public MultiValue(params string[] values) {
            this.options = values;
        }

        // Returns the text of the currently selected value.
        public string SelectedValue {
            get {
                if (options.Length > 0) {
                    return options[_selectedIndex];
                } else {
                    return null;
                }
            }
    ```

```
        }
      }
    }
```

This script may look a little confusing, but it's relatively simple. It needs a little more context to explain though, so read on.

3. Add another class, as follows:

```
#if UNITY_EDITOR
// Overrides how Unity will draw a MultiValue property.
[CustomPropertyDrawer(typeof(MultiValue))]
public class MultiValuePropertyDrawer : PropertyDrawer {

    // Called by Unity when it needs to draw a MultiValue property in
    // the Inspector.
    public override void OnGUI(Rect position,
                SerializedProperty property, GUIContent label)
    {
        // Ensure that the controls found in the GUI class behave
        // properly. This also tells Unity that any edit to any field in
        // here should be recorded for the purposes of Undoing them.
        EditorGUI.BeginProperty(position, label, property);

        // Get a reference to the variables that store the info we need
        var indexProperty =
            property.FindPropertyRelative("_selectedIndex");

        var valuesProperty = property.FindPropertyRelative("options");

        // Calculate the rectangle to draw the first line in. This will
        // hold our toolbar (our list of buttons).
        var firstLinePosition = position;
        firstLinePosition.height =
            EditorGUI.GetPropertyHeight(indexProperty);

        // Use this to calculate the rectangle to draw the second
        // property in. (This will vary, depending on whether the user
        // has elected to expand the list in the Inspector or not.)
        var secondLinePosition = firstLinePosition;
        secondLinePosition.y += 2 + firstLinePosition.height;
        secondLinePosition.height =
            EditorGUI.GetPropertyHeight(valuesProperty);

        // Display the label in front of the toolbar, and get back a new
        // rectangle to draw the toolbar in.
        firstLinePosition = EditorGUI.PrefixLabel(
            firstLinePosition, new GUIContent(property.displayName));

        // Get every string inside the "options" property, as an array
        string[] labels = new string[valuesProperty.arraySize];
```

```
            for (int i = 0; i < labels.Length; i++) {
                labels[i] =
                    valuesProperty.GetArrayElementAtIndex(i).stringValue;
            }

            // Because Toolbar is not in the EditorGUI class, it won't
            // automatically report to the editor that it was updated in a
            // way that the editor can track for the purposes of the Undo
            // system. So, we use BeginChangeCheck before drawing the
            // toolbar, and call EndChangeCheck. If EndChangeCheck returns
            // true, the user made a change.
            EditorGUI.BeginChangeCheck();
            var index = indexProperty.intValue;
            var newValue = GUI.Toolbar(firstLinePosition, index, labels);
            if (EditorGUI.EndChangeCheck()) {
                // The toolbar was changed.
                indexProperty.intValue = newValue;
            }

            // Draw the 'options' list as a regular list. This will also
            // draw things like the expand arrow, the items in the list,
            // and the number of items in the list.
            EditorGUI.indentLevel += 1;
            EditorGUI.PropertyField(secondLinePosition,
                                    valuesProperty, true);
            EditorGUI.indentLevel -= 1;

            // We're done editing this property.
            EditorGUI.EndProperty();
    }

    // Called by Unity to determine the height of the
    // MultiValue property.
    public override float GetPropertyHeight(SerializedProperty property,
                                            GUIContent label)
    {

        // The height of a MultiValue property is the height of both of
        // its two child properties, plus the spacing between them.
        float lineSpacing = EditorGUIUtility.standardVerticalSpacing;

        // Get the child properties
        var indexProperty =
            property.FindPropertyRelative("_selectedIndex");
```

```
        var valuesProperty = property.FindPropertyRelative("options");

        // Calculate the height of this property by getting the height
        // of both properties (including the strings inside the options,
        // if it's been expanded), plus the line spacing
        float indexHeight = EditorGUI.GetPropertyHeight(indexProperty);
        float optionsHeight =
            EditorGUI.GetPropertyHeight(valuesProperty, true);

        return indexHeight + lineSpacing + optionsHeight;
    }

}

#endif
```

This long piece of code creates a new `PropertyDrawer` named `MultiValueProperty Drawer` that defines how something of type `MultiValue`, which we created a moment ago, is drawn in the editor. The code gets a reference to all the necessary bits of the property in question, and then draws the actual UI for the property Inspector.

The `MultiValue` class we created first defines the structure of the property that `MultiValuePropertyDrawer` can actually edit: it contains an array of strings as its possible options, and an `int`, which points to the option that's currently selected. The code in `MultiValuePropertyDrawer` presents the options, and lets the user pick one from the Inspector.

Let's test it out:

1. Create a new, empty game object, and call it "Demo."
2. Create a new C# script called *MultiValueDemo.cs*. Add the following code to it:

```
// A simple component to demo the MultiValueChooser property drawer.
public class MultiValueDemo : MonoBehaviour {

    [SerializeField]
    MultiValue multiValue =
        new MultiValue("One", "Two", "Three", "Four", "Five", "Six");
}
```

Note how the `MultiValue` property looks like Figure 12-12.

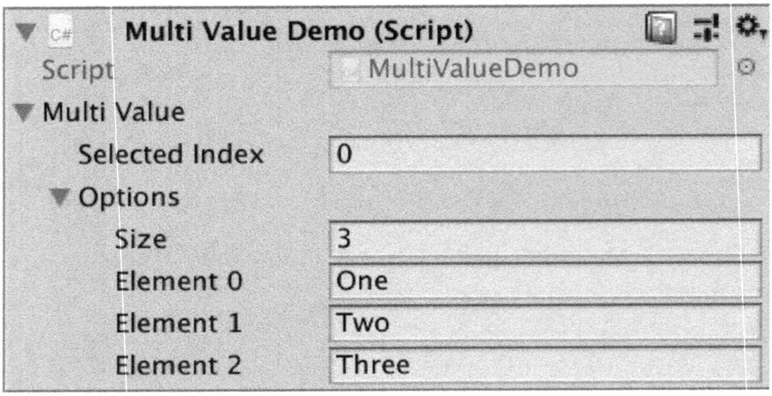

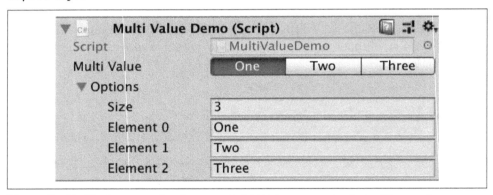

Figure 12-12. *The Inspector for a* MultiValue *property*

When you return to Unity, the Inspector will look like Figure 12-13. You can select a string from the bar at the top of the property, and modify the available strings as well. If you add more properties to the MultiValueDemo class, they will be displayed as you'd expect.

Figure 12-13. *The Inspector for the same* MultiValue *property, but with a custom property drawer*

Discussion

Unity normally draws the child properties of a class in the Inspector. If you want to override this, you need to do all the drawing yourself.

Property drawers cannot use the more advanced EditorGUILayout, but must instead use the EditorGUI. This means you need to calculate and draw the rectangles yourself, as we did in this recipe.

You can learn more about the Unity Editor API in the Unity documentation (*https://oreil.ly/QqFJd*).

12.9 Attribute Drawers

Problem

You want to customize how the Inspector draws a type of variable when a certain attribute is attached to it. For example, the `Header` attribute causes Unity to draw a label above a variable in the Inspector.

Solution

We'll add an attribute that lets you draw a help box above variables, like so:

```
public class HelpBoxDemo : MonoBehaviour {

    [HelpBox(text = "Here's a help box above the variable!")]
    [SerializeField] int integer;

}
```

This code produces the Inspector shown in Figure 12-14.

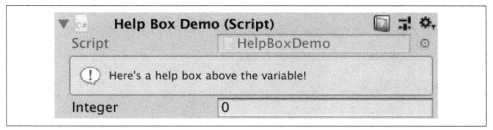

Figure 12-14. The `HelpBox` attribute, which we'll build in this recipe, in action

To create the `HelpBox` attribute, create a new C# script called *HelpBox.cs*, and replace the contents as follows:

```
#if UNITY_EDITOR
using UnityEditor;
#endif

// A HelpBoxAttribute can be placed above a variable to make it display a
// help box above it in the Inspector.

// Note how we define the HelpBoxAttribute class outside the #if
// UNITY_EDITOR areas. This is because code that refers to the HelpBox will be
```

```
// compiled outside of the editor context (that is, with UNITY_EDITOR not
// defined), and it will fail to compile if the class doesn't exist.

public class HelpBoxAttribute : PropertyAttribute
{
    // The text that will appear in the help box.
    public string text;
}

#if UNITY_EDITOR
// The code that draws the help box, as well as the original property.
[CustomPropertyDrawer(typeof(HelpBoxAttribute))]
public class HelpBoxAttributePropertyDrawer : PropertyDrawer {
    public override void OnGUI(
        Rect position, SerializedProperty property, GUIContent label)
    {

        // Let's start by calculating the rectangle in which we'll draw the
        // help box.

        // 'position' is the rectangle that we've been given to draw
        // everything to do with this property. It's calculated by taking
        // the width of the Inspector tab, and the height returned by
        // GetPropertyHeight.

        // The help box will be at the top of the property, so we just take
        // the original position, and reduce the height.
        var helpBoxPosition = position;
        helpBoxPosition.height = HelpBoxHeight;

        // Next, we figure out the rectangle we need to draw the property in.
        // We'll start with the entire available area...
        var propertyPosition = position;

        // Shift it down by the help box's height, plus line spacing
        propertyPosition.y += EditorGUIUtility.standardVerticalSpacing +
            helpBoxPosition.height;

        // And update its height to be however tall the property wants to
        // be, including any child properties.
        propertyPosition.height =
            EditorGUI.GetPropertyHeight(property, includeChildren: true);

        // Get the text from the HelpBoxAttribute.
        HelpBoxAttribute helpBox = (attribute as HelpBoxAttribute);
        string text = helpBox.text;

        // Draw the help box itself.
        EditorGUI.HelpBox(helpBoxPosition, text, MessageType.Info);

        // Draw the original property underneath.
        EditorGUI.PropertyField(
```

```
                propertyPosition, property, includeChildren: true);

    }

    public override float GetPropertyHeight(
        SerializedProperty property, GUIContent label)
    {
        // Calculate the height of the help box, given the editor width
        // (the text might wrap over multiple lines)

        float lineSpacing = EditorGUIUtility.standardVerticalSpacing;
        float propertyHeight =
            EditorGUI.GetPropertyHeight(property, includeChildren: true);

        return HelpBoxHeight + lineSpacing + propertyHeight;

    }

    // Calculates the height of the help box.
    private float HelpBoxHeight
    {
        get
        {
            var width = EditorGUIUtility.currentViewWidth;
            var helpBoxAttribute = attribute as HelpBoxAttribute;
            var content = new GUIContent(helpBoxAttribute.text);
            float helpBoxHeight =
                EditorStyles.helpBox.CalcHeight(content, width);

            // Add a single line's height to ensure that text doesn't get
            // clipped
            return helpBoxHeight + EditorGUIUtility.singleLineHeight;
        }
    }
}
#endif
```

Discussion

You can also call the `HelpBoxAttribute` just `HelpBox` in your code, and it will still work just fine!

It's polite to use help boxes in any editor code that might be used by someone other than you.

You should assume that someone other than you will work with all your code, even if you're a one-person team.

12.10 Asset Processing

Problem

You want to customize how Unity imports certain files.

Solution

Let's set up an asset post-processor that automatically sets up any texture whose filename ends in _n, _nrm, or _normal as a normal map:

1. Create a new C# script called *NormalMapTextureImporter.cs*, and add the following code:

```
#if UNITY_EDITOR
using UnityEditor;

public class NormalMapTextureImporter : AssetPostprocessor
{

    // Called before the texture is imported.
    void OnPreprocessTexture() {

        // Get the name of the file.
        var filename =
            System.IO.Path.GetFileNameWithoutExtension(assetPath);

        // We're looking for texture files that end in any of these
        // suffixes.
        var normalMapSuffixes = new[] { "_n", "_normal", "_nrm" };

        // Check each one
        foreach (var suffix in normalMapSuffixes) {
            if (filename.EndsWith(suffix)) {

                // Get the texture importer that's currently importing
                // this texture
                TextureImporter textureImporter =
                    assetImporter as TextureImporter;

                // Update its type so that Unity is aware that it's a
                // normal map
                textureImporter.textureType =
                    TextureImporterType.NormalMap;

                // Exit here, since we know we don't need to do any more
                // work
                return;
            }
        }
```

```
            }
        }

    }
    #endif
```

This code creates a subclass of `AssetPostprocessor` that we name `NormalMap TextureImporter`, looks for the suffixes we want, checks each file that's being imported for that suffix, and changes the texture type to be a normal map for each one it finds.

2. To test it, take a texture that contains a normal map and rename it so that its name ends with _n.

> If you don't have any normal maps on hand, you can find a useful online generator of normal map textures at NormalMap-Online (*https://oreil.ly/DYd1v*).

3. Import this texture into your project. The file will be imported as a normal map!

Discussion

There are some common, de facto standards in filenames for textures in the game development world: _d for diffuse, _e for emissive, _n for normal, and the like. The asset post-processing system allows you to handle imports based on filename, as well as other parameters.

You can use the `OnPreprocessTexture` function to perform operations before the texture is imported, as we did here. You might want to change something about the texture (for example, modify its alpha value) or change the compression format of the texture.

> You can learn more about Unity's `AssetPostprocessor` class in the Unity documentation (*https://oreil.ly/Erq36*).

There's also an equivalent `OnPostProcessTexture` function, which is called when an asset has finished importing.

The processor not only works with textures, but also with any file Unity might be importing. For example, you could use it to recompress or re-encode sound files.

12.11 Wizards

Problem

You want to create and display a window in the Unity editor that lets the user provide some values, and runs code when the user clicks a button.

Solution

Wizards, a long-standing user interface paradigm dating all the way back to the early 1990s, guides you through a sequence of steps. Wizards can be useful when you have a repetitive process you need to frequently perform while building your game.

Let's create a wizard that creates a cube, and also creates a new material that uses a specified color, all with a single click of a button:

1. Create a new C# script called *CreateCubeWizard.cs*, and add the following code to it:

```csharp
#if UNITY_EDITOR
// This entire class only exists in the editor. It doesn't need to be
// included in built games.
using UnityEditor;

// Create a wizard that generates a new cube, as well as a color.
public class CreateCubeWizard : ScriptableWizard {

    // Create a new entry in the GameObject menu, called "Cube with
    // Color." When it's selected, a CreateCubeWizard will appear. Note
    // that this method must be both public and static for
    // MenuItem to work.
    [MenuItem("GameObject/Cube with Color")]
    public static void CreateWizard() {

        // Create and display the wizard.
        DisplayWizard<CreateCubeWizard>("Create Cube");
    }

    // Stores temporary information about the cube that the user wants
    // to make. These variables are drawn in the window, just like
    // variables in a MonoBehaviour component are.
    [SerializeField] Vector3 size = Vector3.zero;
```

```
[SerializeField] Color color = Color.white;

// Run when the Create button is clicked.
private void OnWizardCreate()
{
    // Create a cube
    var newCube = GameObject.CreatePrimitive(PrimitiveType.Cube);

    // Scale it
    newCube.transform.localScale = size;

    // Create a new material, using the Standard shader (which
    // is the default)
    var tintedMaterial = new Material(Shader.Find("Standard"));

    // Give it a color
    tintedMaterial.color = color;

    // Materials need to be saved to disk. To do this, we need to
    // figure out where we can save the file.
    // GenerateUniqueAssetPath will give us a path that's
    // guaranteed to not already have a file present.
    var desiredPath =
        AssetDatabase.GenerateUniqueAssetPath("Assets/Tinted.mat");

    // Create and save the new asset.
    AssetDatabase.CreateAsset(tintedMaterial, desiredPath);
    AssetDatabase.SaveAssets();

    // Visually "ping" the asset, as though we'd selected it in the
    // Editor. This will show the user that a new file has been
    // created, and where to find it.
    EditorGUIUtility.PingObject(tintedMaterial);

    // Finally, make the new cube use this new material.
    newCube.GetComponent<MeshRenderer>().material = tintedMaterial;

    }
}
#endif
```

We're defining a `ScriptableWizard` called `CreateCubeWizard` that adds a new menu item called "Cube with Color," allowing us to trigger the wizard easily, and then creates a new cube, asking the user to supply `Vector3` for size and a `Color` for color.

2. Open the GameObject menu and note that you'll see a new menu entry: Cube with Color. Click it.

3. Enter your cube size and color, and click Create.

4. A new cube will be added to the scene, a new material will be created with the color, and the cube will be set up to use the new material.

Discussion

Creating editor tools, such as wizards, is an essential part of a more complex Unity workflow. Wizards are a great way of creating custom UI to make your life as a game developer easier.

The Unity Editor API lets you build lots of useful things to make your common workflows easier. If you notice yourself doing something more than a handful of times, it's often a great idea to use the Unity Editor API to make it easier on yourself. The automation possibilities are extensive!

You can learn more about the Unity Editor API in the Unity documentation (*https://oreil.ly/Jj53x*). There are a lot of possibilities, and a lot of ways you can automate repeated workflows.

CHAPTER 13

Files, Networking, and Screenshots

Rich, complex, visual computer programs, like the sort of thing you might make with Unity, also need to do mundane, traditional computer things, like saving, loading, and parsing files. We've saved the most thrilling chapter for last: here you'll find recipes for saving screenshots, state, and textures, as well as for importing files using a custom pipeline. Utterly thrilling (not really), but utterly essential (really!).

13.1 Saving Files

Problem

You want to know where you can save files that your project generates, like screenshots and saved games.

Solution

Use the `Application.persistentDataPath` property to get the location of a folder to which you can save data:

```
public string PathForFilename(string filename) {

    // Application.persistentDataPath contains a path where we can
    // safely store data
    var folderToStoreFilesIn = Application.persistentDataPath;

    // System.IO.Path.Combine combines two paths, using the current
    // system's directory separator ( \ on Windows, / on just about
    // every other platform)
    var path = System.IO.Path.Combine(folderToStoreFilesIn, filename);
```

```
    return path;

}
```

Discussion

The directory provided by `persistentDataPath` is not guaranteed to be exposed to the user; for example, it won't be exposed on mobile platforms where the user doesn't have direct access to the filesystem.

13.2 Saving an Image File of Your Game to Disk

Problem

You want to capture an image of your game (a screenshot), and save it to disk.

Solution

You can capture a screenshot by using the `ScreenCapture.CaptureScreenshot` method:

```
// Capturing a screenshot at current resolution
ScreenCapture.CaptureScreenshot("MyScreenshot.png");
```

When you call `CaptureScreenshot`, Unity will save the resulting image in the directory indicated by `Application.persistentDataPath`.

The screenshot will be the same size as the screen or window that the game is rendering to. You can also request that the screenshot be larger by providing a scaling factor as a parameter. For example:

```
// Capturing a screenshot at double resolution (e.g., if the screen
// resolution is 1920x1080, the resulting file will be 3840x2160)
ScreenCapture.CaptureScreenshot("MyScreenshotDoubleSized.png", 2);
```

Discussion

When you call `CaptureScreenshot`, the capture doesn't happen immediately. Instead, Unity waits for the end of the frame when all rendering has completed; at that point, the screenshot is captured and saved to disk.

 This means that you can capture only one screenshot per frame. Each call to `CaptureScreenshot` is effectively a "request" to capture a screenshot later, and only one request will be stored at a time.

In addition to saving the screenshot as a file, you can save it as a texture by using the CaptureScreenshotAsTexture method:

```
// Capturing a screenshot as a texture.
// Note that this captures the screenshot immediately, and it may not
// contain what you expect.
Texture2D capturedTexture =
    ScreenCapture.CaptureScreenshotAsTexture();
```

Unlike CaptureScreenshot, CaptureScreenshotAsTexture *does* capture the screenshot immediately, because it needs to return the captured texture. This means that the texture may not contain the final image that you expect.

To make it capture at the end of the frame, you need a coroutine that waits for the end of the frame before capturing the texture, such as in this example:

```
IEnumerator CaptureScreenshotAtEndOfFrame() {

    // Wait until the very end of the frame, after all rendering has
    // completed
    yield return new WaitForEndOfFrame();

    // Capture the screenshot
    Texture2D capturedTexture =
        ScreenCapture.CaptureScreenshotAsTexture();

    // capturedTexture now contains the contents of the screen, after
    // everything in the frame has rendered
}
```

You can run this coroutine by calling it with StartCoroutine, as follows:

```
// Begin the coroutine
StartCoroutine(CaptureScreenshotAtEndOfFrame());
```

13.3 Loading Textures from Disk

Problem

You have an image file stored on disk, and you want to display it in the game.

Solution

You can load any texture from a file that's stored in a PNG or JPEG image. In this example, we'll place an image in the project folder (not the *Assets* folder, the folder above it) called *ImageToLoad.png*:

1. In the script that you want to use to perform the loading, add the following code to the top of the file:

```
using System.IO;
```

The `System.IO` namespace contains a number of useful classes for working with files on the disk.

2. Add the following method to the class in which you want to load texture files:

```
// Loads a texture file from disk
public Texture2D LoadTexture(string fileName) {
    // Create the path to this file

    // Application.dataPath is the path to where the built application
    // is; in the editor, it is in the project's root folder (the one
    // that contains the Assets folder)
    var imagePath = Path.Combine(
        Application.dataPath,
        fileName
    );

    // Double-check that a file exists
    if (File.Exists(imagePath) == false) {
        // Warn that there's no file there and give up
        Debug.LogWarningFormat("No file exists at path {0}",
                               imagePath);
        return null;
    }

    // Load the file data.
    var fileData = File.ReadAllBytes(imagePath);

    // Create a new texture. When you create any texture, you specify
    // the width and height; however, when you load a texture, it will
    // automatically resize itself
    var tex = new Texture2D(2, 2);

    // Upload the image data. Unity will decompress it from PNG into raw
    // pixels.
    var success = tex.LoadImage(fileData);

    if (success) {
        // We now have a texture!
        return tex;
    } else {
        // Warn that we can't read this file
        Debug.LogWarningFormat("Failed to load texture at path {0}",
                               imagePath);

        return null;
    }

}
```

You can now use this method to load a texture from disk. Once you have the texture, you can do anything you like with it; for example, here's how to use the `LoadTexture` method to get a texture that's then given to a renderer's material:

```
// Load the texture from disk
var tex = LoadTexture("ImageToLoad.png");

// Check that we got it before we try to use it
if (tex == null) {
    return;
}

// We can now use this texture just like any other!

// For example, here's how we can set the main texture of the renderer
// that this script is on the same object as
GetComponent<Renderer>().material.mainTexture = tex;
```

Discussion

Generally, the textures you use in your game are assets, and you use them directly by dragging and dropping them into the slots in the Inspector. Using this approach for loading texture is only for those situations where you don't have the texture at build time, and need to load it from somewhere else. It takes more time to load and decompress an image file from disk than it does to use an asset that's directly built into the game.

13.4 Saving and Loading a Game's State

Problem

You want to be able to save the state of the project to a file, and load that state later.

Solution

Saving and loading is one of those processes that sounds simpler to implement than it really is. In reality, it's a complex thing, and the specifics of how you implement saving and loading depend on the needs of your project. How much data do you need to store? How often will you be saving data? Do you need to save the fine-grained state of a game, or is it enough to just store simple information, like which level your player has reached?

Overview of the saving system

In this recipe, we'll present and discuss one approach, which allows certain `Mono Behaviours` to save and load their state into a JSON file. It doesn't save the *entire* state of the scene; rather, it allows objects to choose what data they need saved, and what to do with data that's been loaded.

We'll do all of our saving and loading using JSON, for two reasons:

- JSON is a text format, which makes it a bit easier to look at the generated result and diagnose problems.
- JSON doesn't rely on a fixed schema, which means it takes a little less work to get things working.

The overall strategy for this saving and loading system is as follows:

- We'll define a C# interface called `ISaveable`; the `MonoBehaviours` that can save their state implement this interface.
- Saving means finding all `MonoBehaviours` that implement this interface, asking for their save data, and using that data to create the save file.
- Loading means loading the save file, looking up every `MonoBehaviour` that implements `ISaveable` using its ID, and giving that object the information to use to restore it.

The specifics of what each `ISaveable MonoBehaviour` provides when it's asked to provide its save state, and what it does when it receives the saved state, are up to it.

To understand how the saving system works, it's helpful to see what a save file looks like. Here's an example of one; we've added comments to explain each part:

```
{
    // "objects" is a list of objects that stores the data of each saved
    // ISaveable. This saved game contains only a single saved object,
    // but you can have as many as you like.
    "objects" : [
        {
            // Each object has a unique Save ID, which is used to find
            // the object later when the game is loaded.
            "$saveID": "805133b3-fad9-41ed-a253-fce07e3c4672",

            // The data inside each saved object is determined by the
            // object itself.
            "localPosition": {
                "x" : -1.97000002861023,
                "y" : 0.0,
                "z" : 0.0
            },
            "localRotation": {
                "x" : 0.0,
                "y" : 0.0,
```

```
                    "z" : 0.0,
                    "w" : 1.0
                },
                "localScale": {
                    "x" : 1.0,
                    "y" : 1.0,
                    "z" : 1.0
                }
            }
        ],

        // "scenes" contains the list of scenes open when the game was saved.
        "scenes": [
            "SavingLoadingGameState",
            "SavingDemoExtraScene"
        ],

        // "activeScene" is the name of the currently active scene. The
        // active scene is the one into which new objects are instantiated,
        // and controls the lighting settings for the game.
        "activeScene": "SavingLoadingGameState"
    }
```

Downloading LitJSON

To read and write our JSON, we'll be using a third-party open source library called LitJSON.

 Unity provides a tool for working with JSON—the JsonUtility class—but it doesn't meet our needs for saving and loading, because it sits on top of Unity's existing serialization tool. That's not to say that it's entirely useless—in fact, we use it for part of this serialization system to save us some work—but it's not a general-purpose JSON library.

To install LitJSON, follow these steps:

1. Make a new folder in your *Assets* directory called *LitJSON*.
2. In your browser, go to the GitHub page for the latest release of LitJSON (*https://oreil.ly/D_s-u*).
3. Download the source code as a ZIP file.
4. Unzip the ZIP file. It will contain a folder called *src*.
5. Copy the contents of the *src* directory into the *LitJSON* folder you created.

Implementing the saving service

We're now ready to start writing the code that implements the saving system. This will be implemented as a `static` class, which contains methods for saving and loading the scene:

1. Create a new C# script called *SavingService.cs*.

2. Open the file, and delete the `SavingService` class—we'll replace it with our own.

3. Add the following code to the top of the file:

```
using LitJson;
using System.IO;
using System.Linq;
using UnityEngine.SceneManagement;
```

We're bringing in a number of namespaces here to use in our saving system:

`LitJson`
> To read and write JSON data

`System.IO`
> To handle the file input and output

`System.Linq`
> To simplify the task of finding all saveable scripts in the scene

`UnityEngine.SceneManagement`
> To handle loading a new scene (since loading the game means loading a new scene)

> Using LINQ allocates memory, which means that the garbage collector will have to run at some point in the future. This causes hitches and should normally be avoided. However, saving the game happens comparatively rarely, and is expected to be a moderately heavy operation anyway (that is, players expect the game to momentarily pause). Additionally, by calling `System.GC.Collect` when we're done, we do much of the cleanup that would otherwise happen at some unpredictable time in the future. Try to avoid using LINQ during gameplay.

Next, we'll define the `ISaveable` interface. `MonoBehaviours` that implement this interface will be included in the saved game:

1. Add the following code to *SavingService.cs*:

```
// Any MonoBehaviour that implements the ISaveable interface will be
// saved in the scene, and loaded back
```

```
public interface ISaveable {

    // The Save ID is a unique string that identifies a component in the
    // save data. It's used for finding that object again when the game
    // is loaded.
    string SaveID { get; }

    // The SavedData is the content that will be written to disk. It's
    // asked for when the game is saved.
    JsonData SavedData { get; }

    // LoadFromData is called when the game is being loaded. The object
    // is provided with the data that was read, and is expected to use
    // that information to restore its previous state.
    void LoadFromData(JsonData data);
}
```

2. We can now start building our `SavingService` class. Add the following code to *SavingService.cs*:

```
public static class SavingService
{

}
```

 A static class is one whose members must all be static; that is, they belong to the class itself, and not to any instances of the class. static classes cannot be instantiated. In effect, we're using this class as a container for the methods, rather than as something we create instances of (like a MonoBehaviour).

3. Our next step is to define some important strings that will appear in the saved game files. JSON objects work like dictionaries that use strings as their keys; we'll be using these keys to refer to the different parts of the data we're saving. Add the following code to the `SavingService` class:

```
// To avoid problems caused by typos, we'll store the names of the
// strings we use to store and look up items in the JSON as
// constant strings
private const string ACTIVE_SCENE_KEY = "activeScene";
private const string SCENES_KEY = "scenes";
private const string OBJECTS_KEY = "objects";
private const string SAVEID_KEY = "$saveID";

// (use an unexpected character "$" for the Save ID here to reduce the
// chance of collisions)
```

4. We can now create the `SaveGame` method, which performs the work of actually saving the scene. Add the following method to the `SavingService` class:

```
// Saves the game, and writes it to a file called fileName in the app's
// persistent data directory.
public static void SaveGame(string fileName) {

    // Create the JsonData that we will eventually write to disk
    var result = new JsonData();

    // Find all MonoBehaviours by first finding every MonoBehaviour,
    // and filtering it to only include those that are ISaveable.
    var allSaveableObjects = Object
        .FindObjectsOfType<MonoBehaviour>()
        .OfType<ISaveable>();

    // Do we have any objects to save?
    if (allSaveableObjects.Count() > 0) {

        // Create the JsonData that will store the list of objects
        var savedObjects = new JsonData();

        // Iterate over every object we want to save
        foreach (var saveableObject in allSaveableObjects)
        {
            // Get the object's saved data
            var data = saveableObject.SavedData;

            // We expect this to be an object (JSON's term for a
            // dictionary) because we need to include the object's Save
            // ID
            if (data.IsObject) {

                // Record the Save ID for this object
                data[SAVEID_KEY] = saveableObject.SaveID;

                // Add the object's save data to the collection
                savedObjects.Add(data);
            } else {

                // Provide a helpful warning that we can't save this
                // object.
                var behaviour = saveableObject as MonoBehaviour;

                Debug.LogWarningFormat(
                    behaviour,
                    "{0}'s save data is not a dictionary. The " +
                    "object was not saved.",
                    behaviour.name
                );
```

```
        }
    }

    // Store the collection of saved objects in the result.
    result[OBJECTS_KEY] = savedObjects;
} else {
    // We have no objects to save. Give a nice warning.
    Debug.LogWarningFormat(
        "The scene did not include any saveable objects.");
}

// Next, we need to record what scenes are open. Unity lets you
// have multiple scenes open at the same time, so we need to store
// all of them, as well as which scene is the "active" scene (the
// scene that new objects are added to, and that controls the
// lighting settings for the game).

// Create a JsonData that will store the list of open scenes.
var openScenes = new JsonData();

// Ask the scene manager how many scenes are open, and for each one,
// store the scene's name.
var sceneCount = SceneManager.sceneCount;

for (int i = 0; i < sceneCount; i++) {
    var scene = SceneManager.GetSceneAt(i);

    openScenes.Add(scene.name);
}

// Store the list of open scenes
result[SCENES_KEY] = openScenes;

// Store the name of the active scene
result[ACTIVE_SCENE_KEY] = SceneManager.GetActiveScene().name;

// We've now finished generating the save data, and it's time to
// write it to disk.

// Figure out where to put the file by combining the persistent
// data path with the filename that this method received as a
// parameter.
var outputPath = Path.Combine(
    Application.persistentDataPath, fileName);

// Create a JsonWriter, and configure it to 'pretty-print' the
// data. This is optional (you could just call result.ToJson() with
// no JsonWriter parameter and receive a string), but this way the
// resulting JSON is easier to read and understand, which is
// helpful while developing.
```

```
var writer = new JsonWriter();
writer.PrettyPrint = true;

// Convert the save data to JSON text.
result.ToJson(writer);

// Write the JSON text to disk.
File.WriteAllText(outputPath, writer.ToString());

// Notify where to find the saved game
Debug.LogFormat("Wrote saved game to {0}", outputPath);

// We allocated a lot of memory here, which means that there's an
// increased chance of the garbage collector needing to run in the
// future. To tidy up, we'll release our reference to the saved
// data, and then ask the garbage collector to run immediately.
// This will result in a slight performance hitch as the collector
// runs, but that's fine for this case, since users expect saving
// the game to pause for a second.
result = null;
System.GC.Collect();
}
```

SaveGame works by first creating a collection of every MonoBehaviour class that also implements the ISaveable interface. Objects that implement this interface are capable of creating data for storing in a JSON document; for each one we find, we get that data and store it in a JsonData object that will eventually be written to disk.

We also create the list of currently open scenes and store that as well. We also include the name of the currently active scene.

Finally, we convert all of the data into a string containing the textual JSON representation, figure out where to save it on disk, and save the file.

Implementing loading

Now that we know how to save the state of the game, we need to implement the system that loads the data.

Loading the game works like saving the game in reverse: we load the file, parse the JSON, take the list of scenes, load them, go through the list of saved object data, and deliver the loaded data to each appropriate object.

Before we write the LoadGame method, we need to do a little bit of work to deal with an eccentricity in how Unity loads scenes. When you load a scene using Scene Manager.LoadScene, your code waits until Unity has finished loading the scene. However, the scene isn't *quite* done loading when it returns; if you make changes to the objects in the scene right away, they'll be overridden on the next frame. To work around this, we'll register some code that runs after the scene has *really* finished loading. This code will be stored in a variable, which we'll pass to the `SceneManager` after it loads the scenes.

 Because the `SavingService` class is static, any variables it owns must also be `static`. Yes, this is global state, usually considered a thing to avoid, which wouldn't work if we needed to have more than one save/load system in the game. But because systems like saving and loading work by replacing the *entire state of the game*, the idea of having more than one saving system doesn't really apply. So, a little global state is fine to use here.

To implement loading:

1. Add the following variable to the `SavingService` class:

```
// A reference to the delegate that runs after the scene loads, which
// performs the object state restoration.
static UnityEngine.Events.UnityAction<Scene, LoadSceneMode>
    LoadObjectsAfterSceneLoad;
```

2. We can now finally add the `LoadGame` method, which loads the game state from a file. Add the following method to the `SavingService` class:

```
// Loads the game from a given file, and restores its state.
public static bool LoadGame(string fileName) {

    // Figure out where to find the file.
    var dataPath = Path.Combine(
        Application.persistentDataPath, fileName);

    // Ensure that a file actually exists there.
    if (File.Exists(dataPath) == false) {
        Debug.LogErrorFormat("No file exists at {0}", dataPath);
        return false;
    }

    // Read the data as JSON.
    var text = File.ReadAllText(dataPath);

    var data = JsonMapper.ToObject(text);

    // Ensure that we successfully read the data, and that it's an object
    // (i.e., a JSON dictionary)
    if (data == null || data.IsObject == false) {
        Debug.LogErrorFormat(
            "Data at {0} is not a JSON object", dataPath);
        return false;
    }
```

```csharp
    // We need to know what scenes to load.
    if (!data.ContainsKey("scenes"))
    {
        Debug.LogWarningFormat(
            "Data at {0} does not contain any scenes; not " +
            "loading any!",
            dataPath
        );
        return false;
    }

    // Get the list of scenes
    var scenes = data[SCENES_KEY];

    int sceneCount = scenes.Count;

    if (sceneCount == 0)
    {
        Debug.LogWarningFormat(
            "Data at {0} doesn't specify any scenes to load.",
            dataPath
        );
        return false;
    }

    // Load each specified scene.
    for (int i = 0; i < sceneCount; i++)
    {
        var scene = (string)scenes[i];

        // If this is the first scene we're loading, load it and replace
        // every other active scene.
        if (i == 0)
        {
            SceneManager.LoadScene(scene, LoadSceneMode.Single);
        }
        else
        {
            // Otherwise, load that scene on top of the existing ones.
            SceneManager.LoadScene(scene, LoadSceneMode.Additive);
        }

    }

    // Find the active scene, and set it
    if (data.ContainsKey(ACTIVE_SCENE_KEY))
    {
        var activeSceneName = (string)data[ACTIVE_SCENE_KEY];
        var activeScene = SceneManager.GetSceneByName(activeSceneName);

        if (activeScene.IsValid() == false)
```

```
    {
        Debug.LogErrorFormat(
          "Data at {0} specifies an active scene that " +
            "doesn't exist. Stopping loading here.",
          dataPath
        );
        return false;
    }

    SceneManager.SetActiveScene(activeScene);
} else {
    // This is not an error, since the first scene in the list will
    // be treated as active, but it's worth warning about.
    Debug.LogWarningFormat("Data at {0} does not specify an " +
        "active scene.", dataPath);
}

// Find all objects in the scene and load them
if (data.ContainsKey(OBJECTS_KEY)) {
    var objects = data[OBJECTS_KEY];

    // We can't update the state of the objects right away because
    // Unity will not complete loading the scene until sometime in
    // the future. Changes we made to the objects would revert
    // to how they're defined in the original scene. As a result, we
    // need to run the code after the scene manager reports that a
    // scene has finished loading.

    // To do this, we create a new delegate that contains our object-
    // loading code, and store that in LoadObjectsAfterSceneLoad.
    // This delegate is added to the SceneManager's sceneLoaded
    // event, which makes it run after the scene has finished loading.

    LoadObjectsAfterSceneLoad = (scene, loadSceneMode) => {

        // Find all ISaveable objects, and build a dictionary that maps
        // their Save IDs to the object (so that we can quickly look
        // them up)
        var allLoadableObjects = Object
            .FindObjectsOfType<MonoBehaviour>()
            .OfType<ISaveable>()
            .ToDictionary(o => o.SaveID, o => o);

        // Get the collection of objects we need to load
        var objectsCount = objects.Count;

        // For each item in the list...
        for (int i = 0; i < objectsCount; i++)
        {
            // Get the saved data
            var objectData = objects[i];
```

```
        // Get the Save ID from that data
        var saveID = (string)objectData[SAVEID_KEY];

        // Attempt to find the object in the scene(s) that has that
        // Save ID
        if (allLoadableObjects.ContainsKey(saveID))
        {
            var loadableObject = allLoadableObjects[saveID];

            // Ask the object to load from this data
            loadableObject.LoadFromData(objectData);
        }
    }

    // Tidy up after ourselves; remove this delegate from the
    // sceneLoaded event so that it isn't called next time
    SceneManager.sceneLoaded -= LoadObjectsAfterSceneLoad;

    // Release the reference to the delegate
    LoadObjectsAfterSceneLoad = null;

    // And ask the garbage collector to tidy up (again, this will
    // cause a performance hitch, but users are fine with this as
    // they're already waiting for the scene to finish loading)
    System.GC.Collect();
};

    // Register the object-loading code to run after the scene loads.
    SceneManager.sceneLoaded += LoadObjectsAfterSceneLoad;
}

return true;
}
```

The LoadGame method reads the file and first loads the scenes that are specified in the saved game. After that, it creates and saves the code that restores the state of the objects in the scenes, and adds it to the SceneManager's sceneLoaded event. The code itself finds all ISaveable MonoBehaviours, creates a dictionary that maps their Save ID to the object itself, and then uses the loaded object data to both find the appropriate object for the data and deliver the data to that object.

To save the game, you call the SaveGame method on the SavingService class:

```
// Save the game to a file called "SaveGame.json"
SavingService.SaveGame("SaveGame.json");
```

To load the game, you call the LoadGame method:

```
// Try to load the game from a file called "SaveGame.json"
SavingService.LoadGame("SaveGame.json");
```

These methods can be called from anywhere, but be aware that saving the game isn't a lightweight operation. Don't save every frame; save every couple of minutes, at most.

Creating a SaveableBehaviour

The saving system relies on objects having a unique Save ID. This ID is something that you could manually specify, but there's no real reason to—it's never exposed to the user, and each one must be unique. Additionally, the ID must not change between saving the game and loading it again, which means it needs to be stored inside the object itself.

It would be ideal, therefore, to have a system that would take care of this for you, so we'll create one ourselves. We'll subclass the MonoBehaviour class, and add code that automatically generates and exposes the Save ID when necessary. We'll take advantage of the fact that Unity lets you write code that runs when Unity serializes an object into the scene, which happens frequently when you're working with the object in the editor.

Additionally, we'll make this subclass abstract, so that we're implementing only the SaveID property, and leaving the SaveData and LoadFromData methods up to the subclasses.

Create a new C# script called *SaveableBehaviour.cs*, and add the following code to it:

```
public abstract class SaveableBehaviour : MonoBehaviour,
    ISaveable,                        // Marks this class as saveable
    ISerializationCallbackReceiver // Asks Unity to run code when the
                                      // scene file is saved in the editor
{
    // This class doesn't implement SavedData or LoadFromData; that's the
    // job of our subclasses.
    public abstract JsonData SavedData { get; }
    public abstract void LoadFromData(JsonData data);

    // This class does implement the SaveID property; it wraps the _saveID
    // field. (We need to do this manually, rather than using automatic
    // property generation (i.e., "public string SaveID {get;set;}"),
    // because Unity won't store automatic properties when saving the
    // scene file.

    public string SaveID
    {
        get
        {
            return _saveID;
        }
        set
        {
            _saveID = value;
        }
    }
```

```
    }

    // The _saveID field stores the actual data that SaveID uses. We mark
    // it as serialized so that the Unity editor saves it with the rest of the
    // scene, and ask HideInInspector to make it not appear in the Inspector
    // (there's no reason for it to be edited).
    [HideInInspector]
    [SerializeField]
    private string _saveID;

    // OnBeforeSerialize is called when Unity is about to save this object
    // as part of a scene file.
    public void OnBeforeSerialize()
    {
        // Do we not currently have a Save ID?
        if (_saveID == null)
        {
            // Generate a new unique one, by creating a GUID and getting
            // its string value.
            _saveID = System.Guid.NewGuid().ToString();
        }

    }

    // OnAfterDeserialize is called when Unity has loaded this object as
    // part of a scene file.
    public void OnAfterDeserialize()
    {
        // Nothing special to do here, but the method must exist to
        // implement ISerializationCallbackReceiver
    }
}
```

The SaveableBehaviour class's OnBeforeSerialize method is called when the class is being saved into the scene in the editor. If SaveableBehaviour doesn't have a Save ID at this point, it generates one and stores it in a variable that's private (so that other classes can't access and modify the Save ID; they don't need to know it), marked as a SerializeField (so that Unity stores it in the scene file), and set to HideInInspector (so that it doesn't appear in the Inspector, because there's no reason to edit it).

 The class is abstract, which means you can't create instances of SaveableBehaviours directly. Instead, you subclass Saveable Behaviour and implement the SaveData and LoadFromData methods. The SaveID property is taken care of for you.

Creating a Saveable MonoBehaviour

To demonstrate how to build a script that can save its data, we'll build an example, *TransformSaver.cs*, that stores information about the position, rotation, and scale of the game object that it's attached to:

1. Create a new C# script called *TransformSaver.cs*, and add the following code:

```
public class TransformSaver : SaveableBehaviour
{
    // Store the keys we'll be including in the saved game as constants,
    // to avoid problems with typos.
    private const string LOCAL_POSITION_KEY = "localPosition";
    private const string LOCAL_ROTATION_KEY = "localRotation";
    private const string LOCAL_SCALE_KEY = "localScale";

    // SerializeValue is a helper function that converts an object that
    // Unity already knows how to serialize (like Vector3, Quaternion,
    // and others) into a JsonData that can be included in the
    // saved game.
    private JsonData SerializeValue(object obj) {
        // This is very inefficient (we're converting an object to JSON
        // text, then immediately parsing this text back into a JSON
        // representation), but it means that we don't need to write the
        // (de)serialization code for built-in Unity types
        return JsonMapper.ToObject(JsonUtility.ToJson(obj));
    }

    // DeserializeValue works in reverse: given a JsonData, it produces
    // a value of the desired type, as long as that type is one that
    // Unity already knows how to serialize.
    private T DeserializeValue<T>(JsonData data) {
        return JsonUtility.FromJson<T>(data.ToJson());
    }

    // Provides the saved data for this component.
    public override JsonData SavedData {
        get {
            // Create the JsonData that we'll return to the saved
            // game system
            var result = new JsonData();

            // Store our position, rotation, and scale
            result[LOCAL_POSITION_KEY] =
                SerializeValue(transform.localPosition);

            result[LOCAL_ROTATION_KEY] =
                SerializeValue(transform.localRotation);

            result[LOCAL_SCALE_KEY] =
```

```
            SerializeValue(transform.localScale);

            return result;
        }
    }

    // Given some loaded data, updates the state of the component.
    public override void LoadFromData(JsonData data)
    {
        // We can't assume that the data will contain every piece of
        // data that we store; remember the programmer's adage,
        // "be strict in what you generate, and forgiving in what
        // you accept."

        // Accordingly, we test to see if each item exists in the
        // saved data

        // Update position
        if (data.ContainsKey(LOCAL_POSITION_KEY))
        {
            transform.localPosition =
                DeserializeValue<Vector3>(data[LOCAL_POSITION_KEY]);
        }

        // Update rotation
        if (data.ContainsKey(LOCAL_ROTATION_KEY))
        {
            transform.localRotation =
                DeserializeValue<Quaternion>(data[LOCAL_ROTATION_KEY]);
        }

        // Update scale
        if (data.ContainsKey(LOCAL_SCALE_KEY))
        {
            transform.localScale =
                DeserializeValue<Vector3>(data[LOCAL_SCALE_KEY]);
        }
    }
}
```

2. To use this script, add a `TransformSaver` component to your game object. It will automatically be included in saved games, and its state will be restored when the game is loaded.

Discussion

This system doesn't automatically restore any objects that were created after the scene loaded. If you want to support this, you'll need to have an object in your scene that keeps references to objects that it creates, and stores the additional information about

---

those objects when it's asked for its save data. When the object is asked to load, it re-creates the objects.

13.5 Downloading and Parsing JSON from the Web

Problem

You want to be able to download data in JSON format from a web server, such as configuration data.

Solution

There are two steps to solving this kind of problem: first, you need to download the data, and second, you need to parse the data.

 This example makes use of LitJSON, which is the same JSON handling library used in Recipe 13.4. There are many other alternatives out there, like Json.NET (*https://oreil.ly/b7CQi*), or for simple cases, Unity's built-in JSON tools (*https://oreil.ly/I4IZN*).

To download data from the web, use the `UnityWebRequest` class to create a request, and then call its `SendWebRequest` method to start it:

```
// Create the request
UnityWebRequest request = UnityWebRequest.Get("https://httbin.org/get");

// Send the request; we'll get back an operation that represents its
// work-in-progress state
UnityWebRequestAsyncOperation operation = request.SendWebRequest();
```

When you call `SendWebRequest`, it starts talking to the network and immediately returns a `UnityWebRequestAsyncOperation`. This is an object that you can use to get information about the request's progress.

In most cases, you'll want to wait until the operation completes, and then (depending on whether it succeeded or not) take some kind of action.

You can do this using the operation's `completed` event:

```
// Tell the operation that we want it to run some code when it's
// finished:
operation.completed += (op) =>
{
// The operation has finished. Now we'll figure out if it succeeded
// or not.
switch (request.result)
{
```

```
case UnityWebRequest.Result.Success:
// It worked! Log the result so we can see the raw text it
// downloaded.
Debug.Log($"Success!");
Debug.Log(request.downloadHandler.text);
// You can also use downloadHandler.data to get the raw
// bytes.
break;
case UnityWebRequest.Result.ConnectionError:
// We failed to connect. The server address might not be
// valid, or we might not have a working internet
// connection.
Debug.Log($"Connection error: {request.error}");
break;
case UnityWebRequest.Result.ProtocolError:
// We connected, but the server didn't give us data. There
// are many reasons why: file not found, permission denied,
// internal server error...
Debug.Log($"Protocol error: {request.error}");
break;
default:
// Some other event happened. (Nothing good, or else the
// status would have been Success.)
Debug.Log($"Error: {request.result}");
break;
}
};
```

Once you've downloaded the data, you can use LitJSON to parse the JSON and get data out of it.

In this example, we retrieve data from the URL `https://httpbin.org/get`.

 httpbin is a site that's useful for testing HTTP requests, and responds to a number of different URLs with useful information. You can learn more about it at *https://httpbin.org*.

The data that this URL will return looks like this:

```
{
...
"headers": {
...
"host": "httpbin.org"
}
}
```

In this example, we'll fetch the value of the `"host"` value, which is stored inside the `"headers"` value:

```csharp
private void ParseJson(string text)
{
// Given a string containing JSON, turn it into a JsonData.
JsonData data = JsonMapper.ToObject(text);

// Wrap all of our work in a try-catch so that we can correctly handle a
// situation where the data doesn't contain what we expect
try {

// Get the JsonData representing the "headers" object, and then get
// the string value for "host".
string host = (string)data["headers"]["Host"];

Debug.Log($"The host is {host}");
} catch (KeyNotFoundException) {
// We couldn't find either "headers" or "host" in the data. Log an
// error about it.
Debug.LogError($"Couldn't find the host in the downloaded data!");
}
}
```

Discussion

The `UnityWebRequestAsyncOperation` object that you receive by calling `SendWeb Request` on a `UnityWebRequest` can also be used in a coroutine:

```csharp
UnityWebRequestAsyncOperation operation = request.SendWebRequest();
StartCoroutine(WaitForDownload(operation));

// ... elsewhere in your class:

// WaitForDownload is a coroutine that takes a web request operation,
// waits for it to finish, and then takes action based on the
// operation's result.
private IEnumerator WaitForDownload(UnityWebRequestAsyncOperation webOperation)
{
// In a coroutine, you can yield on the operation (because it's an
// AsyncOperation). The coroutine will wait until the operation
// completes, and then resume.
yield return webOperation;

// At this point, the operation is now complete,
// and we can work with the request
var request = webOperation.webRequest;

if (request.result == UnityWebRequest.Result.Success) {
var data = request.downloadHandler.text;
} else {
// Deal with the error
}
}
```

LitJSON's `JsonMapper.ToObject` method parses JSON text into a `JsonData` object, which you can access like a dictionary or an array (depending on the JSON that you parsed). You can find the documentation and API for LitJSON at its official website (*https://litjson.net*).

13.6 Scripted Importers

Problem

You want to write code that lets Unity import a new type of file.

Solution

Not everything in game development revolves around the same file types. Sometimes you need to make custom file extensions. Unity has you covered!

In this example, we'll make a custom importer that allows Unity to recognize text files whose filenames end in *.cube*, which contain JSON data that describes the size and color of a cube.

Let's begin by creating an asset for which we'll then write an importer:

1. Open your favorite text editor, and create a new, empty file. (If you don't have a favorite editor, open Visual Studio, and choose New → File. Make a new, empty file.)

2. Put the following code in the file:

```
{
    "size": {"x":1, "y":1, "z":2},
    "color": {"r":0.5, "g":1, "b":0.5, "a":1}
}
```

3. Save the file as *Test.cube* in your Unity project's *Assets* folder.

4. Go to Unity. Note that while your *Test.cube* file is visible in the *Assets* folder, it's not usable in your project, because Unity doesn't know what to do with *.cube* files! Let's fix that.

5. Create a new C# script called *CubeImporter.cs*, and replace the contents with the following code:

```
#if UNITY_EDITOR
using UnityEditor;

// At the time of writing, asset importers are in the Experimental
// module. By the time you're reading this, the API may have changed, so
// check the documentation.
using UnityEditor.Experimental.AssetImporters;
```

```
// A CubeDescription contains the variables that define our cubes. We'll
// create them by loading them from text files that contain JSON.
public struct CubeDescription {
    public Vector3 size;

    // storing the r, g, b, a values in this 4-component vector
    public Color color;
}

// Indicate to Unity that this script imports files with the file
// extension ".cube," and that this is version 0 of the importer
// (changing the number makes Unity reimport assets of this type).
[ScriptedImporter(0, "cube")]
public class CubeImporter : ScriptedImporter {

    // Called by Unity to perform an import
    public override void OnImportAsset(AssetImportContext ctx)
    {

        // "ctx" contains information about the import that Unity wants
        // us to do; it contains the path to the file, and we'll put
        // the Unity objects into it when we're done

        // "cube" files will contain JSON that describes the color and
        // size of the cube.

        // Create a variable to load the cube description into
        CubeDescription cubeDescription;

        // Attempt to load the JSON.
        try {
            var text = System.IO.File.ReadAllText(ctx.assetPath);

            cubeDescription =
                        JsonUtility.FromJson<CubeDescription>(text);
        } catch (System.ArgumentException e) {
            // We failed to load the JSON. Maybe it's not valid. Report
            // the error.
            Debug.LogErrorFormat(
                "{0} is not a valid cube: {1}",
                ctx.assetPath, e.Message);
            return;

        } catch (System.Exception e) {
            // We caught some other kind of exception, and can't
            // continue. Rethrow the error.
            throw e;
        }
```

```
// Create a generic cube object, which we'll make changes to and
// save as a new asset.
var cubeObject = GameObject.CreatePrimitive(PrimitiveType.Cube);

// Get the last part of the filepath, and use it as the cube's
// name
string name =
    System.IO.Path.GetFileNameWithoutExtension(ctx.assetPath);

// Next, we'll create a cube that's the right size. The default
// cube mesh is 1x1x1; we'll scale it based on the size that was
// passed in.

// Copy the default cube mesh.
var cubeMesh =
  Instantiate(cubeObject.GetComponent<MeshFilter>()
                                      .sharedMesh);

// Create a matrix that scales vertices by the given X, Y, and Z
// amounts.
var scaleMatrix = Matrix4x4.Scale(cubeDescription.size);

// Get a copy of the vertices in the mesh.
var vertices = cubeMesh.vertices;

// For each of these vertices, apply the scale by multiplying
// the matrix against the vertex.
for (int v = 0; v < vertices.Length; v++) {
    vertices[v] = scaleMatrix.MultiplyPoint(vertices[v]);
}

// Store these scaled vertices in the mesh.
cubeMesh.vertices = vertices;

// Tell the cube's MeshFilter to use this new mesh.
cubeObject.GetComponent<MeshFilter>().sharedMesh = cubeMesh;

// Give the mesh a name.
cubeMesh.name = name + " Mesh";

// Create a new material, using the Standard shader (which is
// the default)
var cubeMaterial = new Material(Shader.Find("Standard"));

// Apply the color that we loaded.
cubeMaterial.color = cubeDescription.color;

// Give it a name, too.
cubeMaterial.name = name + " Material";
```

```
    // Tell the cube's MeshRenderer to use this material.
    cubeObject.GetComponent<MeshRenderer>().material = cubeMaterial;

    // Now we store the objects we just created as assets.

    // First, store the GameObject (the collection of components
    // that uses and renders the mesh and material), and mark it as
    // the "main" object.
    ctx.AddObjectToAsset(name, cubeObject);
    ctx.SetMainObject(cubeObject);

    // We also need to store the mesh and material.
    ctx.AddObjectToAsset(cubeMaterial.name, cubeMaterial);
    ctx.AddObjectToAsset(cubeMesh.name, cubeMesh);

    }

}
#endif
```

This looks long and scary, but it's just a long sequence of small steps. It's defining a struct, `CubeDescription`, to describe what a cube is: a `Vector3` and a `Color`. Then it's making a `ScriptedImporter`, called `CubeImporter`, that reads in the JSON of the file in question, and creates a new mesh using the cube information from the file. Magic!

 To learn more about `Vector3` and other mathematical types in Unity, see Chapter 4.

6. Return to Unity. Your *Test.cube* file will now be imported. It now contains three assets usable by Unity: a mesh, a material, and a game object that uses the mesh and material. You can drag the file into the scene, just like any other model.

Discussion

Enabling Unity to understand your custom file types opens a world of possibilities. If you, for example, built an external level editor that exported a level file, this system would allow you to equip the Unity editor with the ability to read your file.

 The Unity community has built importers for lots of common file formats that Unity doesn't necessarily support out of the box. If you're missing a file format feature, search the internet before trying to implement it yourself!

Index

Symbols

2.5D scene, creating, 107
2D blend trees, 210
2D graphics, 89-108
2D physics, creating a sprite with, 93
2D textures, file formats supported by Unity, 19
3D graphics, 109-158
3D objects, 19
3D physics system, 66, 159
    (see also physics)
9-slicing, 339

A

abstract classes, 389, 390
Account button, 5
actions
    binding action to button on gamepad controller, 63
    changing for component using Input Actions field, 64
    making cube able to respond to, 63
Add Component button
    creating script through, 29
    Input -> Player Input, 59
    Physics 2D -> Surface Effector 2D, 100
AddForce method (Rigidbody2D), 98
adding vectors, 73
additively loading a scene, 228
agents, 307
    creating BallAgent example, 307-310
    setting up in Unity editor, 310
    training, 311
AI (artificial intelligence), 281

defining path that AI entities and player can follow, 288-289
enemies detecting where to take cover, 297-302
letting entities in game follow a path, 289-291
albedo (base) color, 111
Alpha Clip Threshold value, 142
    connecting Dissolve Amount to, 140
Alpha value, 142
ambientCG, 116
anchors, 335
angles
    finding angle to a target, 86
    between vectors, working with, 83-84
animation clips, 189
    dragging into blend tree Inspector, 208
    range of, setting, 203
animation curve, 193, 342
Animation pane, 191
    showing keyframes for an animation, 192
animation parameters, 198
animations, 189-223
    animating parts of the UI, 339-342
    animating shader over time, 134-135
    automatically switching cameras, 219
    basic character movement, 194-199
    blended movement, 208
    cinematic camera tracking, 216-219
    controlling speed of animated shader, 136-137
    creating sprite animation, 92
    inverse kinematics, 199-203
    keeping multiple objects in view, 220

forces
    applying manually, 185
    applying to 2D objects, 98-100
forward kinematics, 202
forward property (Transform), 76
Fragment node, 130
    Emission property, 143
frames
    capturing screenshot at end of frame, 375
    creating frame rate–independent behavior,
        32-34
free game art, 337
free motion-capture animations from Unity,
    194
freelook, 160
Freesound, 314
Fresnel Effect node, 129
Fresnel effect, defined, 131

G

game controllers, buttons on righthand side, 63
Game Developer website, 225
game objects
    adding script to, 26-30
    assignment to layers, 168
    faking a dynamic emissive object, 154-155
    finding objects attached to, 36
    setting to be Navigation Static, 288
    storing all children of, 357
    UI elements, 332
    using components attached to, 34-36
    working with, 12
game state, saving and loading, 377-393
Game view, 7
GameObject class
    ReturnToPool extension method, 47
    script managing queue of GameObjects,
        44-52
GameObject menu
    3D Object -> Capsule, 286
    3D Object -> Cube, 68
    3D Object -> Quad, 156
    3D Object -> Sphere, 109
    Create Empty, 59
    Create Empty Child, 12
    Light -> Light Probe Group, 148
    Light -> Reflection Probe, 150
    UI -> Button, 333
    UI -> EventSystem, 65

gameplay, 225-280
    creating a box to drag objects, 251-255
    creating a menu structure, 255-259
    creating a top-down camera, 233-235
    creating a wheeled vehicle, 259-262
    creating camera that orbits its target,
        266-269
    creating orbiting camera that won't clip
        through walls, 269
    creating speed boosts for vehicles, 264-266
    detecting when player completes a lap,
        270-280
    keeping a car from flipping over, 263
    loading new scene file, 225-229
    managing hit points, 229-233
    managing quests, 236-250
garbage collection, 51, 380
Gear icon, using to work with components, 15
Generate Physics Shape setting, 94
GetComponent method, 34
    related methods accessing multiple compo-
        nents, 35
GetKey method (Input class), 55
GetKeyDown method (Input class), 55
GetKeyUp method (Input class), 55
GetObject method, 44
    HideInInspector attribute, 47
gimbal lock, 79
gizmos, 235
Gizmos button (Game view), 8
global illumination (GI) data, 143
Global Volume, 122
glow effect
    creating using Shader Graph, 129-132
    object with glow effect and point light inside
        it, 154
Grab trigger parameter, 205
Grabbing component example, 169-174
groups (audio), 316
    adding audio effects on mixer groups, 320
    using ducking effect, 323
GUILayout, 359

H

Half-Life 2 game, 174
Hand tool, 3, 6
Has Exit Time option (Inspector), 205
HDR (high-dynamic range) rendering, 123
HDRP (High-Definition Render Pipeline), 127

X

.xm files, 19

Y

yield break, exiting coroutines with, 43

yield return, 41, 341
  null result, 42
  using only in methods returning IEnumerator, 41

About the Authors

Dr. Paris Buttfield-Addison is cofounder of Secret Lab, a game development studio based in beautiful Hobart, Australia. Secret Lab builds games and game development tools, including the multiaward-winning ABC Play School iPad games, the BAFTA-winning *Night in the Woods*, the Qantas airlines Joey Playbox games, and the Yarn Spinner narrative game framework. Paris formerly worked as mobile product manager for Meebo (acquired by Google), has a degree in medieval history and a PhD in computing, and writes technical books on mobile and game development (more than 20 so far) for O'Reilly Media. Paris particularly enjoys game design, statistics, law, machine learning, and human-centered technology research. He can be found on Twitter at @parisba and online at *http://paris.id.au*.

Dr. Jon Manning is the cofounder of Secret Lab, an independent game development studio. He's written a whole bunch of books for O'Reilly Media about iOS development and game development, and has a doctorate about jerks on the internet. He's worked on *Button Squid*, a top-down puzzler, and on the critically acclaimed adventure game *Night in the Woods*, which includes his interactive dialogue system, Yarn Spinner. Jon can be found on Twitter at @desplesda and online at *http://desplesda.net*.

Dr. Tim Nugent pretends to be a mobile app developer, game designer, PhD student, and now he even pretends to be an author. When he isn't busy avoiding being found out as a fraud, he spends most of his time designing and creating little apps and games he won't let anyone see. Tim spent a disproportionately long time writing this tiny little bio, most of which was spent trying to add a witty sci-fi reference, before he simply gave up. Tim can be found at @The_McJones on Twitter.

Colophon

The animal on the cover of *Unity Development Cookbook* is the common starling (*Sturnus vulgaris*). These average-sized songbirds live in Europe, the Middle East, North America, and Australia, as well as in northern and southern Africa. They were introduced in Australia and North America in the 19th century and have demonstrated their adaptability by since becoming one of the most common birds in their new home areas, to the point of being considered pests.

Despite their arguable reputation as a nuisance, common starlings are quite beautiful creatures. The plumage of adult common starlings has a remarkable iridescence that occurs when tiny structures within their feathers interact with light, reflecting and refracting it. Typically glossy, with shades of purple and green, starlings' plumage may also feature white spots, especially in the winter, as new feathers grow in. Within a short time, however, the white tips of these new feathers wear off and the birds resume their everyday glossy look (scientists term this unusual phenomenon "wear molt").

For all their noise and beauty, common starlings are maybe best known as the subject of many online videos (*https://oreil.ly/27LiG*) showing their spectacular wintertime "murmurations." For most of the year, starlings travel in small, loose flocks, but in winter they form large flocks of thousands of birds. Taking flight, the birds sometimes fly in a coordinated manner, performing evolving maneuvers that can resemble the movements of a single organism. To achieve this, all birds coordinate their efforts by watching birds near them; a 2013 study found that starlings mass their flocking so cohesively by visually synchronizing their flying to the six or seven birds nearest them. At times the birds seem to undertake murmurations to both harass and evade aerial predators such as falcons or hawks, and a fast-moving bird of prey can often be seen at the outer edges of the feinting, contorting flocks.

The cover illustration is by Karen Montgomery, based on a black-and-white engraving from *General Zoology, or Systematic Natural History* (1800) by George Shaw. The cover fonts are Gilroy and Guardian Sans. The text font is Adobe Minion Pro; the heading font is Adobe Myriad Condensed; and the code font is Dalton Maag's Ubuntu Mono.

Printed in the USA
CPSIA information can be obtained
at www.ICGtesting.com
JSHW050208250624
65297JS00013B/184